LINCOLN CHRISTIAN COLLEGE AND SEMINARY

D0849190

STRESS
RESPONSE
SYNDROMES

Other books by Mardi Jon Horowitz, M.D.

Image Formation and Cognition (later *Image Formation and Psychotherapy*)

Psychosocial Function in Epilepsy

Hysterical Personality (Revised Edition: *Hysterical Personality Style and the Histrionic Personality Disorder*) (editor)

States of Mind: Configurational Analysis of Individual Personality

Personality Styles and Brief Psychotherapy (with Marmar, Krupnick, Wilner, Kaltreider, and Wallerstein)

Psychodynamics and Cognition (editor)

Introduction to Psychodynamics: A New Synthesis

Nuances of Technique in Dynamic Psychotherapy

Person Schemas and Maladaptive Interpersonal Patterns (editor)

Psychic Structure and Change in Psychoanalysis (editor with Kernberg and Weinshel)

Formulation as a Basis for Planning Psychotherapy Treatment

Cognitive Psychodynamics

Essential Papers on Post Traumatic Stress Disorder (editor)

STRESS
RESPONSE
SYNDROMES
Fourth Edition

MARDI JON HOROWITZ, M.D.

JASON ARONSON INC.
Northvale, New Jersey
London

This book was set in 12pt. Bembo and printed and bound by Book-mart Press, Inc. of North Bergen, NJ.

Fourth Edition Copyright © 2001 by Mardi J. Horowitz

10 9 8 7 6 5 4 3 2 1

All rights reserved. No part of this book may be used or reproduced in any manner whatsoever without written permission from Jason Aronson Inc. except in the case of brief quotations in reviews for inclusion in a magazine, newspaper, or broadcast.

Library of Congress Cataloging-in-Publication Data

Horowitz, Mardi Jon, 1934–
  Stress response syndromes / by Mardi Jon Horowitz.—4th ed.
    p. ; cm.
  Includes bibliographical references and index.
  ISBN 0-7657-0313-0
  1. Post-traumatic stress disorder. 2. Post-traumatic stress disorder—Case studies. I. Title.
  [DNLM: 1. Stress Disorders, Post-Traumatic. 2. Adjustment Disorders. 3. Grief. 4. Psychotherapy. WM 170 H817s 2001]
  RC552.P67 H67 2001
  616.85'21—dc21   00-052205

Printed in the United States of America on acid-free paper. For information and catalog write to Jason Aronson Inc., 230 Livingston Street, Northvale, NJ 07647-1726, or visit our website: www.aronson.com

For those strangers who,
roused by a shared sense of humanity,
help those overcome by events,
providing compassion, restoration, and hope

And, more personally,
for my mother,
Lillian Horowitz,
and in memory of
my father, Morris Horowitz

108704

Contents

III. INDIVIDUAL VARIATIONS

IV. CLINICAL EXAMPLES

From the Foreword
to the First Edition

This book by Dr. Mardi Horowitz on the psychological understanding and the psychotherapeutic amelioration of specifically circumscribed psychopathological entities, the Stress Response Syndromes, is an exciting and long-needed investigation that reflects the creative interplay of psychotherapy, research, and practice. It is, after all, of the essence of the clinical medical and health disciplines, the so-called healing arts, of which psychotherapy partakes, that continuing advance in understanding and in practice should accrue from the effective and creative interplay of formal research, basic investigation—in theoretical structure, in experimental laboratory, or in field observation or survey—in interplay with the clinical experience and clinical reflection of the bedside, or in our instance, the consulting room. It is this creative interplay between research and practice, leading to the enhancement of *both*, which has been so underdeveloped in our "peculiar" science with its heretofore essentially one-sided development, sparked by the innovative genius of a Freud, of clinical insight and understanding without the signal benefit of concomitant growth from the formal and systematic research side of any comparable insight and understanding.

Mardi Horowitz's book is a multifaceted model, or rather a series of models, paradigmatic of a new genre, that brings psychotherapy research meaningfully into the clinical picture; that is, where each influence furthers the other. What is the nature then of these models? There is first a model of *problem setting* and *problem delineation* in the field of psychological understanding and psychological intervention. Through a sequence (1) of typical clinical *case history* in sufficient detail; (2) of equally detailed and at the same time wide-ranging *field observation* and survey drawing upon disaster and extreme circumstance, whether wartime military combat or peacetime fire or shipwreck, whether such inhumane extreme circumstances as concentration camps and nuclear holocaust or more "everyday" circumstances of rape, severe illness, death and bereavement; and (3) of equally meticulous attention to the varieties of ingenious analogies to these stress situations, to the extent that they can be ethically re-created within the *experimental laboratory* and there be safely studied via controlled manipulation of critical dimensions; through this sequencing and drawing of common threads, this book serves as a model for the use of consulting room, of field observation, and of experimental laboratory to throw complementary and therefore incremental illumination upon the essential problem of psychotherapy, the understanding and the possibilities for intervention into the psychological dysfunctions of people.

This volume is secondly a model for the rational description of the *natural history* of a psychopathological syndrome or state, a description, that is, of what Dr. Horowitz calls the "general theory," the psychological explanation of sequentially unfolding phases and the general principles of psychological management and psychotherapeutic intervention specifically and differentially appropriate to the specific developmental phase and state of the disorder. This effort brings some rational order out of what so often looks like a chaotic welter of conflicting claims and competing approaches all vying for consumer acceptance in the unregulated psychotherapy marketplace. And thirdly, really as corollary to the "general theory" that accounts for the understanding and the psychotherapeutic modification of the naturally unfolding stress response syndrome, is the model for differentiated understanding and intervention based on the differing enduring character dispositions of the various *personality types or styles* as they differently mesh with the impositions and implications of the disease state and the requirements and possibilities of the intervention strategies.

Robert S. Wallerstein, M.D.
Professor of Psychiatry
University of California, San Francisco

Preface to the Fourth Edition

The 1976 publication of the first edition of this book was followed by establishment of the diagnostic category Post Traumatic Stress Disorder in 1980. That official action by the American Psychiatric Association did a great deal to spur research on PTSD and other stress response syndromes. Revised editions have been necessary to incorporate new knowledge, but I am also pleased that this work has stood the test of time as well as it has.

For this latest edition, two chapters have been entirely rewritten. One of these, Chapter 9, can be used separately as a manual for treatment of stress response syndromes.

As in the previous editions, this book asserts a biopsychosocial model, but focuses on psychosocial meanings.

Mardi Horowitz
San Francisco

Acknowledgments

In my introduction to the first edition, I thanked my high school chemistry teacher, Mr. Toon, for giving me the gift of wanting to study science, and Jurgen Ruesch for pointing the way in psychiatric research. Many other mentors and colleagues have guided me since then. In this edition I cannot list all the colleagues, teachers, patients, and students who have made vital contributions. But certainly important among these are my colleagues Nancy Kaltreider, Charles Marmar, Robert Wallerstein, Daniel Weiss, Nancy Wilner, George Bonnano, Nigel Field, Hansbjorg Znoj, Are Holen, Charles Stinson, Connie Milbrath, and Bryna Siegel.

My own efforts at stress research would not have been possible without the support of the Langley Porter Psychiatric Institute and grants from NIMH and the John D. and Catherine T. MacArthur Foundation. I especially thank William Bevan, John Conger, Murray Gell-Mann, and Jonas Salk for their continued vision and encouragement.

Jack Block, Jerome Singer, Richard Lazarus, Irving Janis, Alan Skolnikoff, Norman Mages, George Kaplan, Jerome Oremland, Seymour Boorstein, and Richard Lieberman provided essential consultations. And of course, this book owes much to those colleagues indicated in the Contents.

My children, Ariana, Jordan, and Joshua, and my wife, Carol, helped with the manuscript at various times but above all softened my own stress responses throughout the time of the work. My thanks to all.

Introduction: A Paradigm

Psychotherapy needs theory, anchored to observables, that is concerned with the relationship between a patient's habitual "style" and his current state and needs. This theory must include the following:

1. A statement of the maladaptive states being considered.
2. A statement of at least some typologies of patient styles that organize and process thought and emotion during such states.
3. A clarification of the relationship between the patient's style and state and various modalities of psychotherapy (e.g., even extending to different ways of giving the same interpretation). This clarification must include a theory of how interventions work and why a mode of therapy useful with one patient's style might not be useful with another.

Stress response syndromes are chosen as the state of maladaption for the following reasons:

1. The relevant external events are known and recent. Therefore, memories and fantasies can be compared with a consensual reality.
2. The general human response tendencies are also known, phasic, and recognizable. Clinical and experimental studies indicate the existence of general stress response tendencies, which take two seemingly opposite forms. One is manifested

1

by intrusive and repetitive thoughts, emotions, and behavior, and the other shows ideational denial, emotional numbing, and behavioral constriction. These general tendencies vary among persons according to cognitive, emotional, and regulatory styles but can be found in some form in patients of any diagnostic or characterologic category.

3. The course of treatment is often short, and the patient's states vary during treatment, allowing clinicians to view the change.

4. The symptoms formed and dissipated after stress events are important throughout psychopathology. They include loss of control over thought and emotion, denial and numbing, repetitious or maladaptive behavior, assault, extremes of anxiety, general tension, suicidal preoccupation, impaired relationships, and psychophysiological disorders.

5. Psychotherapy is frequently the treatment of choice. There have been various procedures advocated and also called erroneous if badly timed or used with the wrong person (e.g., abreaction versus support and permitted denial).

6. We can thus ask: (a) How does the external stress event interact with the patient's personality? The development of clear connections between observation and inferences about the patient's identity, relationships, and habitual defenses? (b) Where is the patient having difficulty in completing the assimilation of and accommodation to the stress event? (c) How does the patient's relationship with the therapist modify the working-through or warding-off process?

PRELIMINARY TACTICS

We shall divide the information about a patient into the following three categories:

1. The current phase of the patient's response to stress, current symptoms and/or problems, and the relation of current events to past events.
2. The patient's disposition regarding personality structure, habitual defenses, cognitive and coping style, behavior patterns, and the relationship of these with his family, society, and biology.
3. The appropriate treatment options.

To serve these ends this book is divided into sections. Part I describes the investigations into the characteristics of stress response syndromes. Part II explains these general response tendencies and describes the principles of treatment for stress-induced symptoms and signs. Part III elaborates on these principles, contrasting three patient types. After describing the relatively universal tendencies and the stylistic variations of these tendencies, Part IV presents five case histories, including transcripts of sections of the psychotherapeutic process, to further illustrate how personality factors and preexisting conflicts form a patient's reaction to a stressful life event.

I

STRESS RESPONSE SYNDROMES

1

INTRUSION AND DENIAL: A PROTOTYPICAL CASE

Intrusive repetitions and denial are labels for two extremes of response to stressful life events, and their meanings are the concern of this book. Because we must use abstract statements and generalizations to explore these meanings, we shall begin with a concrete example, the case of Harry. His unbidden images of a dead woman's body illustrate the intrusive repetition of a horrible sight, and his temporary inability to acknowledge how moved he was by his involvement in her death illustrates a period of denial. Harry is a fictional character, and his history is a composite of characteristics found in studies of real persons. The events of his life are held constant while his character style is molded in various ways in order to contrast the response of different personality styles to the same circumstance.

HARRY

Harry was a 40-year-old truck dispatcher who had worked his way up in a small trucking firm. One night he took a run himself because he was shorthanded. The load consisted of steel pipe, carried in an old truck, and although the truck had armor between the load bed and the driver's side of the forward compartment, it did not fully protect the passenger's side.

Late at night Harry passed an attractive woman hitchhiking alone on a lonely stretch of highway. Impulsively deciding to break the company's rule against passengers of any sort, he picked her up, reasoning that if he did not she might otherwise be molested.

A short time later a car veered across the divider line and entered his lane, threatening a head-on collision. Harry pulled across the shoulder of the road into a clear area but then crashed into a pile of gravel. The pipe shifted, came through the cab of the truck on the passenger's side, and impaled the woman. Harry crashed into the steering wheel and windshield and briefly became unconscious. When he regained consciousness, he was met with the grisly sight of his dead companion.

The highway patrol found no identification on the woman, the other car had driven on, and Harry was taken by ambulance to a hospital emergency room. No fractures were found, his lacerations were sutured, and he remained overnight for observation. His wife, who sat up with him, found him anxious and dazed, talking of the events in a fragmentary and incoherent way.

The next day he left the hospital, and against his wife's wishes and his doctor's recommendation to rest, he returned to work. From then on, for several days, he continued his regular work as if nothing had happened. Harry met with his superiors and with legal advisers and was reprimanded for breaking the rule about passengers but was also reassured that otherwise the accident was not his fault and that he would not be held responsible. It was no secret that other drivers also often broke the no-passenger rule.

During this phase of relative denial and numbing of emotional responses, Harry thought about the accident from time to time but was surprised to find how little emotional effect it seemed to have on him. He was responsible and conscientious in his work, but his wife reported that he thrashed around in his sleep, ground his teeth, and seemed more tense and irritable than usual.

Four weeks after the accident he had a nightmare about mangled bodies and he awoke with an anxiety attack. For the next several days he had recurrent, intense, and intrusive images of the dead woman's body. These images, together with his ruminations about her, were accompanied by more and more severe anxiety attacks. Harry even developed a phobia about driving to and from work, and his regular habits of weekend drinking increased to a nightly use of growing quantities of alcohol. He lost his temper over minor frustrations and had difficulty concentrating at work and even while watching television. Harry tried unsuccessfully to dispel his feeling responsible for the accident, and, worried about his complaints of insomnia, irritability, and increased alcohol consumption, his doctor referred him for psychiatric treatment.

This phase illustrates intrusive repetition in waking and dreaming, thought and emotion. In his psychiatric evaluation, Harry at first was reluctant to talk about the accident. But this resistance subsided relatively quickly, and he reported recurrent intrusive images of the woman's body.

BACKGROUND

Harry's family lived in a central California city with a population of approximately 100,000. His father worked as a hardware store manager and had a middle-class income. His mother married his father after graduating from high school and had been a housewife and mother since then. Harry had two older sisters and one younger sister.

Harry's father, a strict and moralistic man, had a constricted outlook on life. He had been out of work during the Depression and remained occupied with trying to save money. When this was not possible, he became irritated or worried. Besides his work and family, Harry's father valued his men's club activities and his trout fishing. He was never overtly affectionate but did praise the children when they were good. He also took Harry on occasional fishing trips but remained fairly remote. He consistently displayed a rigorous sense of morality and was a strict disciplinarian. As we shall see, Harry internalized these standards of behavior, which contributed to his guilty feelings after the accident.

Harry's mother struggled to provide a good home for her children, making sure that the house was clean, the meals were on time, and the laundry was done. She sometimes cried and belittled herself when she was unable to complete these tasks. Harry felt that his father did not appreciate his mother and that his father did not help her enough. While his father sat in a chair during the evening, his mother continued working, with Harry sometimes helping. Harry's mother favored him and generally was lenient about what he did.

One older sister resented Harry's favored position with their mother and periodically teased and tormented him. But the other two sisters shared their mother's feeling that he was the special one. Harry felt especially close to his younger sister but was not closely attached to the others.

Harry was one of the more intelligent and gifted children in his high school class, and some of his teachers encouraged him to go to college. But he fell in love with a girl in his class, and gradually, with considerable guilt over each new step in their sexual intimacy, they had an affair. Late in their senior year of high school, she became pregnant. They decided they were in love and should therefore get married and have the child. Harry found a job working for a local store, which led to his entering the truck-driving field. Periodic promotions followed until he reached the position of chief dispatcher a few years before the accident. He worked hard, valued the esteem of the other men, but felt bored and limited. His resulting desire for something more contributed a certain impulsiveness to his life, such as his readiness to break the rules to pick up the hitchhiking woman.

Harry and his wife had three children, two boys and a girl. Although Harry occasionally felt dragged down by the amount of time the children demanded from him in the evenings and on weekends, he was an attentive and loving father. He worked at this and consciously wanted to be a better husband and father than his father had been. His resentment of his wife occasionally surfaced, however, for he also wanted independence from what he saw as her demands. He believed that if he had not had to marry her, he could have gone to college, developed his potential, and found more interesting and remunerative work.

For two years, Harry had served in the military, and his wife and family were able to accompany him to a stateside base. He remembered this as one of the happier periods of his life because of the variety of experience and the camaraderie with other men. He had felt occasionally depressed since then.

When he was feeling morose, instead of coming home for dinner, Harry would go to a local bar with some of the men from work. He generally returned home three or four hours later, moderately intoxicated. His wife reacted with coldness, tears, or an angry attack. He counteracted by feeling either upset, guilty, apologetic, or angry in return, criticizing his wife's faults and shortcomings. Once he hit her during such an altercation; she threatened to leave him, and the physical abuse was never repeated. After the accident he feared that his wife would react to his picking up the woman with similar coldness, accusation, and anger.

Following such outbursts, Harry tended to carry a grudge against his wife for several weeks. But to his surprise, she recovered the same day. Her main grievance was that she felt unappreciated for all her devotion as his wife and the mother of his children. Although their sex life was intermittently active, she accused him of being less interested in her, and herself of being less interesting. Even though Harry did not tell her, he agreed. He had been sexually interested in women at work, but this had not gone beyond flirtations and kissing at office parties. But his sexual fantasies had been activated by seeing the woman alone on the highway.

Harry's main leisure activities were picnicking and camping with his family and trout fishing with his father. The two had developed a kind of distant but affectionate relationship around this activity. In addition, Harry liked to read. He tended to select recent novels and had also purchased a set from a "great books" series that he was determined to read from beginning to end.

TREATMENT

During his psychotherapy, Harry worked through several complexes of ideas and feelings linked associatively to the accident and his intrusive images. The emergent conflictual themes (see Table 1–1) included guilt over causing the woman's death, guilt over sexual ideas about her that he had fantasied before the accident, guilt that he felt glad to be alive when she had died, and fear and anger that he had been involved in an accident and her death. There was also a magical belief that the woman had "caused" the accident by her hitchhiking, and his associated anger toward her that then fed back into his various guilt feelings.

His symptoms gradually diminished. At first he was able to sleep better, and gradually he felt less anxious, tense, and irritable. He reduced his alcohol intake to an occasional social drink. Later, the image symptoms stopped, and his relationships returned to about the same level as before the accident, except that he felt closer to his wife, whom he credited with helping him through a difficult period.

All of the complexes of ideas and feelings were activated not only by the accident but also by Harry's state before the conflict. Friction and lack of sexual interest in his wife had led to fantasies about other women and activities that resulted in themes of guilt. Such guilt was connected with these feelings after the accident, just

Table 1–1. Themes Activated by the Accident

CURRENT CONCEPTS	Incongruent with ⟶	ENDURING SCHEMAS OR BELIEFS ⟶	EMOTION
A. Self as "aggressor"			
1. Relief that she and not he was the victim.	Social morality	Guilt	
2. Aggressive ideas about the woman.	Social morality	Guilt	
3. Sexual ideas about the woman.	Social morality	Guilt	
B. Self as "victim"			
1. Damage to her body could have happened to him.	Invulnerable self	Fear	
2. He broke rules.	Responsibility to the company	Fear (of accusations) and shame	
3. She instigated the situation by hitchhiking.	He is innocent of any badness; the fault is outside	Anger	

as his anger with his wife was related to the theme of his anger with the woman hitchhiker. Thus the stress event led to a period of stress that combined internal and external elements.

We shall consider these various elements and combinations as the case of Harry evolves in subsequent chapters. What is important here is the concrete illustration of Harry's signs and symptoms after the accident. The recognition of such signs as the denial period, the free interval when Harry functioned well at work after the accident, and the symptom of intrusive images is enhanced by a knowledge of the theory of the psychological response to stress and how this relates to clinical psychopathology. Without this knowledge, the free period might look like normal adaptiveness, and the intrusive images might not have been explored or might have been regarded as unimportant.

2

CLINICAL OBSERVATIONS AND DIAGNOSES

The major efforts at agreeing on psychological stress response syndromes began with observations of signs and symptoms following disasters such as train wrecks and wars that exposed many to the same type of experience. "Railroad spine," for example, was a common painful disability after railway accidents a hundred years ago (Trimble 1981). Although the threat of litigation was a motivation, it became quite clear to neurologists that conscious malingering was not the reason for many of the functional symptoms that persisted long after the disasters.

Post-traumatic conditions concerned not only the clinical problem of diagnosis and etiological formulation but also the legal problem of compensation when the traumatic events were seen as the potential responsibility of others. That is why the industrial era, with its development of railroad systems run by transportation boards, led to a clearer observation of post-traumatic disorders. There were many legal arguments among experts on both the plaintiffs' and the defendants' sides. In the latter part of the nineteenth and into the twentieth century, these arguments concerned the degree to which

19

a patient's distress and functional impairment was related to (1) aims to get compensation; (2) somatic conversion reactions precipitated by trauma; (3) physical impairments in various organ systems such as the brain, spine, and peripheral nerves; and (4) stress specific responses such as special psychological signs and symptoms induced by psychic trauma.

The implication of nonconscious, psychological motivational factors in symptom formation was a topic of considerable controversy. Hysterical somatic conversion reaction had a history of 4,000 years and was thought to be a syndrome based on heredity, emotional predisposition, and psychological responses to current situations, including stressful life events (Luisada et al. 1974, Veith 1965, 1977). Charcot demonstrated the unconscious derivation of hysterical symptoms and suggested its relation to trauma. He also discussed its presence in men as well as in women. But the clearest relationship between hysterical symptoms and earlier psychological and physical traumas was presented by Breuer and Freud in their "Studies on Hysteria" (1895).

Using the early methods of psychoanalysis, Breuer and Freud explored hysterical symptoms in terms of associated memories and fantasies and found that earlier psychological traumas provided the contents that were reenacted symbolically or indirectly in the symptoms of hysteria. These traumatic events often involved a sexual situation in which the person was involuntarily aroused, in which such excitement was both excessive and incompatible with moral standards. Emotions and impulses to act were strong, yet warded off by defenses. The pressure for expression, together with defensive distortions of expression, was seen as the cause of symptoms that emerged long after the evocative life situation. An emotionally charged recollection of the traumatic memories and a working-through of previously incompatible ideas relieved the symptoms.

Breuer and Freud noted the psychological traumas that could precipitate such diverse hysterical symptoms as recurrent visual hallucinations, emotional outbursts, paralyses, compulsive movements, and other sensory or motor disturbances. They also discovered that there was frequently a latent period between the occurrence of a stressful event and the onset of symptoms. Once symptoms formed, however, there was a remarkable tendency toward recurrence or persistence long after the event's termination and its immediate effects. In addition, there was often a bland denial of the meaning of symptoms, which was called *la belle indifférence.*

Freud made many theoretical revisions after the initial psychoanalytic discoveries of the traumatic basis of hysterical symptoms. He was at first dismayed to find that memories of childhood seduction, the primary trauma in his theory, were not always true memories but occasionally fantasy elaborations of childhood situations (E. Jones 1953). Thus, the traumatic event did not always represent an external stress alone. It also involved internal components and might produce virtually any symptomatic picture, not just hysterical syndromes (Freud 1920).

Through the elaborations and corrections of the theory, the concept of trauma became generalized. And as psychoanalysis developed, trauma and familial strain were regarded as the causes of various symptoms, conflicts, fixations, character traits, defenses, and adaptive and maladaptive cognitive and affective developments (Bibring 1943, Fenichel 1945). This generalization of trauma as an explanatory concept necessitated the description of its many variations. An array of terms resulted, including multiple, strain, cumulative, screen, bad-object, fantasy, and retrospective traumas (Fairbairn 1954, Freud 1937, Furst 1967, Glover 1929, Greenacre 1952, Sachs 1967, Sears 1936, and Stern 1961). Despite this diffusion of terminology and theory, clinicians did agree on some key findings. One of these discoveries was the phenomenon that after a traumatic event there is a compulsive tendency to repeat some aspect of the experience (Freud 1914b, 1920, Schur 1966). This involuntary repetition includes the recurrence of thoughts and especially images about the stress event, of feelings related to the original experience, and of behavioral reenactments of parts of the experience itself. Repetitions in thought may take many forms, including nightmares, dreams, hallucinations, pseudohallucinations, recurrent unbidden images, illusions, and recurrent obsessive ideas.

Harry's images of the dead woman's body, as discussed in Chapter 1, are one example. Emotional repetitions may occur with or without clear conscious awareness of their conceptual associations. Behavioral reenactments range from compulsive verbalizations of the event through recurrent expressions of it in gesture, movement, or artistic productions, to patterning of interpersonal relations. The trauma may be symbolically repeated over and over again. Finally, there are several repetitive physiological responses to stress: behavioral or cognitive repetitions may include recurrence of stress-related physiological responses such as sweating, tremor, palpitations, or other autonomic symptoms.

Involuntary repetitions may occur despite conscious efforts to avoid and suppress them, but they are not necessarily static replicas of the original experience. A series of successive revisions in content and form is frequently noted in clinical studies. Such repetitions may eventually lose their intrusive and involuntary nature; the change in content and reduced intrusiveness indicates that there has been a progressive mastery of the experience. But unfortunately this does not always happen, and in some persons these intrusive repetitions persist indefinitely.

The involuntary repetition of stress-relevant contents may be a sharp contrast with its ostensible opposite: the massive ideational denial of the event and general emotional numbness. Menninger (1954) called this hypersuppression the most normal and the most prevalent of defenses. Warding off thoughts about the stress event or its implications may alternate with intrusive repetitions in a variety of phasic relationships. Denial and numbness may occur over a given time span of hours or days, alternating with phases of ideational intrusion and emotional pangs. There also may be intrusive repetitions of one aspect of a stress event, with simultaneous denial and numbing of another implication of the event (intrusion of fearful themes, for example, with inhibitions of the experience of guilty themes).

The very early writings on psychological stress and trauma contained the essential elements later amplified in the modern literature, which will be cited in later chapters. To recapitulate, early studies indicated that major stress events tend to be followed by involuntary repetition in thought, emotion, and behavior. Such responses tend to occur in phases and to alternate with periods of relatively successful warding off of repetitions, as indicated by ideational denial and emotional numbness. The common clinical observations of posttraumatic response tendencies are summarized in Table 2–1.

SYMPTOMS

During *intrusive* states, mental images in any sensory modality (visual, auditory, olfactory) may form as if they were real perceptions (Horowitz 1983). A variety of imagery experiences are quite important in stress disorders (Brett and Ostroff 1985). In a *hallucinatory* experience, the person has sensations that he or she interprets as real but that have no external basis. In a *pseudohallucination*, the person sees the vivid subjective images as false signals of external reality but nonetheless responds emotionally as if they were real. These *unbidden images*, whether hallucinatory, pseudohallucinatory, illusory, or mnemonic, include sensing the presence of others who may have died during the traumatic event. And these images may be the source of paranormal phenomena, such as seeing or hearing ghosts of the deceased.

Such unbidden images tend to occur most frequently when the person relaxes, lies down to sleep, or closes her eyes to rest. Vivid sensory images occurring during periods of rest or relaxation constitute a *hypnagogic* phenomenon. A similar occurrence when awakening is called a *hypnopompic* phenomenon. These frightening experiences may lead to *anticipatory anxiety* about their recurrence or

Table 2-1. Common Clinical Observations in Post-Tramatic Reactions

	Denial States	Intrusive States
Perception and attention	Daze Selective inattention Inability to appreciate significance of stimuli	Hypervigilance, startle reactions Sleep and dream disturbances
Consciousness of ideas and feelings related to the event	Amnesia (complete or partial) Non-contemplation of topics that ought to be considered because of implications of the stressor event	Intrusive-repetitive thoughts, emotions, and behaviors (illusions, pseudo-hallucinations, nightmares, unbidden images, and ruminations) Feeling pressured, confused, or disorganized when thinking about event-related themes
Information processing	Disavowal of meanings of current stimuli in some way associated with the event Loss of realistic sense of appropriate connection with the ongoing world Constriction of range of thought Inflexibility of purpose Major use of fantasies to counteract real conditions	Overgeneralization of stimuli so that they seem as if related to event Preoccupation with event-related themes with inability to concentrate on other topics
Emotional attributes	Numbness	Emotional "attacks" or "pangs" of affect related to the event or to reminders
Action patterns	Frantic overactivity Withdrawal Failure to decide how to respond to consequences of event	Compulsive repetitions of actions associated with the event or of search for lost persons or situations
Somatic attributes	Avoidant sleeping; lethargy; hibernative states	Altered activities, usually hyper-arousal of the autonomic nervous system with felt sensations such as bowel pain, diarrhea, constipation, fatigue, headache, muscle pain, cramps, tremors, intense startle reactions, palpitations, high pulse rate, hypertension, restlessness

to *secondary anxiety* if the subject interprets the phenomenon as a sign of losing control or "going crazy."

Patients can immediately be reassured that hypnogogic phenomena and other unbidden perceptual and other imagery experiences are not serious portents of psychosis but are common in those who have experienced traumatic events. Reassurance is especially useful if denial states have created a latency period before the onset of an intrusive phase of response. In such instances, intrusive experiences come as a major surprise to a person who believes that she has already "mastered" the stressful life event.

In regard to perception and attention, the daze and selective inattention of the denial states contrast with the excessive alertness and startle reactions of the intrusive states. Denial experiences may include staring blankly into space, and even avoiding the faces of others who can provide emotional support. There may also be a narrowing of focus and a failure to react appropriately to new stimuli, with a sometimes stubborn adherence to tasks and stimuli considered important before the new and drastic changes in the life situation occurred. As well, there may be an accompanying inner sense of clouding of perception, with a feeling that the world has become gray, less colorful than before. This clouding of consciousness may include a diminished awareness of bodily sensations, even a feeling of being "dead in life" (Lifton 1967).

This brings us to two important symptoms: (1) the sense of numbness that may be present during the denial phase and (2) its opposite, pangs of strong emotion that may characterize an intrusive phase. Numbness as a symptom is not simply an absence of emotions; it is a sense of being "benumbed." The individual may actually feel surrounded by a layer of cotton or insulation. This emotional blunting may alter patterns of interaction with support systems, affecting family life, friendship, and work relationships. Members of the support network may be offended by this alteration in the nature of their relationship with the patient and so withdraw, reducing the person's support just when she most needs it.

These kinds of experiences or signs do not sharply differentiate the normal or abnormal responses to serious life events. Rather,
along with the diagnosis of mental disorder, they are a matter of
degree and, to some extent, of personal as well as social value judg-
ment and labeling. Table 2–2 illustrates the relationship among common routes of response to serious life events and the pathological
intensifications of each phase, which lead, in some instances, to the
diagnosis of a mental disorder such as Post-Traumatic Stress Disorder. Note that the route indicated suggests a general phasic tendency between denial and intrusions, across populations and types
of stress events. This general tendency toward phases of response is
reinforced by empirical findings when studied in groups but has
many individual and situational variations (Horowitz et al. 1980a,
Zilberg et al. 1982).

The frequency and intensity of these intrusive and denial signs
and symptoms can be examined quantitatively, by obtaining a self-
report form, using common assertions, and asking any new subject

Table 2–2. Phases of Response to Stress

Stress Response States	Pathological Stress
Event	
Outcry	Panic; exhaustion; dissociation; reactive psychosis
Denial — Excessively intense or prolonged	Maladaptive avoidance (suicide, drugs, counterphobic acts); delayed stress reaction; depression
Intrusion	Prolonged post-traumatic reaction
Working through → Blocked	Psychosomatic reaction; maladaptive behavior pattern
Completion → Not reached	Personality disorder or constriction with inability to act or love

to agree whether or not that assertion could be made about her experiences during the past week. Clinicians can also judge the presence or intensity of a sign or symptom by using a rating scale. The Impact of Event Scale (Horowitz et al. 1979, Zilberg et al. 1982) measures the former, and the Stress Response Rating Scale (Horowitz et al. 1980, Weiss et al. 1984) measures the latter.

Using these instruments on a series of sixty-six consecutive cases in our clinic treatment of stress response syndromes, we summarized the comparative frequencies and intensities of the various intrusive and denial experiences and manifest patterns. These data are summarized in Tables 2–3 and 2–4.

Both the self-report and the clinician's rating scale allow separate scores for intrusive and avoidance or denial experiences. In another study, we compared the mean scores of thirty-eight patients for whom the inciting serious life event for a stress response syndrome was exposure to violence directed at the self and forty-three cases for whom the inciting event was the death of a close relative or very close friend. There were no significant differences in the group mean scores on intrusion or avoidance in these groups, thus agreeing with the assertions made in this book that these are general stress response tendencies. But there were a few differences on specific items: The group exposed to violence reported more efforts to remove the event from conscious remembrance and more efforts not to allow their thoughts to turn to the event. The group who had experienced deaths often reported that they felt as if the event had not been real, or at least not completely real. Similarly, on the clinician's ratings, the group exposed to actual or severely threatened violence was rated as having more symptoms of hypervigilance, startle reactions, and more impairing bad dreams. Again, on most items there were comparably high scores that did not differentiate the groups. The data for these findings are presented in Tables 2–5 and 2–6. The scales are worded exactly as given to patients and clinicians. The stress response rating scale has been expanded to forty

Table 2–3. Impact of Event Scale: Experiences Reported by Sixty-six Subjects with Stress Response Syndromes (from Horowitz, Wilner, Kaltreider, et al., 1980)

		GROUP	
	%[a]	MEAN[b]	SD
Intrusion Items			
I had waves of strong feelings about it.	88	3.8	1.9
Things I saw or heard suddenly reminded me of it.	85	3.7	1.9
I thought about it when I didn't mean to.	76	3.3	2.2
Images related to it popped into my mind.	76	3.2	2.2
Any reminder brought back emotions related to it.	76	3.0	2.1
I have difficulty falling asleep because of images or thoughts related to the event.	64	2.6	2.4
I had bad dreams related to the event.	44	1.7	2.2
Avoidance Items			
I knew that a lot of unresolved feelings were still there, but I kept them under wraps.	71	3.0	2.2
I avoided letting myself get emotional when I thought about it or was reminded of it.	70	2.8	2.1
I wished to banish it from my store of memories.	65	2.8	2.3
I made an effort to avoid talking about it.	61	2.2	2.0
I felt unrealistic about it, as if it hadn't happened or as if it wasn't real.	58	2.2	2.3
I stayed away from things or situations that might remind me of it.	53	2.2	2.3
My emotions related to it were kind of numb.	59	2.1	2.1
I didn't let myself have thoughts related to it.	50	1.8	2.2

a Percent positive endorsement.
b On a scale of intensity where 5 is severe; 3, moderate; 1, mild; 0, not at all (within the past seven days).

Table 2–4. Stress Response Rating Scale: Signs and Symptoms Reported by Clinicians for Sixty-six Subjects with Stress Response Syndromes (from Horowitz, Wilner, Kaltreider, et al., 1980)

	%[a]	GROUP MEAN[b]	SD
Intrusion Items			
Pangs of emotion	95	3.1	1.3
Rumination or preoccupation	90	2.9	1.4
Fear of losing bodily control or hyperactivity in any bodily system	82	2.6	1.5
Intrusive ideas (in word form)	77	2.3	1.5
Difficulty in dispelling ideas	74	2.1	1.6
Hypervigilance	69	1.6	1.4
Bad dreams	54	1.6	1.7
Intrusive thoughts or images when trying to sleep	51	1.6	1.8
Reenactments	57	1.5	1.5
Intrusive images	51	1.4	1.6
Startle reactions	34	0.6	1.0
Illusions	26	0.6	1.1
Hallucinations, pseudohallucinations	8	0. 2	0.8
Denial Items			
Numbness	69	1.8	1.5
Avoidance of associational connections	69	1.7	1.4
Reduced level of feeling responses to outer stimuli	67	1.7	1.5
Rigidly role adherent or stereotyped	62	1.5	1.5
Loss of reality appropriateness of thought by switching attitudes	64	1.4	1.2
Unrealistic narrowing of attention, vagueness, or disavowal of stimuli	52	1.2	1.3
Inattention, daze	48	1.2	1.5
Inflexibility or constriction of thought	46	1.0	1.2
Loss of trains of thought	44	0.9	1.2
Loss of reality appropriateness of thought by sliding meanings	41	0.8	1.2
Memory failure	34	0.8	1.2
Loss of reality appropriateness of thought by use of disavowal	25	0.6	1.2
Warding off trains of reality-oriented thought by use of fantasy	15	0.3	0.8

a Percent positive endorsement.

b On a scale of intensity where 5 is major: 3. moderate; 1 minor; 0, not present (within the past seven days).

Table 2–5. Impact of Event Scale: Self-Reports

On _____ you experienced _____.
    (date)   (life event)

Below is a list of comments made by people after stressful life events. Please check each item, indicating how frequently these comments were true for you *during the past seven days*. If they did not occur during that time, please mark the "not at all" column.

| | MEAN ENDORSEMENT | |
	VIOLENCE GROUP (n = 38)	DEATH GROUP (n = 43)
1. I thought about it when I didn't mean to.	3.39	3.64
2. I avoided letting myself get upset when I thought about it or was reminded of it.	3.32	2.88
3. I tried to remove it from memory.	3.50	1.95[a]
4. I had trouble falling asleep or staying asleep.	3.00	2.67
5. I had waves of strong feelings about it.	3.95	3.60
6. I had dreams about it.	1.87	1.09[b]
7. I stayed away from reminders of it.	2.66	2.12
8. I felt as if it hadn't happened or it wasn't real.	1.18	2.05[a]
9. I tried not to talk about it.	2.59	2.33
10. Pictures about it popped into my mind.	3.35	3.39
11. Other things kept making me think about it.	3.29	3.53
12. I was aware that I still had a lot of feelings about it, but I didn't deal with them.	3.16	3.52
13. I tried not to think about it.	3.34	2.40[a]
14. Any reminder brought back feelings about it.	3.78	3.77
15. My feelings about it were kind of numb.	2.26	2.53

Note: Intrusion subset = 1, 4, 5, 6, 10, 11 ,14; avoidance subset = 2, 3, 7,8, 9, 12, 13, 15. Mean scores on each item are based on a 5-point scale, where 0 = not experienced, 1 = rarely experienced, 3 = sometimes experienced, and 5 = often experienced during the last week.
a Value significantly different from value in violence group.
b Value marginally significantly different from value in violence group.

Table 2–6. Stress Response Rating Scale: Clinicians' Ratings

Directions: Please judge the degree to which the following signs and symptoms describe the patient *within the last seven days only*. Do not spend too much time deciding about any one item. Base your judgments on either the history as reported, or your own observations. Check the appropriate line for each item. If you have absolutely no information for a particular item, and the not-present response might inaccurately describe the subject's condition, then use the no-information response, but use it sparingly. Scores are based on degree of presence with 0 = not present, 1 = minor, 3 = moderate, 5 = major.

| | MEAN ENDORSEMENT | |
| | VIOLENCE GROUP | DEATH GROUP |
SYMPTOM	(n = 38)	(n = 41)
1. *Hypervigilance*: Excessively alert, overly scanning the surrounding environment, overly aroused in perceptual searching, tensely expectant.	2.38	0.56[a]
2. *Startle reactions*: Flinching after noises, unusual orienting reactions, blanching or otherwise reacting to stimuli that usually do not warrant such responses.	1.09	0.42[a]
3. *Illusions or misperceptions*: A misappraisal of a person, object, or scene as something or someone else (e.g., a bush is seen for a moment as a person; a person is misrecognized as someone else).	0.57	0.52
4. *Intrusive thoughts or images when trying to sleep*: Unwelcome and unbidden mental contents that may be difficult to dispel; include trains of thought that begin volitionally but develop an out-of-control quality.	2.22	1.43
5. *Bad dreams*: Any dreams experienced as unpleasant, not just the classical nightmare with anxious awakenings.	2.11	1.13[a]
6. *Hallucinations, pseudohallucinations*: An emotional reaction to imagined stimuli, experienced as if it were real, regardless of the person's belief in its reality. "Felt presences" of others as well as sensations of smell, taste, touch, movement, sound, and vision are included, along with out-of-body experiences.	0.29	0.75
7. *Intrusive images while awake*: Unbidden sensations which occur in a nonvolitional manner either in visual or other sensory systems. Awareness of these images is unwanted and occurs suddenly.	2.06	2.31

(continued)

Table 2–6. (Continued)

| SYMPTOM | MEAN ENDORSEMENT | |
	VIOLENCE GROUP (n = 38)	DEATH GROUP (n = 41)
8. *Intrusive thoughts or feelings while awake*: Unwilled entries of simple ideas or trains of thought and feeling taking unwilled directions.	2.08	2.68
9. *Reenactments*: Any behavior that repeats any aspects of the serious life event, from minor tic-like movements and gestures to acting out in major movements and sequences, including retelling the event. Repeated enactments of personal responses to the life event, whether or not they actually occurred at the time of the event.	0.94	0.77
10. *Rumination or preoccupation*: Continuous conscious awareness about the event and associations to the event that go beyond ordinary thinking through. The key characteristic is a sense of uncontrolled repetition.	2.77	2.90
11. *Difficulty in dispelling thoughts and feelings*: Once a thought or feeling has come to mind, even if it was deliberate, awareness of it cannot be stopped.	2.2	2.68
12. *Pangs of emotion*: A wave of feeling that increases and then decreases rather than remaining constant.	2.89	3.08

a Value significantly different from value in violence group.

signs and symptoms. The additions go beyond intrusive items to include denial items and general stress reactivity. Table 2–7 lists the additional items.

COMMON THEMES

Any event is appraised and assimilated in relation to the past history and the current cognitive and emotional set of the person who experiences it, and therefore it produces idiosyncratic responses.

Table 2–7. Other Symptoms of Stress for Clinician Rating on the Stress Response Rating Scale

13. *Fears or sensations of losing bodily control*: Sensations of urinating, vomiting, or defecating without will, fear of suffocating, fear of being unable to control voluntary behavior as well as somatic responses such as sweating, diarrhea, tachycardia.
14. *Inattention, daze*: Staring off into space, failure to determine the significance of stimuli, flatness of response to stimuli.
15. *Memory failure*: Inability to recall expectable details, sequences of event, or specific events.
16. *Loss of train of thought*: Temporary or micromomentary lapses in continuation of a communication, or report of inability to concentrate on a train of thought.
17. *Numbness*: Sense of not having feelings, or being "benumbed." (*Note*: Either patient report or your inference is acceptable here.)
18. *Sense of unreality*: Experiences of depersonalization, derealization, or altered sense of time and place.
19. *Withdrawal*: Feelings or actions indicating social isolation, or experiences of being isolated and detached.
20. *Misdirection of feelings*: Displacement of positive or negative feelings.
21. *Excessive use of alcohol or drugs*: Avoidance of implications of the event by increased usage. Alcohol: excessive usage. Drugs: abuse of prescription agents, as well as abuse of other drugs, legal and illegal.
22. *Inhibition of thinking*: Attempts to block thinking about the event. Success or awareness of the attempt is not a consideration.
23. *Unrealistic distortion of meanings*: Effects of the event on day-to-day living are inaccurately appraised.
24. *Excessive sleeping*: Avoidance of implications of the event by increased sleeping as well as by simply staying in bed.
25. *Avoidance of reminders*: Staying away from certain places, foods, or activities; avoiding photographs or other mementos.
26. *Seeking of distracting stimulation or activity*: Avoidance of the implications of the event by seeking excessive exposure to external stimuli or activities such as television, loud music, fast driving, sexual activity, voracious reading, or other diversions.
27. *Hyperactivity*: Fidgeting, markedly increased pace of activity, inability to slow down or stop sequences of actions; periods of frenzied activity.
28. *Retarded pace of actions*: Psychomotor retardation; clear slowing, either continuous or episodic, of thought or behavior.
29. *Tremors or tics*: Tremors or tics, including about the eyes and mouth. (*Note*: Basis of tremor or tic as neurological or characterological is irrelevant.)
30. *Clumsiness or carelessness*: Dropping objects, bumping into furniture, actions that are more than awkward.

(*continued*)

Table 2–7. (*Continued*)

31. *Autonomic hyperarousal*: Sweating, palpitations, frequent urination, altered skin color, altered pupil size, or other autonomic signs.
32. *Troubled sleep*: Inability to fall and stay asleep; bad feelings about or during sleep.
33. *Restlessness or agitation*: Report of inner sensations of agitation or action and behavior which is restless or agitated.
34. *Excited states*: Thought and action are dominated by excessively high rate of arousal, information processing, and expression. May include excessively high levels of sexuality, creativity, productivity, exercise.
35. *Self-hatred*: Uncontrollable suicidal preoccupation or gestures, self-loathing, or hostility toward a part of the body.
36. *Rage at others*: Uncontrollable hostility and anger, even if the target is unclear.
37. *Panic or disintegration*: Periods of high pressure, confusion, chaos, anxiety, and purposelessness.
38. *Sadness*: Uncontrollable sadness or grief; floods of despair, longing, pining, or hopelessness.
39. *Guilt or shame*: Out-of-control experience of remorse, sense of wrongdoing, or exposure of personal evil or defectiveness.
40. *Irritability or touchiness*: Relations with peers, children, or strangers that are either inwardly irritating or outwardly abrupt, hostile, and bristling.

Human beings are as similar as they are different, however, and there seem to be certain fairly universal conflicts between wishes and realities after stress events such as accidental injuries, illnesses, and losses. Clinical studies reveal at least nine themes as common problems during the process of working through stressful life events. Such thematic contents may occur as intrusive ideas, deliberately contemplated ideas, or warded-off ideas.

Fear of Repetition

Any event that occurs once may recur; yet the anticipation of repeating painful stress events conflicts with the wish to avoid displeasure. Persons not only fear a real repetition; they also fear repetition in thought and emotion.

States of mind colored by fear are much like states of mind colored by anxiety, as observed in bodily sensations and felt emotions. The main difference between the two sets of states is the nature of the thoughts and how they appraise external situations. When an external situation is judged in reality to be very threatening or dangerous, then the emotional quality may be labeled as fear; when the situation is judged as not really threatening, the affect is labeled as anxiety. Matters become complex because persons fear anxiety and are anxious about fear. And they become even more complex in regard to who judges how threatening the external situation really is to the particular individual or to the average individual.

It is in this context of the fear of repetition that problems of diagnosing develop. Many of the same signs and symptoms that characterize a phobic disorder may be found in a post-traumatic stress disorder. The fear of repetition leads persons to develop a phobic anxiety with any stimulus that can be associated to the previous traumatic event and to engage in a variety of marked withdrawal procedures. A person who has had an accident on the street may develop a phobic reaction not only to the specific street corner but also to any street corner and to traffic and may even withdraw into her home and be labeled as agoraphobic.

Sometimes a peripheral stimulus present during the traumatic event, such as the fragrance of flowers that was noticed at the scene of a previous attack in the park, may trigger a sudden fear response when the fragrance is smelled again. This may lead to a panic attack, with full-blown symptoms of pounding heart, weak knees, and choking sensations. At other times, there is no sudden acceleration of alarm responses but, rather, a constant sense of foreboding, impending doom, and a nameless dread constituting chronic anxiety. Sometimes the specific fear of repetition is relatively unconscious; only the dread seeps into conscious awareness. Then the anxiety is not associated with the memory of the stressful life event or the concern that it might be repeated.

Fear of Merger with Victims

Like the fear of repetition, there can also be a fear of the reen-actment of events in which the injured person is now the self rather than the other person. For example, if one sees a suicide, one may fear committing suicide oneself.

Shame and Rage over Vulnerability

The expectation of personal omnipotence or total control is unrealistic but is nonetheless a universal hope and sometimes a deeply felt personal belief. Both the failure to prevent a stress event such as an accident and the weakness that may follow an event such as an illness are regarded as a loss of control and conflict with the wish for power and mastery. Persons who have had a heart attack or back injury, for example, may apologize profusely because they cannot carry out garbage cans, or they may unwisely carry them out to avoid a sense of shame for either shirking their duty or feeling useless. After a fire has burned down the family house, parents may feel deflated in the eyes of their children because their life is now uncomfort-able, with smaller quarters and economic difficulties. Magical think-ing often extends such irrational attitudes so that the inability to master a stressful event is regarded as equivalent to a regression to infantile helplessness.

Rage at the Source

Rage is a natural response to frustration. One important theme after stress events is anger with any symbolic figure who can be construed as responsible, however irrational this may seem. A pa-tient may become angry with a doctor who tells him the bad news that a diagnostic study has revealed a serious and unexpected ill-ness. A mother who cuts her finger while slicing meat may feel an impulse to say to a nearby child, "See what you made me do." Asking why it happened and why me, after a stress event, is usually associated with the need to find out who is to blame and who should be punished.

Rage frequently will conflict with a sense of social morality. For instance, a person may feel rage toward a friend who has fallen ill; this rage conflicts with the recognition that the illness is not the friend's fault and that he needs help, not blame.

A less obvious but often important instance of rage at the source is the theme of resentment toward a person who has died. At an unconscious level, the deceased may be regarded not as a passive agent who has died but, rather, as an active agent who has deliberately abandoned the survivor. Thoughts directed toward the deceased are expressed as "How could you have left me now?" Knowing consciously and intellectually that the death was not deliberate may not prevent such an emotional and transient response. These themes may be based in part on unconscious views from childhood that parental figures will always be there, are omnipotent, and so can prevent bad things from happening to themselves if they really wanted to.

Rage at Those Exempted

If one has suffered a loss, perhaps the death of a loved one, it is possible to feel angry with those others—no matter how sympathetic they may be—whose loved ones remain alive. Such responses can range from envy to hatred and destructive wishes, even though such ideas seem irrational, undesirable, and unthinkable to the person who experiences them.

Fear of Loss of Control of Aggressive Impulses

There is another conflict between the destructive fantasies mentioned above and the wish to remain in control, and that is the fear that one will impulsively act out one's fantasies in an out-of-control manner. For example, a soldier traumatized by repeated combat experiences often fears, upon his return to civilian life, that he will physically attack persons who only slightly provoke him.

Guilt or Shame over Aggressive Impulses

The rage alluded to above often extends to destructive fantasies directed toward anyone symbolically connected to the stressful event. When violence is a part of the event, this itself seems to stimulate generalized aggression. The aroused hostility conflicts with a sense of conscience and leads to feelings of guilt or shame.

The urgent need to stare at a potential threat is another impulse that can evoke guilt or shame. This instinctive investigative gesture would seem to be free of conflict, but when other persons are the victims, it is not. For example, there may be severe bodily damage to others killed in an accident, in which both social convention and natural revulsion dictate looking away from maimed bodies or covering them up. Staring at dead bodies seems, to the person who does it, to be an unwarranted aggression. The memory of such episodes of compulsive looking can lead to anxiety or guilt if the person feels that he was morbidly curious and thus fails to recognize the presence of an intrinsic need to gain information about a potential threat.

Guilt or Shame over Surviving

When others have been injured or killed, it is a relief to realize that one has been spared. Once again, at a level of magical thinking there is a common irrational belief that destiny chooses an allotment of victims, as in the placation of primitive gods through human sacrifice. If one has eluded the Fates, it may seem to have been unfairly at the expense of other victims. The wish to be a survivor conflicts with moral attitudes toward sharing social pain, leading to self-castigation for being selfish.

Sadness over Losses

Any painful stress event contains an element of loss that conflicts with the universal wish for life permanence, safety, and satisfaction. The loss may be another person, an external resource, or an aspect of the self. Naturally, some losses are both symbolic and real. A person who has been laid off from work, not for personal reasons, but because a plant has closed, may suffer a loss of self-esteem because she has been prevented from working.

The frequency of these stress-related themes can be determined for stressed populations by defining their ideational and emotional components and independently rating their occurrence in clinical material (Krupnick and Horowitz 1981). Such studies indicate these themes' presence in many kinds of traumatic life events.

As mentioned earlier, these nine themes provide the ideational and emotional contents that are commonly warded off in periods of denial or are intrusive in periods of compulsive repetition. Any one of these themes merges the current stress event with earlier conflicts over previous stress events. Guilt over hostile impulses is too common in everyone's past history to be a theme unique to a current trauma. Rather, the current event will be emotionally associated to previous memories and fantasies of guilt over excessive hostility. Such blending of themes leads to a diagnostic dilemma requiring determination of how much of a given problem is due to the recent life event, however stressful, and how much is due to earlier developments.

DIAGNOSTIC PROBLEMS

Investigations of syndromes occurring after stressful life events demonstrate the intermingling of elements from earlier unresolved conflicts with response elements related to the recent experience

(Greenacre 1952, Murphy 1961, Solomon et al. 1971, Windholz 1945). Given that all psychological manifestations are determined by multiple causes, the question of diagnosis becomes one of the relative weights of possible etiological factors. The main problem is the existence, nature, and etiological importance of general stress response tendencies, as contrasted with idiosyncratic or person-specific variations in response to stress. This problem has proved to be so difficult that before *DSM-III* there was no really adequate diagnostic category for Traumatic Neuroses in the formal nomenclature.

In the official (1952) American psychiatric nomenclature (*DSM-I*) and in the 1968 revision (*DSM-II*), neuroses that followed major external stress events were classified according to their presenting symptoms, as were other types of neuroses, such as anxiety neurosis, obsessive compulsive neurosis, or hysterical neurosis. In *DSM-I*, symptomatic responses to very stressful experiences could also be classified as Gross Stress Reactions, but this category was later deleted in the *DSM-II* of 1968. The appropriate categorization became Transient Situational Disturbances, with subheadings of adjustment reaction of adult, adolescent, or childhood life.

Despite such vague official diagnostic definitions in the psychiatric literature, courtrooms, and case conferences, the diagnosis of traumatic neurosis was used frequently, and most agreed on what the term meant (Keiser 1969). For example, in Hinsie and Campbell's *Psychiatric Dictionary* (1960), traumatic neurosis was defined as having the following features:

> (1) fixation on the trauma with amnesia for the traumatic situation which may be total or partial; (2) typical dreamlife (dreams of annihilation, aggression dreams where the patient is the aggressor but is defeated, frustration or Sisyphus dreams, and occupational dreams in which it is the means of livelihood rather than the body-ego which is annihilated); (3) contraction of the general level of functioning, with constant fear of the environment, disorganized behavior, lowered efficiency, lack of coordinated goal activities, and profoundly altered functioning in the autonomic motor and sensory

nervous system; (4) general irritability; and (5) a proclivity to explosive aggressive reactions. [p. 497]

The term "fixation on trauma" in the preceding definition refers to the same phenomena that are labeled in Moore and Fine's *Glossary of Psychoanalytic Terms* (1968) as "repetition compulsion," in the following psychoanalytic definition of traumatic neurosis:

> A neurosis in which overwhelming tension and painful affects, such as anxiety or guilt related to a traumatic experience, can be mastered by the usual defenses of the ego. Pathological and archaic ego mechanisms are set in motion which determine a clinical picture dominated by somatic features and a repetition compulsion forcibly bringing to mind the original trauma. Symptoms include marked emotional lability, with uncontrollable discharges of anxiety, fear, or rage; severe disturbances of sleep, with typical dreams in which the trauma is painfully re-experienced; and mental repetitions in the waking state of the traumatic situation, in whole or in part, in the form of fantasies, thoughts, or feelings. Psychological mastery of the trauma is usually accompanied by recession of the traumatic elements and increasing prominence of psychoneurotic symptoms. [p. 94]

These kinds of clinical summations and the first edition of this work (Horowitz 1976) led to the *DSM-III*'s inclusion of the diagnosis of Post Traumatic Stress Disorder. The diagnostic criteria, as revised for *DSM-IV*, are summarized in Table 2–8. The criteria for acute stress are included for comparison purposes. The most frequently cited diagnosis in the set of categories applicable to stress response syndromes is PTSD. In a future revision of *DSM* it will be part of Stress Response Syndromes instead of Anxiety Disorders, along with Acute Stress Disorder, Adjustment Disorder, Complicated Grief Disorder, and others.

Intrusive thoughts and feelings are not unique to Post Traumatic Stress Disorder. They are a sign of strain to psychological systems and may occur in a variety of disorders. Some diagnostic issues are illustrated in the following case vignette.

Table 2–8. Post Traumatic and Acute Stress Disorders

Post Traumatic Stress Disorder	Acute Stress Disorder
A. The person has been exposed to a traumatic event in which both of the following were present: 1. The person experienced, witnessed, or was confronted with an event or events that involved actual or threatened death or serious injury, or a threat to the physical integrity of self or others. 2. The person's response involved intense fear, helplessness, or horror. *Note:* In children, this may be expressed instead by disorganized or agitated behavior.	A. The person has been exposed to a traumatic event in which both of the following were present: 1. The person experienced, witnessed, or was confronted with an event or events that involved actual or threatened death or serious injury, or a threat to the physical integrity of self or others. 2. The person's response involved intense fear, helplessness, or horror.
B. The traumatic event is persistently reexperienced in one (or more) of the following ways: 1. Recurrent and intrusive distressing recollections of the event, including images, thoughts, or perceptions. *Note:* In young children, repetitive play may occur in which themes or aspects of the trauma are expressed. 2. Recurrent distressing dreams of the event. *Note:* In children, there may be frightening dreams without recognizable content. 3. Acting or feeling as if the traumatic event were recurring (includes a sense of reliving the experience, illusions, hallucinations, and dissociative flashback episodes, including those that occur on awakening or when intoxicated). *Note:* In young children, trauma-specific reenactment may occur. 4. Intense psychological distress at exposure to internal or external cues that symbolize or resemble an aspect of the traumatic event.	B. Either while experiencing or after experiencing the distressing event, the individual has three (or more) of the following dissociative symptoms: 1. A subjective sense of numbing, detachment, or absence of emotional responsiveness 2. A reduction in awareness of his or her surroundings (e.g., "being in a daze") 3. Derealization 4. Depersonalization 5. Dissociative amnesia (*i.e.*, inability to recall an important aspect of the trauma)

(continued)

Table 2–8. (Continued)

Post Traumatic Stress Disorder	Acute Stress Disorder
5. Physiological reactivity on exposure to internal or external cues that symbolize or resemble an aspect of the traumatic event.	
C. Persistent avoidance of stimuli associated with the trauma and numbing of general responsiveness (not present before the trauma), as indicated by three (or more) of the following:	C. The traumatic event is persistently reexperienced in at least one of the following ways: recurrent images, thoughts, dreams, illusions, flashback episodes, or a sense of reliving the experience; or distress on exposure to reminders of the traumatic event.

C. Persistent avoidance of stimuli associated with the trauma and numbing of general responsiveness (not present before the trauma), as indicated by three (or more) of the following:

1. Efforts to avoid thoughts, feelings, or conversations associated with the trauma.
2. Efforts to avoid activities, places, or people that arouse recollections of the trauma.
3. Inability to recall an important aspect of the trauma.
4. Markedly diminished interest or participation in significant activities.
5. Feeling of detachment or estrangement from others.
6. Restricted range of affect (*e.g.*, unable to have loving feelings).
7. Sense of a foreshortened future (*e.g.*, does not expect to have a career, marriage, children, or a normal life span).

D. Persistent symptoms of increased arousal (not present before the trauma), as indicated by two (or more) of the following:

1. Difficulty falling or staying asleep
2. Irritability or outbursts of anger
3. Difficulty concentrating-
4. Hypervigilance
5. Exaggerated startle response

D. Marked avoidance of stimuli that arouse recollections of the trauma (*e.g.*, thoughts, feelings, conversations, activities, places, people).

(continued)

Table 2–8. (*Continued*)

Post Traumatic Stress Disorder	Acute Stress Disorder
E. Duration of the disturbance (symptoms in Criteria B, C, and D) is more than 1 month.	E. Marked symptoms of anxiety of increased arousal (*e.g.*, difficulty sleeping, irritability, poor concentration, hypervigilance, exaggerated startle response, motor restlessness).
F. The disturbance causes clinically significant distress or impairment in social, occupational, or other important areas of functioning.	F. The disturbance causes clinically significant distress or impairment in social, occupational, or other important areas of functioning or impairs the individual's ability to pursue some necessary task, such as obtaining necessary assistance or mobilizing personal resources by telling family members about the traumatic experience.
	G. The disturbance lasts for a minimum of 2 days and a maximum of 4 weeks and occurs within 4 weeks of the traumatic event.
	H. The disturbance is not due to direct physiological effects of a substance (*e.g.*, a drug of abuse, a medication) or a general medical condition, is not better accounted for by Brief Psychotic Disorder, and is not merely an exacerbation of a preexisting Axis I or Axis II disorder.

Specify if:
   Acute: if duration of symptoms is less than 3 months
   Chronic: if duration of symptoms is 3 months or more
   With Delayed Onset: if onset of symptoms is at least
   6 months after the stressor

CASE EXAMPLE

Following his graduation from college, a 24-year-old man lived with his mother while working sporadically at jobs that he did not like. He occasionally dated but had never lived with a woman or with other roommates. He and his mother occasionally had loud verbal fights about domestic issues such as who would keep the apartment clean, and on occasion they had even been warned by the landlord that other tenants had complained about the noise.

One evening, after such an argument, his mother had crushing chest pains and shortness of breath. The young man called their family physician but reached an answering service. After some frustration, he was advised to call an ambulance to take his mother to the nearest emergency room. He became increasingly frantic when she lost consciousness and the ambulance had not yet arrived. He therefore took her to an emergency room in his own car and stayed at her side as she was wheeled to the intensive care unit. Shortly after intravenous treatment was started, monitors indicated a cessation of heartbeat. The woman was defibrillated and an airway passed into her trachea. Her son refused to leave and was pushed aside by the resuscitation team. Several urgent medical orders were given and then rescinded, and the young man wondered whether his mother was receiving adequate care.

Despite the resumption of heartbeat with defibrillation, there was again a cardiac arrest, and after a time his mother was pronounced dead. The young man wept, received some support from the emergency room staff, and then returned alone to his apartment.

For the next several days he remained at home by himself, felt sad, and occasionally cried. He then resumed his job and apparently worked well for two months but then began to function less well and was laid off. Within a few weeks he consulted a community mental health center because of depression. After the initial interview, a diagnosis of major depressive disorder was made because he had difficulty sleeping, had lost weight, had no appetite, had a loss of sexual interest, felt morose, and brooded most of the time.

After a few interviews it became apparent that his depressive symptoms seemed to be clearly related to the event of his mother's death. He reported that he had difficulty sleeping because of intrusive and repetitive images of his mother's head being yanked back while a laryngoscope was being forced, as he saw it, down her throat. He was enraged at the emergency room staff, who he felt had provided incompetent care. He blamed himself for not taking his mother more quickly to a better emergency room, without the telephone delay or waiting for an ambulance. In continued psychotherapy, he worked on the conflicted relationship with his mother, in which his ambivalence toward her before her death was also a prominent feature.

He remained angry about the care of his mother in the emergency room, sought legal advice, and brought suit against the hospital. Records of her treatment at the hospital emergency room were subpoenaed, and the defense counsel for the hospital obtained documents about the young man's treatment at the community mental health center, including the process notes of the therapeutic interviews.

In the ensuing trial, the relationship between the patient and his mother, the competency of her care in the emergency room, and the patient's reaction thereafter were the issues of concern. The following is an analysis of each of these points.

It was clear that the young man had had a somewhat turbulent relationship with his mother, with feelings of ambivalence toward her, as she had toward him, in the period before her death. This may have complicated his mourning process. In addition, the young man's personality characteristics, which included difficulty in relating to women, becoming independent, and making decisions, had led to previous episodes of depression, although he had never received a formal psychiatric diagnosis or treatment for a depressive disorder. He had, however, sought previous psychiatric consultations and had made some incomplete starts on psychotherapy in college. His emotional pain following his mother's death was partly due to these pre-event characteristics in his personality and to the ambivalence and guilt in his relationship with his mother.

In the process notes, the therapist at the community health center had recorded an interpretation made to this young man in which she had said that his anger with the hospital emergency room staff was an attempt to displace his anger with himself. This anger with himself was due to guilt over his argument with his mother and his own sense of having failed her. The therapist encouraged him to review more realistically the events leading to the death and to feel an appropriate level of remorse but not an exaggerated guilt. Even though this interpretation may have been accurate, it only indicates that there were complex themes involved in the development of this man's stress response syndrome with its phasic components of intrusion and denial.

The competency of medical care as an issue in the suit included both the degree of damage to the mother's chances of survival and the degree of damage done to the young man as he witnessed the trauma of the treatments as well as his mother's death. In reviewing the mother's treatment in the emergency room, it was established that there had been some procedural errors and omissions but that these had been rapidly corrected and were not deemed to have caused her death. There was some impression of violence in the treatment, as in the passage of the laryngoscope, but the impact of this on the young man was partly due to his refusal to follow the staff's instructions to leave the room. In this case, the actions witnessed contributed to his syndrome but not to his mother's death. Although the perceptions led to memories intrusively recalled, it was felt that the inappropriate actions by the hospital staff were not significant in causing his reaction.

If this case had turned out differently, if the hospital had been found in some way responsible for precipitating some of the young man's psychological responses, an expert opinion might then have tackled the diagnostic problems. There might have been a debate among experts on post-traumatic stress disorders, about whether this patient warranted that diagnosis. After all, his initial diagnosis in the community mental health center was that of a depressive disorder, not a post-traumatic disorder or an adjustment disorder. His experience could also be seen as a simple bereavement, once the connection to the death of his mother was established, as most people do have to sustain at some time the death of one or both parents.

The arguments for this individual's being diagnosed as having Post Traumatic Stress Disorder are that (1) the initial diagnosis of major depressive disorder was not based on the full information, (2) the death of the young man's mother was associated with visual traumatizations that had been shocking to him, and (3) his symptoms of repetitive and intrusive recollection of the emergency room scene were prominent. His reaction did involve pre-event conflicts, invariably the case to some degree, but the context of the event was of sufficient severity to warrant the diagnosis.

From this case, we find that premorbid personality is involved even with reactions to shocking, unusual, and disastrous experiences. It is especially pertinent to how a person works through these experiences and when the person emerges from a period of symptomatology. Life events that seem commonplace, such as the death of a parent, are not necessarily simple bereavements but may have traumatic features for the individual. Finally, diagnoses are not mutually exclusive; a person may satisfy several diagnoses according to the *DSM-IV*'s criteria and clinical criteria.

Post-Traumatic Stress Disorder, Chronic Type

The diagnosis of post-traumatic stress disorder, acute type, is made when the duration of symptoms is less than three months. For example, the emergence of nightmares and unbidden images regarding a rape five months after the assault itself and continuing up to seven months afterward is still considered an acute post-traumatic stress disorder. This should be differentiated from a chronic post-traumatic stress disorder in which the symptoms have lasted for three months or more. The duration of symptoms should also include the period of denial symptoms, when there has been a markedly diminished interest in activities, or feelings of detachment, estrangement, or constricted or numbed emotions. If, for example, the rape occurred in January, with a period of denial and numbing until August, followed by the onset of intrusion in September, continuing and leading to diagnosis because of continued symptoms in December, then the situation is a chronic post-traumatic stress disorder. Despite the label chronic, there may be little difference between the chronic syndrome and an acute post-traumatic stress disorder.

Delayed Post-Traumatic Stress Disorder

A delayed post-traumatic stress disorder, according to the *DSM-IV*, refers to an onset of symptoms at least six months after the trauma. This latency period is common because defensive mechanisms may restrict association to the event until the person feels at some safe distance from it. Paradoxically, this sense of now being safe, often coupled with some perceptual reminder of the event, can trigger the onset of an intrusive phase of symptoms. This period may emerge first in the form of dreams about the event and then spill over to unbidden images in the daytime. Diagnosis is made more complicated because the person's wish to deny the association to the event may impede full expression of the association of ideas and feelings, so that the current symptomatology may not be related clearly to the event now more distant in time.

Chronicity

Despite the *DSM-IV*'s differentiation of acute, chronic, and delayed post-traumatic stress disorders, the actual clinical experience of them may be similar, whether or not the symptoms reach prominence within the first six months following the trauma, the second six months, or thereafter. Anniversary reactions, exactly one year after the event, may also evoke the beginning of an apparent post-traumatic stress disorder. The issue of chronicity arises when the disturbance goes on for several years or emerges after a delay of several years. In such instances, there is an even more complex compounding of personality characteristics and the response to the particular serious life event, and very severe life events may lead to further character changes beyond those that occur during adolescence and early adulthood. When a decade or so has passed since a single traumatic event, especially when time has passed since a string of traumatic experiences (as in combat or concentration camps), then the syndrome may be so complex that multiple diagnoses need to be made and carefully formulated in order to understand that individual.

Organic Brain Syndromes

In making both differential and comprehensive diagnoses, it is important to consider the possibility of concussion in acute physical traumas or malnutrition in prolonged stress responses. Very mild concussions may leave no immediate apparent neurologic signs but have residual long-term effects on mood and concentration (Trimble 1981). Malnutrition during extended stressful periods may also lead to organic brain syndromes.

Persons with post-traumatic stress disorders commonly cope in ways that may lead to other disorders, such as turning to an excessive use of tobacco, alcohol, narcotics, sedatives, or food. If they present a mixed syndrome combining organic and psychological factors, one should make a diagnosis of each disorder concurrent with the diagnosis of post-traumatic stress disorder.

Adjustment Disorders

Adjustment disorders are defined by the *DSM-IV* as maladaptive reactions to identifiable psychosocial pressures. For this to be the correct diagnosis, signs and symptoms should emerge within three months of the onset of the change in life circumstances. The signs and symptoms include a wide variety of disturbances in interpersonal and work functions as well as maladaptive extremes of anxiety, depression, rage, shame, and guilt. According to the *DSM-IV*, if these signs and symptoms meet the criteria for another Axis I mental disorder, such as anxiety disorder or depressive disorder, the diagnosis of adjustment disorder should not be made.

The identifiable psychosocial pressures that may precipitate adjustment disorders include such changed life circumstances as divorce, difficulties with child rearing, illness or disability, financial difficulties, a new form of work, graduation, moving, retirement, and cultural upheaval.

The *DSM-IV* lists subcategories for adjustment disorders, organized by the patient's predominant complaint about her subjective experience. Among the subtypes are depressed or anxious mood, other out-of-control emotional states (i.e., rage, shame), disturbance of social conduct, work or academic inhibition, and withdrawal from others. This is an open-ended diagnostic entity, with subtypes classified by surface phenomena.

Neither post-traumatic stress disorder nor adjustment disorder should be regarded as a minor mental disorder. In either instance, suicidal ideation may be high and severe dysfunction found in such areas as work, social life, and parenting. Although both disorders may cause high levels of personal distress, the prognosis for full recovery is usually excellent.

Brief Psychotic Disorder

Another diagnosis related to traumatic events is that of brief psychoses. These conditions have a sudden onset immediately following exposure to stressful events. They may last for a few hours or for as long as two weeks. The clinical picture includes emotional turmoil and the presence of at least one gross psychotic symptom such as expressed delusions. This is what primarily differentiates a brief reactive psychosis from a post-traumatic stress disorder and an adjustment disorder.

To be diagnosed as having a brief psychosis, the patient should have experienced a recent traumatic life event that lies outside the range of usual human experiences. Observations suggest that brief stress-induced psychoses are less common than are post-traumatic stress disorders.

Bereavement

Many persons react to bereavement in a resilient manner. But for others, bereavement leads to a period of turbulent distress lasting up to two or more years (Osterweiss et al. 1984). At some time during the year following a death, a person may episodically experience signs and symptoms that would constitute a major depressive disorder were they not transient and clearly connected to grief. For these reactions, professional treatment may be indicated.

Medical disorders may be part of the bereavement reactions. Clinicians should take a careful history for increased alcohol consumption, being alert for cirrhosis of the liver, organic brain syndrome, and accident proneness. They should also ask about suicidal impulses, increased cigarette smoking and its cardiorespiratory consequences, and the use of sedatives or tranquilizers with their potential for habituation, paradoxic wakefulness, and other side effects.

Some circumstances are likely to increase the severity or duration of grief reactions, including a preexisting high dependency on the deceased, preexisting frustration or anxiety in relating to the deceased, unexpected or torturous deaths, a sense of alienation or antagonism to others, a history of multiple earlier or simultaneous losses that have not been integrated, and real or fantasied responsibility for the suffering or death itself. When several of these factors are present, a complicated bereavement reaction may result.

Complicated Grief Disorder

Recent research, based on reliable clinician–observer ratings and utilizing latent class model analyses and signal detection statistical analyses, have indicated the validity of a diagnosis of complicated grief disorder (Horowitz et al. 1997). Subjects selected by an algorithm for the set of symptoms did not significantly overlap with diagnoses of Major Depressive Disorder, which are often applied in disturbances due to excessive, distorted, or prolonged grief (see also Prigerson et al. 1997). The most sensitive symptoms specific to this disorder, over a year after the loss event, include intrusive symptoms, pangs of severe emotion, and distressingly strong yearnings, all related to the lost relationship. They also include feeling far too personally empty, staying socially isolated, disturbed sleep, and loss of interest in career, social, caretaking, and recreational or creative activities to a maladaptive degree. Criteria for a new diagnostic entity, Complicated Grief Disorder, from this research are found in Table 2–9.

Table 2–9. Criteria for Complicated Grief Disorder

Event
  Bereavement at least a year ago.
Signs and Symptoms Criteria:
  Any *three* of the following seven symptoms, experienced during the recent month, and for at least a month, with a severity that interferes with daily functioning:
Intrusive Symptoms:
1. Unbidden memories or intrusive fantasies related to the lost relationship.
2. Strong spells or pangs of severe emotion related to the lost relationship.
3. Distressingly strong yearnings or wishes that the lost one was there.
Signs of Avoidance and Failure-to-Adapt:
4. Feelings of being far too much alone or personally empty.
5. Excessively staying away from people, places or activities that remind the subject of the deceased.
6. Unusual interference with sleep.
7. Loss of interest in work, social, caretaking, or recreational activities to a maladaptive degree.

3

FIELD STUDIES ON THE IMPACT OF LIFE EVENTS

With Nancy Wilner

The clinical studies are of patients who present themselves spontaneously for treatment, and field studies are necessary to determine the generality of phenomena. Without field studies, one cannot know if the clinical observations are pertinent only to rare instances of "falling ill" or indicate general response tendencies.

MILITARY COMBAT

Field studies of stress require the natural occurrence of the same kind of disaster in a more or less extensive population. War, unfortunately, provides such conditions. The threat of death, maimed bodies, and the loss of comrades are common, and people often commit acts of violence and/or witness the consequences for others. Oddly enough, even though there have been so many wars, psychological stress response syndromes were not fully recognized until World War II, as they had to be forced past considerable resistance. Physical causes were preferred as a basis for the theory, because psychological causation sounded too much like weakness, cowardice, or a lack of patriotism.

But the immense number of psychological casualties among combat soldiers, sailors, and airmen in World War I forced the recognition of some type of syndrome. Earlier observations had been made, such as De Costa's description of "soldier's heart" in the American Civil War, but they lacked psychological descriptors. Instead of calling them coronary symptoms due to the strains of combat, in World War I the presence of daze, fear, trembling, nightmares, and inability to function were sometimes attributed to brain damage. The cause was postulated to be cerebral concussions and the ruptures of small blood vessels caused by exploding shells, hence the then common term for traumatic war neuroses of *shell shock*. This organic focus led to a concentration on expectable symptoms such as those known to characterize acute and chronic brain syndromes. Earlier, at the end of the nineteenth century, traumatic neuroses after derailments and other train wrecks had been attributed to spinal concussions (Trimble 1981).

Multiple observations eventually revealed that physical traumas were not invariably antecedents of combat reactions. Anyone exposed to constant death threats and terrible sights might respond with prolonged symptoms, even if he emerged physically unharmed and was exposed only once. Symptoms also appeared frequently in persons exposed to extended combat, with antecedent physical traumas not necessarily the cause.

The vast populations presenting symptomatic responses to psychologically traumatic events in World War II forced phenomenological studies of the symptoms' relative frequency (Archibald and Tuddenham 1965). A good example is the study of combat reactions by Grinker and Spiegel (1945), whose summary of the nineteen most common symptoms that persisted long after the soldiers were removed from combat are shown by rank order in Table 3–1. The organization of tabulation, as in most phenomenological studies, is according to frequency of occurrence.

Table 3–1. Most Common Signs and Symptoms of Operational Fatigue as Found by Grinker and Spiegel (1945) (in rank order by frequency)

1. Restlessness	11. Tremor
2. Irritability or aggression	12. Difficulty concentrating,
3. Fatigue on arising, lethargy	confusion
4. Difficulty falling asleep	13. Alcoholism
5. Anxiety, subjective	14. Preoccupation with combat
6. Frequent fatigue	15. Decreased appetite
7. Startle reactions	16. Nightmares
8. Feeling of tension	17. Psychosomatic symptoms
9. Depression	(e.g., vomiting, diarrhea)
10. Personality change and memory	18. Irrational fears (phobias)
loss	19. Suspiciousness

These symptoms are typical of those found in other studies of military combat. After World War II, Lidz (1946a,b), Fairbairn (1952), and Brill and Beebe (1955) each described nightmares as significant signs of combat neuroses. Later work by Haley (1974) on patients' reports of atrocities described Vietnam veterans who were depressed, anxious, sad, rageful, and despairing. He saw their delayed reactions as including denial and leading toward intrusions, which also took the form of sleep disturbances and nightmares.

De Fazio (1975) also pointed to nightmares as a frequent psychological problem for Vietnam veterans. In 1982, Langley reported symptoms of guilt, depression, alienation, irritability, high stress, nightmares, flashbacks, and startle response in a group of Vietnam combat veterans who developed the additional problems of substance abuse and marital, legal, and vocational difficulties. In 1984, Silver and Iacono reported a study of 405 Vietnam veterans that supports the *DSM-III*'s Post Traumatic Stress Disorder symptoms of intrusions, sleep disturbance, and difficulty concentrating. Similar important findings were also compiled by Figley (1978, 1979, Figley and Leventman, 1982) and Kolb (1982, 1983, 1984).

The categories of symptoms that Grinker and Spiegel slated for observation and codification may reflect the theory of that time. In his studies of post-traumatic neuroses of World War I veterans, Freud (1920) emphasized nightmares, one form of intrusive and repetitive thought, but had played down a similar phenomenon—recurrent unbidden images of frightening scenes that occur in waking thought:

> Now dreams occurring in traumatic neuroses have the characteristic of repeatedly bringing the patient back into the situation of his accident, a situation from which he wakes up in another fright. . . . I am not aware, however, patients suffering from traumatic neurosis are much occupied in their waking lives with memories of their accident. Perhaps they are more concerned with *not* thinking of it. [p. 13]

Freud was partly incorrect, for recurrent memories such as unbidden images while awake are a much more common occurrence than he believed.

Wilson and Krauss (1982) made a systematic study of Vietnam veterans with and without post-traumatic stress disorder (see also Hendin and Haas 1984, see also Wilson 1980). Their results indicate that the best predictor of a post-traumatic stress disorder in Vietnam veterans is knowing the degree to which the person was involved in combat, felt stress during combat, was exposed to injury and death, and felt psychologically isolated upon returning home from the war (see also Van der Kolk et al. 1984). In a multiple regression analysis of the best predictors of seven post-traumatic symptoms such as intrusive imagery, depression, and problems of anger and rage, Wilson and Krauss found that the best predictive exponential variables for subsequent intrusive imagery were exposure to scenes of injury and/or death and psychological isolation upon coming home. Psychological isolation, but not injury and death, was the best predictive variable for the other six symptoms of post-traumatic stress disorder. This indicates that the intrusive and repetitive imagery from experiences of violence and death threats is often a specific stress response.

The expression "everyone has his breaking point" evolved from experience with reactions to combat. It suggests that every person, when exposed to enough stress, may show an acute stress response syndrome. Persons with certain latent neurotic conflicts or predispositions to certain stress triggers and alarm reactions may respond to lower levels of external stress (Hendin and Haas 1984, Hendin et al. 1983). Persons with a higher stress tolerance will not "break down" until the level of stress is higher. Brill (1967) observed that soldiers with preexisting neuroses had a seven-to-eight-times greater chance of psychiatric reactions than did those with more normal predispositional characteristics.

In a lengthy review of the literature, Hocking (1970) verified the hypothesis that individuals adjust differently to differing degrees of stress. In his view, prolonged, extreme stress results in neurotic symptoms in virtually every person exposed to it. He noted that of 303 individuals in military combat during World War II, more than half suffered from subsequent depression, insomnia, nightmares, anxiety, tension, irritability, startle reactions, impairment of memory, and obsession with thoughts of wartime experiences. Significant numbers of men were also observed to deny trauma by channeling their emotional difficulties into psychosomatic symptoms (see also the comprehensive review by Lewis and Engel [1954]).

Despite efforts to distinguish among the symptoms and signs of acute and chronic reactions (Kardiner and Spiegel 1947), extended field studies indicate that these stress responses are not necessarily disparate, the main difference being the temporal onset or maintenance of the syndrome. It is clear that the phases of symptoms and signs may begin shortly after the stress event, may persist for a long period, or may begin only after a long latency period (Archibald and Tuddenham 1965, Archibald et al. 1962, Baker and Chapman 1962, Cobb and Lindemann 1943, Davis 1966, Friedman and Linn 1957, Horowitz et al. 1980, Parkes 1964, Popovic and Petrovic 1965).

CONCENTRATION CAMPS

Additional evidence regarding the duration of stress responses and the frequency of occurrence of stress symptoms arose from the most deplorable circumstances imaginable. Studies of concentration camp victims indicated that profound and protracted stress may have chronic or permanent effects no matter what the predisposition of the prestress personality. This evidence was found in the decades of studying the survivors of the Nazi concentration camps (Eaton et al. 1982). Study after study, as reviewed in two workshops (Krystal 1968, Krystal and Niederland 1971), confirm the occurrence of stress response syndromes, persisting for decades, in major proportions of those populations who survived protracted concentration camp experiences. As just one example, 99 percent of the 226 Norwegian survivors of a Nazi concentration camp in World War II had some psychiatric disturbances when intensively surveyed years after their return to normal life. Of the total population studied, 87 percent had cognitive disturbances such as poor memory and inability to concentrate, 85 percent had persistent nervousness and irritability, 60 percent had sleep disturbances, and 52 percent had nightmares (Eitinger 1969). It should be noted that the hideousness of these concentration camps also meant severe malnutrition and physical maltreatment that could have caused brain injury.

In addition to such general stress symptoms as recurrent intrusive memories, concentration camp survivors may have special symptoms and signs because of the protracted duration of their stress and the intensity of their dehumanization by the Nazis. Such signs as the synecdoche of success, the bleaching away of childhood memories, and the altered schemas of self- and object relationships may distinguish the survivor syndrome of concentration camp victims from stress response syndromes in general (Furst 1967, Krystal 1968, Lifton 1967, Ostwald and Bittner 1968).

The effects of being a victim of a concentration camp can lead to changes in personality and so to changes of interpersonal patterns, including those of parenting. The result is that the effects of the concentration camp may be visited onto the children of the victims and perhaps to succeeding generations (Krystal 1985). These generations of families thus become carriers of conscious and unconscious values, myths, fantasies, and beliefs as well as actual interpersonal transactive styles that may have been forcibly changed by the violent life experiences of one generation (Danieli 1982).

To recapitulate: though not negating the powerful influence of prestress personality configurations, findings from large groups of persons indicate that stress response syndromes are not limited to any subgroup of the exposed populations. There is no doubt that some general stress response tendencies can be found.

THE CONCEPT OF PHASES
OF STRESS RESPONSE

War and concentration camps produce extraordinary strain, but even so there seem to be phases of response in which denial or intrusive symptoms and signs may predominate.

Shatan (1973), in a study of Vietnam veterans twenty-four months after combat, noted the presence of intrusiveness in the form of insomnia, nightmares, and restlessness that may not have surfaced during combat and demobilization, when denial and numbing may have predominated. Shatan observed that the delay in the manifestation of these symptoms caused the government physicians to assume that the Vietnam War produced fewer psychiatric casualties than may actually have been the case. Horowitz and Solomon (1975, 1978) described the differences between soldiers under great protracted combat stress during World War II and those in Vietnam. Soldiers in combat in World War II went initially into a period of denial and numbing, but they did, nonetheless, remain at the front. The stress mounted, and when it exceeded the person's ability to

maintain denial, then experiences characteristic of intrusive and repetitive feelings emerged.

In Vietnam, because of repeated rotation to relative safety,
Horowitz and Solomon presumed it was possible for many soldiers
to enter and remain in the denial phase. Other elements, such as
the availability of drugs, the lack of group fidelity, and the opposition to the war, contributed to a state of alienation characterized
by depersonalization and isolation.

Upon return to the United States, there would be a period of
relief and well-being, and the denial and numbing would continue
for a while. Ultimately, with the relaxation of defensive and coping operations, the person might then enter the painful phase of
intrusive recollection (Egendorf et al. 1981).

For whatever combination of reasons, during the combat period of the Vietnam War, there was a general impression that levels
of traumatic disorders were lower than they were during World
War II. A period of controversy followed the combat period as to
the prominence of Post Traumatic Stress Disorders in veterans,
succeeded by a growing recognition of relatively widespread problems in the veterans. One issue was the emergence, after the Vietnam War, of a new official nosology, *DSM-III*, with the diagnostic
composition of Post Traumatic Stress Disorder, as we have discussed.

It may be more useful in some cases to think in terms of Post
Traumatic Character Disorders, although there is no official inclusion of such a term in the nomenclature. The reason is that wars
are often fought by combat troops in late adolescence or very early
adulthood. Identity is not completely consolidated, and the traumatic experiences of the war become incorporated into self schemas
and concepts of the relationship of self to the world. A confusing
situation, including the domestic unpopularity of the war, faced the
veterans returning from Vietnam and alienated many of them. This
situation combined with predisposition before the war, the war itself,
and atrocities observed or committed to alter personality while it
was being formed and re-formed during an important developmental

phase. Problems in self-definition, self-coherence, and self-articulation to domestic society resulted.

Excessive adherence to official diagnostic labels may inhibit individualized case formulations along these lines. Character development occurs throughout adult life, and massive trauma or prolonged strain affects this process. Prolonged denial or intrusion phases become, in some, new features of personality.

Concentration camp survivors sometimes exhibit such effects. Chodoff (1970) observed a sequence of reactions to concentration camp life in his studies of these victims and described this sequence in terms of stages. First was the universal response of shock and terror upon arriving at the camp. This fright reaction was generally followed by a period of apathy and often by a longer period of mourning and depression. The apathy was psychologically protective, by providing a kind of emotional hibernation. Lifton (1967) suggested that this kind of depression might, in part, be characterized as a delayed mourning reaction, as the victims were unable to engage in a ceremonial mourning for their dead. Gorer (1965), too, emphasized the connection between ritual and mourning and the maladaptions that may result if distress is not worked through in this personal and expressively social form.

As an adaptive measure, regression was a stage noted in many prisoners of war, as the result of overwhelming pressures. Docility and submissiveness were the products of the victims' dependency on their masters. Some identification with the aggressor was observed, and irritable behavior was discharged in petty fights with other prisoners.

The most important defenses among concentration camp inmates during their imprisonment were denial and isolation of affect. Chodoff named the most distinctive, long-term consequence of Nazi persecution observable over a thirty-year period as the "concentration camp syndrome." Invariably present in this syndrome is some degree of felt anxiety, along with irritability, restlessness, apprehensiveness, and startle reactions. These anxiety symptoms are worse at night, accompanied by insomnia and nightmares, which are simple or slightly disguised intrusive repetitions of the traumatic experience.

Lifton pointed out the significance of psychic numbing in the behavior of Jews in Nazi camps, stating that anyone encountering such massive death will experience a cessation of feeling, a desensitization or psychic numbing. An element of this kind of denial is the need to "see nothing," for if it is not "seen," it is not happening. Added to this is the severing of human bonds of identification. "I see you dying, but I'm not related to you in your death." Lifton also described two kinds of numbing—the apathy of the "walking corpse," or the "know nothing" who acts as though death does not exist.

From this a collaborative numbing emerges, an equalizer between the victim and the victimizer, in which the Jew, the victim, does not exist, and the Nazi, the victimizer, is omnipotent but denies the human consequences of his actions. Such numbing and denial may be followed, even years later, by a phase of the intrusive repetition of ideas and feelings related to the earlier warded-off events.

NUCLEAR HOLOCAUST

Based on interviews with seventy-five survivors, made seventeen years after the United States dropped an atomic bomb on Hiroshima, Japan, Lifton (1967) described the experience as a permanent encounter with death, consisting of four phrases. The first was an overwhelming immersion in death, a "death in life" feeling similar to that of the concentration camp victims. This phase was dominated by elements of extreme helplessness in the face of threatened annihilation and surmounted by an extremely widespread and effective defense mechanism that Lifton called "psychic closing off," a cessation of feeling within a very short period of time. The unconscious process was described as closing oneself off from death, the controlling fantasy being "If I feel nothing, then death is not taking place." It is thus related to the defense mechanisms of denial and isolation, as well as to the behavioral state of apathy, and is distinguished by its global quality, a screen of protection against the impact of death in the midst of death and dying. This response to an overall exposure to death merges with longer-term feelings of depression and despair, mingled with feelings of shame and guilt. The guilty fantasy "I am responsible for his death; I killed him" is interwoven with the shameful fantasy "I should have saved him or helped him."

The second phase of the Hiroshima encounter with death is called the "invisible contamination," in which symptoms of radiation sickness appeared at unpredictable intervals of weeks or months after the bomb had been dropped. There was a fear of epidemic contamination, a sense of individual powerlessness in the face of an invisible agent, and a denial of illness when the symptoms did appear.

The third phase, which occurred after many years with the experience of later radiation effects, was an undercurrent of imagery of an endless chain of potentially lethal impairments which, if not evident that year or five years later, would appear in the next generation.

The fourth phase was that of a lifelong identification with death and dying, which Lifton explained as the survivors' means of maintaining life. Because of the burden of guilt they carry for having survived, the survivors' obeisance before the dead is their best means for justifying and maintaining their own existence and is a continued preoccupation.

Lifton also described the survivors' residual problems, especially those of psychological imagery, which manifest themselves in various ways. Among them he noted a profound impairment of the sense of invulnerability; a sense of being among the "elite" who have mastered death and a sense of vulnerability to it at any time. Many victims carried with them, seventeen years later, intrusive images of the horror of that day and the days immediately after and talked of still seeing pictures in their minds of people walking slowly in the streets, their skin peeling off.

A profoundly ambivalent pattern emerged of both seeking help and resenting it. Working through this event, Lifton felt, was a reformulation, a way of establishing an inner ideology as a means of dealing with overwhelming feelings, creating a new reality within which the victims could understand and master their experiences and their feelings of shame and existential guilt. Faced with this form of guilt, with resistance to establishing trust in the human order, the survivors of concentration camps, of atomic bombing, and of Vietnam need a new identity, a sense of connection with people, and meaning and significance for their life in order to come to terms with the past disaster and the world in which they continue to live.

DISASTERS

The term *post-traumatic neurosis* was coined by those physicians who studied and treated victims of railway accidents late in the nineteenth century. The general signs and symptoms that followed derailments were more severe than those noted in persons knocked down in the streets by horses or carts, despite the absence of neurologically diagnosed physical injury, and this was thought to be due to the unusual fear and dread involved. As well reviewed by Trimble (1981) the term *traumatic neurosis* was first used in this situation by Oppenheim (1905), who wrote a major text on neurology, noting that the syndrome might appear after any injury or surgical operation. He wrote that traumatic neurosis was clearly different from hysteria, although this differentiation was disputed by other leading physicians. Gradually, studies of natural and man-made disasters indicated that although stress might precipitate a variety of syndromes, including post-traumatic psychoses and dissociative episodes, the post-traumatic stress disorders were noted in discrete, neurotic-level forms (Keiser 1968).

The signs and symptoms characterizing both the denial and the intrusion phases of stress response syndromes have been noted in modern studies of disaster (Green 1982). These symptoms are found more frequently and prominently in those persons exposed to a disaster who have had the greatest levels of shock, injury, or loss (Green et al. 1987). Treatment by psychotherapy helps reduce these symptoms (Lindy 1987). Premorbid culture and the social environment—whether supportive or neglectful, benign or hostile—also influence the course of recovery from stress response syndromes (Boehnlein et al. 1985, Green et al. 1985).

For example, the skywalk of a prominent hotel in Kansas City fell to crush, injure, or threaten hundreds below in a crowded social gathering. Wilkinson (1983) studied the 102 survivors during the five months following the disaster. Of these, 88 percent had a significant degree of intrusive episodes of thought and feeling. Repeated recollections of the disaster were reported as symptoms in 83 percent of the 52 men and in 94 percent of the 50 women studied. Recurrent feelings, usually of anxiety and depression, were found in 54 percent of the sample, again more in women (60 percent). Difficulty concentrating was found in 44 percent of the sample. The victims and observers of the falling skywalk suffered more often from such symptoms as intrusion and ease of startle than did those persons in the sample who served as rescuers. Themes of survivor guilt were prominent in the bereaved, and many needed to talk over and over again about what happened. Post-traumatic symptoms may also be found in secondary disaster victims, those who recover and sort human remains (Jones 1985).

Similar findings were noted in several studies of the survivors of the Buffalo Creek Disaster. The Buffalo Creek Disaster occurred when a large upstream body of water was suddenly released, forming a gigantic wave that tore through a West Virginia town, killing 125 people and rendering the entire population of 5,000 homeless.

Erickson (1976) described these survivors in some of the same terms used by Lifton to describe the survivors of Hiroshima. Some were demoralized, disoriented in terms of life plans, and apathetic. In a separate study of some of the same people, Titchner and Kapp (1976) found post-traumatic neurotic symptoms in 80 percent of the group interviewed, with a prominence of unresolved grief, survivor shame and guilt, and feelings of impotent rage and hopelessness even two years after the traumatic event.

Children, with their varied mind development at rapidly changing stages, may have some of the same, or different, characteristics of responses. An example is Terr's (1981, 1983) reports on the responses of the Chowchilla survivors. This study is about 23 to 25 of the 26 children who in 1976 were kidnapped from their Chowchilla, California, school bus. Three kidnappers drove them for about eleven hours in two vans with blackened windows and then buried them alive in a truck-trailer under the ground in a covered hole. The children and their bus driver remained there for sixteen hours, uncertain of their fate, until two of the kidnapped boys dug a tunnel out to summon help. Terr was able to follow these children and to report their status four years later.

Every one of the 25 child victims suffered from persistent fears, although after four years, 19 reported spontaneous resolution of some of these fears. Eighteen of the 25 youngsters, mostly between 10 and 15 years of age, suppressed any thoughts about the kidnap experience. Although the children had visual memories of the events, they were like daydreams and not accompanied by signs of acute distress or a sense of intrusiveness (except when they occurred as nightmares or hallucinations). Misperceptions and perceptual over-generalizations led to startle reactions.

Unexpected, sudden reminders could evoke sensory memories and precipitate extreme anxiety in some of these children. Although five children had terrifying dreams in the first year after the kidnapping, 12 described them in later follow-up interviews, after more than two years had passed. Sometime during the four years,

18 of the children had played out repetitively some theme clearly related to the traumatic events. Some of the children denied the post-traumatic symptoms, but, Terr felt that every child she studied suffered from a post-traumatic stress response syndrome but that the numbing, amnesias, and intrusive, dysphoric flashbacks seen in traumatized adults were not prominent in this population.

Because there are variations in predisposing character and culture, post-traumatic social and environmental influences, and age and status, it is hard to predict how many members of a given population will develop what type of stress response syndrome after a disaster. Some indication is offered, however, by epidemiological studies that sample a large population containing persons who have and have not been exposed to a given event. Robins and colleagues (1985) studied a group of 43 persons exposed to flood, tornado, or toxic contaminations and compared their responses to those of a well-selected group of 325 similar people who had not been exposed. Over half of the exposed persons had three or more symptoms of Post Traumatic Stress Disorder, although only 2 of the 43 warranted a diagnosis as circumscribed in *DSM-III*. This contrasted with 10 persons, about 3 percent, of the sample of unexposed persons, one of whom warranted the diagnosis of Post Traumatic Stress Disorder. Of the exposed group, 8 percent warranted the diagnosis of phobic disorder, compared with 4 percent of the unexposed group. In addition, 27 percent of the exposed group reported their health to be only fair to poor, contrasted with 8 percent of the nonexposed group. The more directly exposed persons in such samples, as already mentioned, tend to exhibit greater morbidity (Smith et al. 1985). The best predictors of post-trauma symptoms were degree of exposure and the number of symptoms the individual subject experienced before the event. Sex differences were not noted.

In similar studies, Shore and colleagues (1985) found that persons involved in the Mount St. Helens volcanic eruption disaster had significant elevations in the frequency of three psychiatric disorders when compared with an epidemiologically similar group. These disorders were Post Traumatic Stress Disorders, Generalized Anxiety Disorders, and single epidoses of Major Depressive Disorder. In this sample females showed higher incidences of the conditions than did males, and morbidity increased between year one and year three after the disaster. Women between 36 and 50 years of age seemed the most susceptible.

To recapitulate, such field studies confirm the findings of clinical investigations of the psychological response to external stress events. As in clinical observation, a phasic tendency was noted. Intrusive repetitions may coexist or alternate with periods of denial and numbness. Like repetitions, the periods of numbness and denial are relatively involuntary. Finally, these phases are perhaps most clearly seen in bereaved persons, whether the bereavement comes from the loss of another or the threat of one's own death.

BEREAVEMENT

Much of the literature on bereavement was summarized by Parkes (1964), later expanded through his own studies (1970, 1972, Parkes and Weiss 1983), and has been reviewed by Raphael (1983) and Osterweiss and colleagues (1984). Bowlby (1961, 1969, 1980) has also reviewed the material.

Parkes referred to the now-classic paper by Lindemann (1944) on the varieties of reactions to bereavement found in a mixed group of psychiatric and nonpsychiatric patients. He noted that Lindemann did not show the relative frequency of the various syndromes that he described, nor did he indicate how long after bereavement his interviews took place. Lindemann defined acute grief as a definitive syndrome with psychological and somatic symptomatology, which may appear immediately after a crisis or may be delayed. He described it as uniform, in that it is expressed by waves of anxiety and panic that are defended against by denial of the event and by avoidance (i.e., of visits from others, of mentioning the deceased, or of expressions of sympathy by others). He explained the use of denial as motivated by fear of loss of control and emphasized the importance of the possibility of underreaction as well as overreaction.

Parkes felt that although Lindemann's studies gave a fair picture of the overall reaction, they failed to reveal the relationships between the phases described and the variations of each phase over a period of time. They particularly did not explain how long the various phases of grief could be expected to last, nor did they delineate what was a pathological, as opposed to a normal, variant of grief.

To answer some of these questions, Parkes (1970) interviewed 22 London widows at three-month periods for thirteen months after their bereavement. These widows were felt to be showing typical grief reactions: of the 22, only 6 felt that they had fully accepted the news when they were told that their husbands would die; 8 frankly disbelieved it. As a result of these interviews, Parkes was able to find phases of reaction.

Denial-Numbing

The initial, immediate reaction is described by Parkes as a state of numbness, often preceded by an expression of great distress. Although this sense of numbness was a relatively transient phenomenon, some form of denial of the full reality of what had happened often persisted. One year later, 13 widows said there were still times when they had difficulty believing in the reality of their husbands' deaths. Bowlby, too (Bowlby and Parkes 1970), had revised his classification of the phases of mourning to introduce numbness as the initial phase. This is reflected, in Parkes's study, in affective reports of one group that showed little or no affect in the first week, not much in the second, but moderate-to-severe disturbance by the third month.

A second group showed a steady increase in affect over a period of time, and a third group, which showed moderate or severe affect in the first week, tended to remain disturbed during the first two months but improved thereafter. Each widow seemed to have her own way of mitigating her feelings. These included a blocking out or denial of affect, partial disbelief, an inhibition of painful thoughts and evocation of pleasant ones, and an avoidance of reminders.

In 1960, Lindemann noted another form of mitigation that he called *selective forgetting*. In this phenomenon the image of the deceased person is lost from consciousness. This observation was supported by Parkes and illustrated by a woman in his sample who could not recall the face of her husband during the first month after his death, although in ensuing months she had a clear visual memory.

Intrusive Repetitions

Parkes indicated the presence of intrusive thinking, often in the form of misidentification illusions (seeing the deceased in a stranger) or of hypnogogic hallucinations (Marris 1958). For example, one woman felt initially stunned and angry after the death of her husband. For the next few days she kept busy, and then, five days later, she said that something invaded her; a presence almost "pushed [her] out of bed." It was her husband, and the experience was "terribly overwhelming." During this period, the widows' feelings were seldom admitted fully to consciousness, and their minds were often distracted from the loss, but there were periodic breakthroughs.

Bowlby called the second phase, the one following numbing, "yearning" or "protest." Parkes emphasized this phase as well, indicating four components: (1) pining and preoccupation, (2) direction of attention toward places and objects associated with the lost person, (3) development of a perceptual set for the deceased, and (4) crying for that person. Parkes pointed out, too, that hallucinations and illusions occurred and noted that they have always occupied a prominent place in folklore, especially in the form of ghosts and in the concept of being haunted.

Parkes postulated that a widow who had fully accepted bereavement and made a good adjustment would be able to look back on the past with pleasure and into the future with optimism. But after thirteen months, only 3 widows satisfied his criteria.

In Lindemann's earlier account (1944) he stated that after eight to ten interviews within a period of four to six weeks, in which psychiatrists facilitated grief work, it was possible to complete the working-through of ordinary, uncomplicated grief reactions. He was referring to families of victims of the Coconut Grove fire, who suffered no anticipatory grief, who participated in "group mourning," and received much sympathy and support. Lindemann's statement had caused Parkes to underestimate the duration of uncomplicated and oftentimes anticipatory grief; he ultimately determined that it was necessary to follow the bereaved for a two- to three-year period.

Parkes (1970) interpreted his study as confirming Bowlby's belief that grief is a phasic process, although transitions from one phase to another are seldom distinct. In 1972, Parkes distinguished seven phases of mourning: (1) initial denial and avoidance of loss; (2) alarm reactions such as anxiety, restlessness, and physiological complaints; (3) searching, an irrational urge to find the lost person; (4) anger and guilt; (5) feelings of internal loss; (6) adoption of traits or mannerisms of the deceased; and (7) acceptance and resolution, including appropriate changes in identity.

Grayson (1970) found a similarity between the grief reactions to the loss of real objects and the loss of intangibles, particularly missed experiences and relinquished hopes. The process of diminishing the force of these wishes requires the same working through to completion as does the mourning process (Lewis 1961, Rees 1970). Grayson found abreaction and catharsis to be valuable discharges of affect without which decathecting would take longer and be less complete. He emphasized the need for persons to break through the phase of denial in order to face the painful reality of the missed experience.

Gorer (1965) also agreed with the theory of phases, having studied 35 bereaved people who sought psychiatric help because they suffered from prolonged grief, delayed reaction, vivid nightmares, or an absence of grief that signified that all was not well. Gorer described the most characteristic feature of grief not as prolonged depression but as acute and episodic pangs or episodes of severe anxiety and psychological pain that begin within a few hours or days after bereavement and reach a peak of severity within two weeks. At first they are frequent and spontaneous, but as time passes, they become less frequent and occur only when something brings the loss to mind.

Gorer noted the phenomenon of searching that fills the gap between aim and object and gives a sense of the deceased's continued presence. He explained avoidance of the full reality of the loss as a way of mitigating the pain of grieving and as a necessary part of distancing so that implications could be slowly worked through and dealt with cognitively. Gorer also observed the presence of two opposing tendencies: an inhibitory tendency that, by means of repression, avoidance, and postponement, holds back or limits the perception of disturbing stimuli; and a facilitating or reality tendency that enhances perception of and thoughts about disturbing stimuli. He pointed out that over a period of time, an individual will often oscillate between the two tendencies so that periods of intense feeling will alternate with periods of conscious or unconscious avoidance. He also found no clear ending to grief but, rather, a turning point that reflects the abandonment of old modes of thought and behavior.

Glick and colleagues (1975) found that widows in the first year after their husbands' deaths usually could not enter into a new relationship without concomitant feelings of disloyalty toward the dead spouse. This indicated a sex difference, as the widowers in their study did not feel that a new relationship would conflict with the memory of commitment and fidelity to the deceased wife. Instead, widowers often established a new quasi-marital relationship within a few months of their wife's death and expected sympathy from the new companion for their continued grieving for their dead wife.

In addition to sexual differences, there are cultural differences in response to bereavement that may be related to different views of the meaning of death, different patterns of attachment, different rituals and responses to loss, and other factors (Eisenbruch 1984, Windholz et al. 1985). Nonetheless, tendencies toward intrusive experiences, including hallucinatory experiences of the deceased, and toward denial experiences, including denial of the fact of death itself, are found in some individuals cross-culturally. Across cultures, intense grief and mourning responses are expected to last up to a year after the death, often with a ritual at that time to mark a return to social availability (Rosenblatt et al. 1976).

Life events questionnaires, as reviewed by Horowitz and colleagues (1977), are a way of surveying the distress experienced by groups of individuals after a variety of events. The most devastating life event is usually thought to be the death of a child. As just one example of many studies, marital discord and divorce were reported in 50 to 70 percent of families whose child died from cancer (Kaplan et al. 1976, Strauss 1975).

DEATH OF A PARENT

By selecting a specific type of bereavement, such as the death of a parent, it is possible to compare the experiences of persons who do and do not seek help in dealing with the trauma and their responses to it. The death of a parent is a common event, one that most adult children of living parents come to expect with the advancing age of their mothers and fathers. Yet such deaths have an impact, as both the current loss and the past meaning of the relationship are reconsidered, with concomitant reflection on self-concepts. In some persons, intrusive and denial phases may be prominent.

In a series of papers, our own research group reported on the quantitative and clinical studies of field subjects who experienced a parental death and went through 2-, 6-, and 13-month evaluation sessions of their responses, and of patients who sought brief psychotherapy because of neurotic-level symptoms precipitated by the death of a parent (Horowitz, Krupnick et al. 1981; Horowitz, Marmar, Krupnick et al. 1984; Horowitz, Marmar, Weiss et al. 1984; Horowitz, Weiss et al. 1984; Horowitz, Wilner et al. 1980b; Kaltreider et al. 1984; Kaltreider and Mendelson 1985).

In the initial evaluations, intrusion levels were high on the self-report in 33 percent of the field subjects and at medium levels in 39 percent. High levels were defined clinically as the level of signs and symptoms that merited concern, that diagnostic, evaluative, or treatment procedures were clearly warranted, and that the person was more likely to be in a problem or pathological category. Medium levels were defined as a clinical level of concern with complaints or signs that gave a global indication of a condition that warranted further diagnostic, evaluative, or treatment procedures, even though the severity was not marked. Though the patient sample had higher levels of distress, as shown in Table 3–2, there was a subpopulation among the field subjects that was also high in distress, as shown in Table 3–3. Table 3–4 shows the same data 13 months after the death of the parent.

Those persons who felt in some way responsible for, guilty over, or ashamed of the events leading up to, during, and following the parental death had more prolonged symptoms. The loss of the mother produced more prolonged symptoms over time than did the death of the father. The more the persons experienced other negative life events, the more they tended to have persisting symptoms related to the themes of the parental death. Those persons judged to have more developed self-organizational capacities had the sharpest rate of decline in symptoms over time.

Table 3–2. Differences between Groups at First Evaluation

| PRIMARY DISTRESS VARIABLES[a] | MEAN (SD) | | *t* | *P* | ω^{2} [b] |
	PATIENTS (N = 31)	FIELD SUBJECTS (N = 36)			
Self-rating					
Intrusion (IES)	21.52 (7.99)	13.83 (9.05)	3.66	.001	.16
Avoidance (IES)	20.74 (9.64)	9.69 (9.66)	4.67	.000	.24
Depression (SCL-90)	1.75 (1.00)	0.81 (0.78)	4.30	.000	.21
Anxiety (SCL-90)	1.22 (0.84)	0.69 (0.78)	2.62	.011	.08
Total symptoms (SCL-90)	1.12 (0.63)	0.57 (0.59)	3.68	.000	.16
Clinician rating					
Intrusion (SRRS)	18.53(11.05)	8.36(10.72)	3.79	.000	.17
Total neurotic signs and symptoms (BPRS)	16.48 (4.68)	10.64 (6.83)	4.13	.000	.19

a IES indicates the Impact of Event Scale; SCL-90, the Symptom Checklist-90; SRRS, the Stress Response Rating Scale; and BPRS, the Brief Psychiatric Rating Scale.
b This is an index of the proportion of variance accounted for by group variance.
Source: Horowitz, M. J., Krupnick, J., Kaltreider, N., et al. Initial psychological response to parental death. *Archives of General Psychiatry* 38:316–323, 1981.

PERSONAL ILLNESS, DYING, AND THE THREAT OF DEATH

In her study of 400 dying patients in a Chicago hospital, Kübler-Ross (1969) pioneered investigations into the psychological effects of the process of dying. After first having difficulty in getting these people to talk to her, she discovered the denial of impending death not only by the patients but also by the doctors and nurses. The medical staff coped with the difficulty of confronting the dying patient by the defensive maneuvers of selective withdrawal and inaccessibility. Thus when human contact was needed most, it was less available because of avoidance behavior. According to Kübler-Ross's report, patients go through five stages between their awareness of serious illness and their death:

Table 3–3. Percentages of Persons at Three Levels of Distress on Initial Evaluation after the Death of a Parent

PRIMARY DISTRESS VARIABLES[a]	PATIENTS (N = 31)			FIELD SUBJECTS (N = 36)			x^2	P
	LOW	MEDIUM	HIGH	LOW	MEDIUM	HIGH		
Self-rating								
Intrusion (IES)	3	36	61	28	39	33	8.98	.011
Avoidance (IES)	10	32	58	61	17	22	19.02	.001
Depression (SCL-90)	7	32	61	46	31	23	15.23	.001
Anxiety (SCL-90)	23	26	51	65	6	29	13.32	.001
Total symptoms (SCL-90)	23	23	54	66	17	17	13.68	.001
Clinician rating								
Intrusion (SRRS)	17	40	43	67	19	14	16.91	.001
Total neurotic signs and symptoms (BPRS)	3	52	45	42	47	11	17.56	.001

[a]IES indicates the Impact of Event Scale; SCL-90, the Symptom Checklist-90; SRRS, the Stress Response Rating Scale; and BPRS, the Brief Psychiatric Rating Scale.

Source: Horowitz, M. J., Krupnick, J., Kaltreider, N., et al. Initial psychological response to parental death. *Archives of General Psychiatry* 38:316–323, 1981.

Table 3–4. Percentages of Persons at Three Levels of Distress at 13 Months

PRIMARY DISTRESS VARIABLES[a]	PATIENTS[B]			FIELD SUBJECTS[b]			x^2	p
	LOW	MEDIUM	HIGH	LOW	MEDIUM	HIGH		
Self-rating								
Intrusion (IES)	57	33	10	69	19	12	1.72	NS
Avoidance (IES)	73	17	10	75	19	6	.31	NS
Depression (SCL–90)	55	26	19	66	22	12	.87	NS
Anxiety (SCL–90)	68	19	13	85	6	9	2.88	NS
Total symptoms (SCL–90)	77	13	10	81	13	6	.26	NS
Clinician rating								
Intrusion (SRRS)	53	37	10	90	7	3	10.04	.007
Total neurotic signs and symptoms (BPRS)	43	47	10	47	53	0	3.17	NS

a IES indicates the Impact of Event Scale; SCL–90, the Symptom Checklist 90; SRRS, the Stress Response Rating Scale; and BPRS, the Brief Psychiatric Rating Scale.
b Numbers vary from 32 to 30.

Source: Horowitz, M. J., Krupnick, J., Kaltreider, N., et al. Initial psychological response to parental death. *Archives of General Psychiatry* 38: 316–323, 1981.

1. *Shock and denial* when told that they have a serious illness, with a few maintaining this defense until the very end. Aldrich (1974) mentioned the impact of ambivalence on anticipatory grief. The dying person grieves in anticipation of the loss of her loved ones and resents being the one to die. The dying person finds it difficult to cope with this ambivalence, which increases the likelihood of denial. Aldrich noted that denial will prevail until the patient's disengagement and withdrawal have progressed to a point from which she can face death and loss with relative equanimity.

2. *Anger*, directed toward family, nurses and doctors, and those who epitomize health, functioning, and life itself, and remind them of what they are attempting to deny. The patients are, in effect, asking "why me?" and, by expressing their rage or anger, receive some comfort.

3. *Bargaining for time*, for example, to see a son graduate from college or a grandchild born. The patient is now saying, "Yes, me, *but* . . ."

4. *Depression*, which may be of two kinds: one is a reactive depression manifested by simultaneous crying and talking about the loss that lies ahead; the other is a quiet depression in which there is crying but no talk. Encouraging the grieving and mourning over the impending loss allows for the emergence of anticipatory grief and leads the patient into the last phase.

5. *Acceptance*, a period when the patient separates from those people he or she will leave behind. The unfinished business has been finished.

RAPE

Rape, or attempted rape, is a different kind of event from those previously discussed, although it, too, can be life threatening. It is not anticipated, there is no long period of time to deal with its possibilities, but it certainly demands a period of time to work through its effects (Veronen and Kilpatrick 1983). Its victims also indicate a phasic response to this kind of episode.

In a study of "rape trauma syndrome," during a one-year period, Burgess and Holmstrom (1974) followed 146 women who were seen at the emergency ward of Boston City Hospital. Their results were essentially similar to those of an earlier study of 13 women by Sutherland and Scherl (1970) in which they noted phasic responses. The rape trauma syndrome is described as "an acute phase and a long-term reorganization process that occurs as a result of forcible rape or attempted forcible rape" (p. 508). These behavioral, somatic, and psychological responses are an acute stress reaction to a life-threatening situation. In the acute phase, there may be a wide range of emotions, characterized by disorganization of the victim's lifestyle. Shock and disbelief are often expressed, and two emotional styles emerge in equal number. One is the expressed style, in which feelings of fear, anger, and anxiety are evidenced by crying, smiling, restlessness, and tension. The other is the controlled style, in which feelings are masked or hidden and the victim appears calm.

In the second phase, which was found to begin about two or three weeks after the attack, motor activity changes, and nightmares and phobias are especially evident. Dreams and nightmares are very upsetting and are of two types, one in which the victim is being attacked, wishes to do something, but wakens before acting. In the second type of dream, also of an attack, which occurs after a longer period of time, the victim masters the situation and fights off the assailant. There were some instances in which the victim woke up crying, though she had been unable to cry during daytime hours. There was also a phobic reaction to this traumatic situation, much like the "traumatophobia" described by Rado (1948) in his paper on the treatment of war victims. The phobia develops as a defensive reaction to the stressful event. There were fears connected with the setting in which the rape occurred (outdoors, indoors, being alone), sexual fears, fears of crowds, and fears of being followed.

In a later publication on crisis intervention with victims of rape, Sutherland-Fox and Scherl (1975) described a third phase in which the patient feels depressed and wants to talk. It is during this phase that two central issues must be worked through: the victim's feelings about herself and her feelings about the assailant. Some go through a period of guilt and self-punishment as a first step toward integrating the experience. Initial feelings of anger or denial—suppressed or rationalized during the second phase—now reappear for resolution. The third phase is relatively brief, and if, after several weeks, the experience has not been integrated and taken its appropriate place in the past, Sutherland-Fox and Scherl suggest that further help be sought.

A "silent rape reaction" was also observed. A number of women in the sample stated that they had been raped or molested at earlier periods of their lives and that the current rape reawakened their reaction to the earlier experience. It became clear that because they had not talked about and worked through the effects of the previous rape, the syndrome had continued to develop and remained unresolved. Emphasis was placed on the victim's need for support and comfort, for a working through from the acute phase to reorganization to completion, and a return to normal functioning as quickly as possible.

In a monograph sponsored by the American Psychiatric Association Committee on Women, Hilberman (1976) described four clinical phases of response to such a crisis: (1) an anticipatory or threat phase in which there is a need to protect the illusion of invulnerability; (2) an impact phase that includes anxiety, numbness, disorganization of thought, and loss of control; (3) a recoil phase in which the individual becomes more aware of adaptive or maladaptive responses to the stress and can experience either increased self-confidence or damage to self-esteem, depending on her perception of her behavior during the stress; and (4) a post-traumatic phase in which a successful response indudes assimilation of the experience and spontaneous re-covery, whereas a maladaptive response may result in a permanently impaired self-concept with evidence of continuing anger, guilt, night-mares, and impaired capacity to function.

Burgess and Holstrom (1976) elaborated on the fourth phase in explaining the victim's coping strategy before and during the assault as an issue to be confronted after the assault. For example, they asserted that there might have been intense guilt for the woman who submitted to rape in response to physical threats, whereas the victim who was beaten to insensibility and then raped may have suffered differently. Rape, of course, is used here as an extreme example of many other types of assault such as mugging, battery, burglary, and bullying. Any of these episodes of violence, threat, or fright can lead to stress response syndromes.

MEDICAL ILLNESSES

Medical illnesses and disabilities can also instigate the life events that lead to stress response syndromes. Kaltreider and colleagues (1979) found that a substantial minority of women who have had a hysterectomy manifested a related stress response syndrome in the months that followed the operation. Mourning problems may also occur after an abortion. Often a new pregnancy diminishes the mourning process, and reactions may not occur until after the birth of a healthy baby (Bourne and Lewis 1984). During the period between a perinatal death and a subsequently healthy pregnancy, the person may be relatively unwilling to look at all the implica-tions of the perinatal death.

Life-threatening illnesses such as myocardial infarctions are even more likely to be associated with early denial and later intrusive thinking. The early denial may even ameliorate certain problems, as it can reduce emotional arousal at a time of cardiac irritability, when arrhythmias, with fatal consequences, may occur (Biodeau and Hackett 1971, Hackett and Cassem 1970). Broncoscopy, burn treatment, spinal cord malfunction, renal dialysis, stroke, chronic pain, and other illnesses all may provide a major stressor with profound psychological as well as physical consequences (Krueger 1984).

Even the news of being at risk for premature death may set in motion a stress response syndrome. Interventions to inform people of risk factors are now more and more common; perhaps the most common is telling persons that they are at risk for premature heart disease because of high cholesterol, patterns of heavy cigarette smoking, or elevated blood pressure. In a large study of men so informed, intrusive thinking was found at higher levels in those given repeated reminders than in an informed group with fewer systematic reminders of the causes for early death from heart attacks. Elevated levels of intrusive thinking were found at yearly intervals, including the time period of three years after the news of risk. At the third year, 7 percent of a group of nearly 1,500 men reported they were more than "quite a lot upset" by this news (Horowitz, Simon et al. 1983). An additional 11 percent were at "moderate" to "quite a lot upset" about this news, meaning that 18 percent of men were substantially upset for a period of three or more years after receiving such news. Having intrusive thoughts and being constantly upset about the news is not the same, however, as having a diagnosable stress response syndrome, as indicated in the previous chapter. This suggests that physicians should ask about psychological consequences for a considerable time after a patient has an illness or has been told that he is at risk of illness. Although stress response syndromes are less frequent in such situations than after disasters or personal traumas, they may nonetheless occur and impede adaptation to medical conditions (Dimsdale and Hackett 1982).

Medical procedures can be embedded in a cascading series of stress events that characterize illnesses and modern treatment practices. Pain but, even more, the fear of pain, loss of control, or medical error can add to the psychological stress.

MENTAL ILLNESS AS A STRESS EVENT

Other mental disorders also may create a cascading series of stress events, while at the same time impair coping capacity. The individual who has a psychotic reaction, is hospitalized and treated, and then is to be discharged may also be regarded as having a stress response syndrome involving the memories (and fantasies) along this pathway of experience. If manic behavior occurred at work, there may be memories of the episodes that lead to a dreadful anticipation of social scorn on returning to the work place. If violent or bizarre behavior threatened loved ones during a paranoid reaction, the person who has now recovered to rational levels of interpersonal functioning may still have intrusive thoughts about the illness episodes. Witnessed struggles with staff or demented episodes of other patients in the hospital may also have been stressful events, during a period of relative "copelessness." The kind of brief psychotherapy to work through stressful life events, which will be discussed later, should also be considered as part of the overall approach to patients who have had such psychotic disorders or relevant nonpsychotic medical and psychiatric disorders.

CONCLUSIONS

Phases of stress response found in clinical studies of individuals who seek evaluation and treatment are also found in populations that sustain similar stress events and that are then evaluated as part of field study research. Intrusive thinking and denial characterize these phases. The generality of intrusive thinking as a stress response tendency led to the type of experiments to be described in the next chapter, as a further examination of the generality of this type of response in the experimental laboratory where many variables may be systematically controlled.

4

EXPERIMENTAL
FINDINGS

With Stephanie Becker and Nancy Wilner

Clinical and field studies agree regarding findings of general human responses to stress, which include a central tendency toward intrusive repetition and a counteractive tendency labeled as denial. The idea of a general tendency has another meaning beyond "pertaining to many people," and that is that it may occur after stress events of varying magnitude. Clinical and field studies are of persons after major stress events; minor events do not usually motivate persons to seek help. The study of responses to stress events that range from minor to moderate in intensity can, however, be examined in the laboratory. Such experimental studies are advantageous for several reasons: the degree of generality across kinds of events and kinds of persons can be examined under controlled circumstances, and the precise operational definitions necessary for experimental work may sharpen theoretical reflection.

All experiments summarized here used volunteer subjects who reported their conscious experiences before and after viewing a variety of stressful films. The findings indicated that intrusive and repetitive thought tended to follow this more moderate, nontraumatic kind of stress and that positive affect-inducing films and depressing films produced effects equivalent to those elicited by a film that threatened bodily injury. These data will be summarized in this chapter; the details have been published previously.

EXPERIMENTAL BACKGROUND

Films afford a well-studied and replicable laboratory device for providing visual stress events (Goldstein et al. 1965, Lazarus 1966, Lazarus and Opton 1966, Nomikos et al. 1968). Intrusive and repetitive thought can be defined and then quantified using self-report and content analysis procedures. Aside from the stress film method, the experimental literature on stress research provides few leads relevant to this paradigm (Higbee 1969). Fortunately, there is now a return to measuring conscious experience fostered by dream and hallucinogen research and more recently by interests in altered states of consciousness (Barr et al. 1972, Hartman 1967, Tart 1969). Lazarus (1966) developed a cognitive paradigm for experimental research on the impact of stressful films. Several teams have studied the effects of stress films on subsequent dreams (Breger et al. 1971, Cartwright et al. 1969, Witkin 1969, Witkin and Lewis, 1965). In brief, these studies indicate that the stressful experience incurred while awake is repeated later while in dreaming sleep. The repetition often occurs in covert forms. Contrary to clinical observations of response to traumas, nightmares were not noted. This omission of observation was due perhaps to the mildness of the experimental stress events or the heightened defensiveness of subjects in a laboratory setting. Intrusive thoughts were not measured in these studies.

METHODS

A Series of Experiments

The hypothesis states that after a visually perceived stress event imposed by film, subjects from a variety of population groups, given a variety of instructional sets, will report more intrusive thoughts, more repetitions of film contents, and more visual images than after a less stressful contrast film. This hypothesis was first tested in a pilot study, and when significant positive results were found, a series of replications with additional controls was conducted. The series varied the subject populations, the instructions and demand set given to the subjects, and the contents and order of the stress films. An outline of sequence and references is found in Figure 4–1.

Design

In a prototypic experiment, groups of subjects saw a stress film and a neutral contrast film in counterbalanced order. Before and after each film, measurements were taken to obtain baseline, postneutral film (referred to as neutral), and poststress film (referred to as stress) scores on selected variables.

Subjects

The volunteers in the different experiments were college students and enlisted men in military service.

Film Stimuli

The stress films were (1) *Subincision*, which depicts circumcision as part of a puberty rite; (2) *It Didn't Have to Happen*, a film showing woodshop accidents; and (3) an auto accident film. The neutral contrast film used was *The Runner*, which shows a man run-

References for details of particular experiments

a. Horowitz (1969)
b. Horowitz (1970)
c. Horowitz & Becker (1971a)
d. Horowitz & Becker (1971b)
e. Horowitz & Becker (1971c)
f. Horowitz, Becker & Moskowitz (1971)

g. Horowitz, Becker, Moskowitz & Rashid (1972)
h. Becker, Horowitz & Campbell (1973)
i. Horowitz & Becker (1973)
j. Horowitz & Wilner (1976)
k. Wilner & Horowitz (1975)

Figure 4–1. The Sequential Organization of the Series of Experiments

ning through the countryside meeting people along the way. All films were silent and edited to run from six to nine minutes.

Signal Detection Task and Mental Content Reports

The periods for reporting mental contents were interspersed between segments of a signal detection task that, though boring, demanded continuous attention as subjects judged whether a tone was higher, lower, or the same as the preceding tone. At the end of each segment, during a two-minute break, subjects wrote a report of their mental contents, defined as any thoughts, feelings, visual images, other images, observations, "flashes," memories, or anything else that occurred in the mind during the tone task (Horowitz 1969, 1970, Horowitz and Becker 1971c).

Self-Ratings of Affect

The affect ratings consisted of 11 mood words that the subjects rated on a 9-point scale to indicate their feelings at different points in the experiment. The negative affect words were anger, contempt, disgust, fear, nervousness, pain, sadness, and surprise, and the positive affect words were happiness, interest, and pleasantness.

Quantification of Data on Conscious Experience

The raw data from the mental contents reports were content analyzed by judges for intrusive thoughts, film references, and several other variables of less relevance here. The Spearman rank difference correlations for the two or three judges used in the separate experiments ranged from 0.85 to 0.94 for intrusions and 0.91 to 0.99 for film references.

Briefly, an *intrusive thought* was defined as any thought that implies nonvolitional entry into awareness, requires suppressive effort or is hard to dispel, occurs perseveratively, or is experienced as something to be avoided. A *film reference* was defined as any thought that refers directly to the film, film setting, or film experience, and it includes anticipations of seeing the film.

Instructional Demand

The different experiments varied according to the demand sets incorporated into instructions to subjects, because in studying con-

scious experience, such variables have been found to exert significant effects (Orne 1962, Rosenthal 1966). The main instructional
variances, as indicated in Figure 4–1, were to suggest to some subjects that intrusive images were minor equivalents of a pathological
process, such as that leading to hallucinations, and to other subjects
that such images were an unconsciously motivated normal process
aimed at mastering a stress event.

Data Analysis

Computer implementation of the Finn Multivanate Analysis
of Variance for a nonorthogonal design enabled the cross-experi-
mental data analysis reported here (Finn 1972). The analysis was
divided into stages, because not every variable was scored for every
experiment and not every design included baseline, neutral, and stress
conditions. The main variables, scored for every experiment, were
subjected to an analysis of variance for 133 subjects who had data
in all three conditions. Included as potential sources of variance for
this analysis were the subject groups; the demand set incorporated
in the instructions; the order in which films were viewed; the
baseline, neutral, and stress conditions; interaction effects; and variances among and within subjects.

RESULTS

The hypothesis that intrusive and repetitive thought would
occur most frequently in the stress condition was confirmed.

Intrusions and Film References

Tables 4–1 and 4–2 report an ANOVA and adjusted means
for the effects of all factors and conditions on intrusions and film
references. The population consisted of 133 subjects in various

Table 4–1. Analysis of Variance Data for Intrusion and Film References Considering All Factors and Conditions for 133 Subjects

INTRUSIONS				
Sources of Variance	*MS*	*df*	*f*	*p*
Among Subjects				
Population of Sample	7.46	2	1.01	<.37
Instructional Demand	16.16	3	2.18	<.09
Sex	16.84	1	2.27	<.13
Order of Films	1.14	1	.15	<.70
Among-subjects Error	7.42	117		
Within Subjects				
Condition	57.51	2	20.69	<.001
Cond. X Pop.	6.39	2	2.30	<.10
Cond. X Instruc.	1.67	3	.60	<.50
Cond.X Sex	3.13	1	1.13	<.30
Cond. X Order	1.05	1	.38	<.50
Within-subjects Error	2.78	234		
Film References				
Among Subjects				
Population	32.75	2	2.11	<.13
Instruct	1.16	3	.07	<.97
Sex	1.73	1	.11	<.74
Order	4.52	1	.29	<.59
Among-subjects Error	15.51	117		
Within Subjects				
Condition (s)	146.51	2	49.08	<.001
Pop. X Cond. (s)	14.04	2	2.57	<.10
Instruc. X Cond. (s)	6.93	3	1.27	<.20
Sex X Cond. (s)	5.72	1	1.05	<.30
Order X Cond. (s)	12.01	1	2.20	<.20
Within-subjects Error	5.47	234		

Table 4–2. Combined Means on Intrusions and Film References as Adjusted According to Report Length

Factor	N	INTRUSIONS			FILM REFERENCES		
		Base	Neutral	Stress	Base	Neutral	Stress
Population							
Military Inpts.	23	−.44	−.16	.41	−1.69	−.88	−.08
Civil. Students	82	−.83	−.40	1.38	−2.14	−.23	1.51
Health Students	28	−.50	−.11	.39	−1.53	.08	1.61
Sex							
Male	99	−.66	−.33	.55	−1.81	−.13	.98
Female	34	−.80	−.20	2.33	−2.29	−.69	2.05
Instructional Demand							
Normal	24	−.72	−.30	1.73	−2.26	−.53	2.44
Abnormal	25	−.63	.02	1.79	−1.96	−.25	1.65
Specific	16	−.49	.01	.93	−1.70	.07	.86
General	68	−.76	−.49	.49	−1.86	−.28	.78
Order							
Stress 1st	51	−.67	−.20	.57	−1.82	.16	.86
Neutral 1st	82	−.71	−.36	1.27	−2.00	−.55	1.50
Overall	133	−.69	−.30	1.00	−1.23	−.29	1.23

experiments who each had data on the variable in all conditions (baseline, neutral, and stress). At the $p < .05$ cutoff level, only the change in conditions exerts a significant effect on both intrusions (MS=57.5, df=2, F=20.70, $p < .001$) and film references (MS = 146.5, df=2, F=49.1, $p < .001$). Population differences (health sciences students, college students, military personnel), film order (stress or neutral first), sex of subjects, and instructional demand (general, specific, abnormal, normal slants) did not exert a significant influence. Intrusions and film references correlated positively in the stress condition ($r = .51$, $p < .001$, $n = 133$).

The adjusted means in Table 4–2 indicate deflections of a content analysis item from a norm of zero, with zero computed as the expectable level based on word length alone. Positive scores indicate the number of intrusions per subject above expectation, and negative scores indicate lower than expectable levels. The significant condition effect for intrusions is accounted for by the stress film. Baseline film references are, of course, especially low because no film has yet been seen, and only occasional anticipatory remarks have been made. The neutral and stress condition film reference levels are significantly different. Overall, 77 percent of the subjects were scored by two or three judges as having at least one episode of intrusions in the stress condition.

Intrusions Correlating with Degree of Reported Stress

In the stress condition, persons who rated themselves high on negative emotions tended also to report high levels of intrusions. The adjusted intrusion scores, in 133 subjects who made the same affect report measure during the stress condition, correlated significantly and positively with a composite of negative affects ($r = .27$, $p < .001$) and significantly and negatively with a composite of positive affects ($r = -.16$, $p < .05$) The highest correlation with specific individual affects was with pain ($r = .38$, $p < .001$) and surprise ($r = .35$, $p < .001$). With large numbers of subjects, some low levels of correlation (e.g., $r = -.16$) may reach statistical levels of significance but indicate only a small size of effect.

A group of 77 subjects also rated themselves after the stress film on a 1–100 "thermometer" scale for emotional and physical stress, following Stevens's method (1966). Both scales correlated significantly and positively with intrusion levels. For emotional stress, the correlation was $r = .39$, $p < .01$, and for physical stress, $r = .34$, $p < .01$.

MIXED AFFECT EXPERIMENT

The previous series of experiments indicated that the tendency toward intrusive thought is general in that it occurs even after the mild to moderate stress of seeing a silent film and is thus not restricted to traumatization or overwhelming stress. However, the theme of each stress film used was one of bodily injury, a topic usually evoking fear.

Though fear is highly relevant to the concept of stress and trauma, it is a specific and limited emotion. If intrusive repetitiousness is a general response tendency, it can be expected after the arousal of other types of emotion associated with other sets of information. This includes prediction of intrusive episodes even after arousal of positive affects.

To test this hypothesis, four stimulus conditions were used to evoke fearful, sad, pleasant, and comparatively neutral states. To maintain coherence with the previous series of studies, equivalent designs and measures were used. It was predicted that the three affect arousal states all would lead to intrusive and repetitive thought and that these responses would be significantly greater than those resulting from the comparatively neutral stimulus.

METHODS

Design

The subjects were drawn from the same population pool. They were ranked for emotional responsivity according to pretest data on their usual responses to horror, pornographic, and tragic films. Following their ranked order, they were evenly assigned to view films depicting either the separation of a small child from his parents, nude erotic interactions, bodily injury, or the neutral film used in the previous experiments. After collecting the data, as described earlier, the subjects were informed of an investigator's interest in qualities of thought and were taught how to rate themselves retrospectively for frequency and intensity of intrusive and repetitive thought. The data were analyzed by groups designated according to the particular film stimulus. There were eight film showings, two at each of four experimental sessions. Each of the four films was shown as the first film during one session and as the second film during another session.

Films

All of the films were silent and edited to run between six and nine minutes. The woodshop film provided the bodily injury stimulus, the runner film the neutral stimulus. For a separation theme, *John*, a documentary (Robertson and Robertson 1969), was edited by us and depicts an 18-month-old boy whose mother has just died. His father places him in a foundling home and makes occasional brief visits. The film portrays John's initial gregariousness; his subsequent angry, crying, and searching behavior; and finally, his lethargy, despair, and withdrawal. There are poignant close-ups of his facial expressions, some as he is rejected by his father, but no such shocking scenes as in the other negative affect film with its depiction of bodily injury. The basic theme of this film is the sadness of separation.

Erotic Film

The erotic film depicts a loving heterosexual couple enjoying foreplay and intercourse. The film is pleasurable and erotically arousing, with no hints of perversion. The erotic arousal, supplemented by activation of voyeuristic-exhibitionistic themes, is regarded as stressful because of the absence of immediate means to reduce this arousal.

Subjects

The subjects were 75 health science students.

Data Analysis

The direct means for each subject, derived by averaging the scores given by three judges, were used to analyze the mental content data, as the word length of reports was noted to be consistent among the subject subgroups. Analyses of variance were used to determine the significance of film, order, and sex effects. T-tests were used to examine the significance of differences among particular cells of data.

RESULTS

Film Effects

As predicted by the main hypothesis, intrusions and film references were high after the erotic, separation, and bodily injury films and low after the neutral film. This variation in films contributed the main effect, according to an analysis of variance (see Tables 4–3 and 4–4).

The bodily injury film, least evocative of intrusions of the three stress films, differed significantly from the neutral film ($t = 3.5$, df = 78, $p < .001$). The greatest differences among the three stress films was between the separation film (more intrusions) and the bodily injury film (fewer intrusions), but this difference was not significant. The stress films did not differ significantly for film references. The lowest film reference scores after a stress film were also those after the bodily injury film. This level was significantly higher than that noted after the neutral film ($t = 2.47$, df = 78, $p < .02$). Persons with high levels of intrusions tended to have high levels of film references after the separation film ($r = .61$, $p < .01$), the bodily injury film ($r = .49$, $p < .01$), and the neutral film ($r = .36$, $p < .05$) but not after the erotic film ($r = .16$, $p = NS$).

These content analysis variables had significant and positive correlations with the self-ratings completed by the subjects during

Table 4–3. Intrusions: Analysis of Variance and Means by Sex and Film

Source of Variance	df	MS	F	p
Order (1st or 2nd)	1	6.01	2.24	.14
Sex	1	8.93	3.33	.07
Film (Content)	3	18.31	6.82	.0003
Sex X Film	3	3.91	1.46	.23
Film X Order	3	4.39	1.63	.18
Between S's Error	134	2.68		

COMBINED MEANS	Erotic	Neutral	Separation	Injury	
Males	1.68	.62	1.42	1.58	1.27
Females	1.98	.68	2.98	1.74	1.83
	1.81	.64	2.23	1.65	

NUMBER OF SUBJECTS	Erotic	Neutral	Separation	Injury	
Males	22	27	15	20	84
Females	17	17	16	16	66
	39	44	31	36	150

Table 4–4. Film References: Analysis of Variance and Means by Order and Film

Source of Variance	df	MS	F	p
Order (1st or 2nd)	1	49.54	2.74	.10
Sex	1	25.02	1.39	.24
Film (Content)	3	81.99	4.54	.0046
Sex X Film	3	14.03	.78	.51
Film X Order	3	44.02	2.44	.07
Between S's Error	134	18.06		

COMBINED MEANS	Erotic	Neutral	Separation	Injury	
Order 1	3.94	3.16	5.32	3.12	3.80
Order 2	5.92	1.50	6.28	6.24	5.00
	5.26	2.48	5.72	4.68	

the retrospective phase of the experiments, except for frequency and intensity of film repetitions after the erotic film (see Table 4–5).

Affects

The data on affects conform to what one would expect from the films' themes. In analyses of variance, the film effects dominated and were highly significant for every affect (p values $< .0001$). Pleasantness, interest, and happiness were greatest after the erotic film. Sadness and anger were greatest after the separation film, and contempt was rated equally high for the bodily injury and the separation films. Fear, nervousness, physical sensations, pain, and disgust were greatest after the bodily injury film.

Correlations of selected individual affects with levels of intrusions after the separation film were positive between intrusions and sadness, greater than that of any other affect. Intrusions after the

Table 4–5. Correlation of Content Analysis and Self-report Variables

CONTENT ANALYSIS VARIABLES	SELF–REPORT VARIABLES					
	Frequency of Nondeliberate Film Repetitions			Intensity of Nondeliberate Film Repetitions		
INTRUSIONS	Erotic	Separation	Bodily Injury	Erotic	Separation	Bodily Injury
Erotic	.32[a]			.42[b]		
Separation		.62[c]			49[b]	
Bodily Injury			.71[c]			.68[c]
	FILM REFERENCES					
Erotic	.25			.15		
Separation		.60[c]			47[b]	
Bodily Injury			.54[c]			.36[a]

[a] p $< .05$
[b] p $< .01$
[c] p $< .001$

bodily injury film correlated positively but not significantly with reports of nervousness and physical sensations during the film. Intrusions after the erotic film also correlated positively and significantly with both physical sensations and happiness and nervousness.

Self-report of Intrusions and Repetitions

The self-ratings of nondeliberate film repetitions during the signal detection task, and the intensity of these repetitions, were significantly affected by the kind of film seen before the task (F = 4.15, df = 110, p <.008 for repetitions, F = 4.87, df = 110, p < .003 for intensity). This difference was due to the mild effects of the neutral film, as opposed to the films evocative of strong emotions, as shown in Table 4–6.

CONCLUSION

The tendency toward intrusive and repetitive thought after stressful events was observed in clinical, field, and experimental modes of investigation. This concept is clear and can be quantified. Both the field and experimental studies supplemented the clinical understanding by indicating that the tendency is a general one, found across divergent populations. The experimental studies also revealed another aspect of the generality of this pattern. Intrusive and repetitive thoughts usually occurred after stress that varied in the emotion that was aroused and in the intensity of that emotion in a range from mild to moderate to severe.

Table 4–6. Frequency and Intensity of Film Repetitions by Self-report. Group Means on a 1 (Low) to 9 (High) Scale for Frequency and Intensity

	Erotic	Neutral	Separation	Bodily Injury
Frequency of Repetition	4.23	2.06	3.77	3.75
Intensity of Repetition	4.38	2.11	4.06	4.03

II

GENERAL THEORY

5

EXPLANATION OF SYMPTOM FORMATION

The findings regarding stress response syndromes can be summed up as a list of observations to be accounted for by theory:

1. There are general response tendencies to stressful events. Although people vary in resiliency, areas of vulnerability, and available supports, those subjected to enough stress may be expected to show some stress response symptoms.
2. The response tendencies are also general in that they may appear after a variety of stress events differing in quantity and quality. (Different kinds of stress events may result in additional particular responses.)
3. Many stress responses persist long after termination and resolution of the external event. Some symptoms begin only after an interval of apparent restoration of calm.
4. After termination of the external stress event, one of the main observations is of intrusive repetition in thought, emotion, and/or behavior. A set of related but antithetical

responses, including ideational denial, emotional numbness, and behavioral avoidances, is also frequently noted.

5. These stress response tendencies of intrusion and denial are inclined to occur in temporal phases, at least after major stress events. Phases may overlap, and persons may vary in their entry into and emergence from a phase and in their sequence and termination of phases. One person may function in different phases with regard to different complexes of ideational and emotional responses. Abstracting a general stress response tendency from a wide range of variation in individuals and kinds of stress events, one arrives at the following cognitive and emotional sequence:

   a. Phase of initial realization that a stress event has occurred, often with a sharply accelerated expression of reactive emotion.

   b. Phase of denial and numbness.

   c. Mixed phase of denial and intrusive repetition in thought, emotion, and/or behavior.

   d. Phase of further ideational and emotional processing, working through, and acceptance (or stable defensive distortion), with a loss of either the denial or the peremptory recollection of the stress event.

EARLY PSYCHOANALYTIC EXPLANATION

In his later theoretical model of psychic trauma, Freud (1920) hypothesized that traumas occur when excessive stimuli overexcite the mind. He accounted for the different responses to the same kind of life event by hypothesizing variations in a "stimulus barrier." This barrier against stimulation was a theoretical construct to account for the regulation of the perceptual entry of information and energy from external events into the psychic apparatus. Freud also conceptualized the motive for altering this stimulus barrier. Signals of danger, fear, or anxiety are activated as an external stress event is anticipated or sampled by the initial perception (Freud 1926). As the anxiety increases, the stimulus barrier is raised and so accepts less input.

The term *anxiety*, as used here, is a theoretical construct and not necessarily a felt emotion. The term *stimulus barrier* also refers to a theoretical construct. Though widely used in the early psychoanalytic literature, the term has unfortunate concrete implications. Reduction and augmentation functions are performed by multiple processes at various levels of stimulus processing. The concept of regulation is thus relevant, but to avoid the concrete metaphor of a barrier, I use the term *modulation* of stimulus input. This modulation can occur, as external events are appraised, at any step of the information processing. This regulation includes both inhibitions and facilitations of representation and sequencing.

Freud's theoretical model conceptualized a feedback loop. Suppose that there is a continuous perceptual sampling of an ongoing external stress event and that the degree of processing of this information can be regulated. The degree of this modulation, in turn, depends on the magnitude of aroused emotions such as fear or anxiety. Initially, as the information input increases, signal emotions, such as anxiety, also increase. The anxiety encourages an increase in defensive inhibitions, and so there is a reduction in information processing. And when the anxiety decreases as a result of these controls, the emotional motive for modulation also decreases. With less modulation there is then more information processing and so the anxiety or other emotional arousal increases again. If such a dynamic system is unstable at its extremes, the feedback loop and transactional arrangement may lead to phases in which there is a decrease from higher levels of anxiety and an increase from lower levels. In information-processing models this is called *marginal instability*.

Freud's clinical theory of traumatization was developed during his observation and training with Charcot, the French scholar of hysteria and hypnosis, and in his subsequent work with Breuer on hysteria (Breuer and Freud 1895). The Breuer–Freud theory of the traumatic etiology of hysterical symptoms emphasized not only the role of external stress events but also the importance of repressing certain ideas and emotions triggered by the event and by contributors to the earlier internal stress events. As Breuer and Freud stated, persons with hysterical symptoms actually suffer from reminiscences because they cannot remember and they cannot *not* remember. When they try to remember, they have either partial amnesia or an overwhelming uncontrolled recollection. And when they try not to remember, they have intrusive "breakthroughs" such as unbidden images.

In these early formulations, repression is a control concept, related to memories, associated ideas, and event-reactive emotions and impulses. The difference between Freud's theory of repression and that of the stimulus barrier is that in repression the inhibition is directed against traumatic memory rather than against traumatic perceptions. The classical psychoanalytic theory of control over the contents of consciousness is a system of dual entry of information from internal and external sources with a feedback loop allowing for defensive regulation of both sources. Symptoms of amnesia are explained in this model as the products of overextensive inhibitory control. Intrusions are failures of defensive inhibition in the face of impulsive facilitations. In later formulations this thesis was complicated by the need to include other unconscious defensive operations involved in the formation of symptoms, which earlier had been explained as instances of repressive failure.

INFORMATION PROCESSING EXPLANATION

Evocation of a stress state requires that the person register and interpret incoming stimuli as cues of threat. One reason for the variance in individual responses to stress events is that persons differ in registration and interpretation as well as in styles and capacities for coping with threats. In recent decades psychologists have worked increasingly with cognition and have attempted to model the place of cognitive mediation in the sequence from stress event to stress response.

Lazarus, an influential experimentalist and theoretician in the psychology of cognitive aspects of response to stress (Lazarus 1966, Lazarus and Folkinan 1984), emphasized the importance of appraisal in coping with threat. Very simply, he considers emotions as responses to concept-forming operations. A person views environmental cues as threatening or nonthreatening through primary and secondary appraisals and reappraisals. The degree of threat appraised and reappraised leads to variations in emotions such as fear, anger, depression, euphoria, and elation. Tomkins (1978) views such emotions as ways of increasing the motivation to respond, as amplifications of the response tendencies activated by threats, or as tension reductions.

Lazarus explained that secondary appraisals compare the threat with the coping resources and with several reappraisals of threat to see whether it exceeds the coping capacity. The discrepancy between the degree of threat and the available coping capacity thus accounts for the emotion activated. An initial emotional response such as fear or anger may be reduced when a benign reappraisal of threat is made through cognitive processing.

A cognitive elaboration of the psychoanalytic model of stress response was developed by Janis, another leading psychological theorist and investigator (Janis 1958, 1962, 1967, 1969, Janis and Leventhal 1968, Janis and Mann 1977). Janis and Lazarus agree on the importance of cognitive processing, although Janis emphasized emotions as motives, in contrast with Lazarus, who emphasized cognitive processing as a precursor and cause of emotional responses (Lazarus et al. 1969). But these positions are not incompatible, as there may be many levels of conscious and unconscious information processing, with emotional responses serving as both cause and effect at different levels of representation.

Janis followed and elaborated the classical psychoanalytic model while emphasizing the distinctive motivational properties of what he called "reflective fear." He joined the word *reflective* to fear to obtain a term more precise than the hypothetical construct *signal anxiety*. The word *reflective* indicates that both threat and information from cognitive processing affect the magnitude of this kind of emotional response to danger. When aroused, reflective fear can lead to three modes of adjustment of the stress state. Janis called these adjustments increased needs for vigilance or reassurance or fusions into a compromise of the two divergent tendencies.

Vigilance needs strengthen the cognitive processing of the other cues, relevant or not, and may lead to the misinterpretation of cues and unwarranted increases in reflective fear. Startle reactions are one example. Reassurance needs may motivate thought processes that lead to either appropriately or inappropriately reassuring ideas. In pathological degrees, reassurance needs lead to "blanket reassurance," a reduction in reflective fear, and, hence, to unwarranted and perhaps maladaptive complacency. In extreme forms, then, reassurance contains elements of denial and numbness. In fusions, the person may be in hypervigilant-to-perception states while professing denial and feeling only blunted emotions.

The difference in emphasis on emotions as motives or as responses can be resolved. That is, emotions, thoughts, and controls can be considered as they interact. Emotions are responses to thought processes, thus providing a circuit for the equilibration of levels of emotional arousal.

Additional support for such transactional models and the central importance of ideational processes is found in field studies of response to surgery as related to clinically rated levels of fear before the operation (Cohen and Lazarus 1973, Johnson et al. 1971). The findings failed to replicate Janis's findings that anticipatory fear reduces postoperative distress. Johnson and his colleagues therefore rejected the Janis theory that fear is drivelike in its motivation of cognition, as in his concept of the "work of worrying." Instead, like Lazarus, Johnson and his colleagues modeled emotion as a response. Saltz (1970) supported this model in his review of experimental research on anxiety and threat, showing that the data do not sustain the theories that anxiety functions as a drive (Spielberger 1966, Taylor and Spence 1952).

Nonetheless, emotions such as anxiety can have motivational functions when they influence the controls, which in turn modify the cognitive processes. Low levels of emotion may themselves act as new information, for example, as bodily sensations, and these sensations may increase associations to memories related to similar bodily-sensory states. This may influence and promote a working-through process. Janis's formulations and findings thus remain viable and useful. At high levels of emotional arousal, however, inhibitory controls may be activated, and a reverse effect may occur, constricting the associational width and inhibiting the ideational processing. The reason for this heightened control lies in part in the motives to avoid accelerating anxiety, to avoid entering into highly fearful states of mind, or to be able to exit from them.

TERMINATION OF STRESS STATES BY ACTION

Action is the prototypic terminator of stress states because action changes events. The knight who slays an attacking dragon terminates the threat. He also discharges (or changes) the state of his own rage and rage-action plans as activated by the effrontery of the dragon's attack. The knave who runs faster than the dragon can also cancel the stress of the attack and discharge (or change) his fear and fear-action plan. In either case, successful action terminates the stress event. Emotions such as fear of the dragon or rage at it also are reduced by successful action. Such termination of states of emotional appetite, as Dahi suggested (1977), can be conceptualized in two ways. The traditional view is that there is a discharge of aroused emotions through action. The cognitive view is that there is a reduction of emotion because of the completion of a script, the discharge of an intention, or the modification of schematized belief structures, otherwise called cognitive maps.

With the addition of this concept of terminating external stress events, a model can be developed showing that internalized action plans can be terminated by means of cognitive processing in the absence of externally expressed actions. Such a model is relevant to understanding the symptomatic responses to stress that persist or begin after the external stress events are terminated.

The need to match new information with inner models based on older information, and the revision of both until they agree, can be called a *completion tendency* (Horowitz 1976). The assumption of a completion tendency is not new. Festinger (1957) described similar forms of cognitive processing as part of a need to reduce cognitive dissonance, and French (1952) explained conceptual shifts as ideas passed through integrative fields. Mandler (1964) observed a completion tendency in a complex series of interrupted behavioral responses. After an organized response system has been interrupted, it usually resumes later and continues until the initial plan has been completed. Mandler followed Miller and colleagues (1960) in attributing this effect to a built-in tendency to execute successive steps, as in a computer program. Script theory elaborates this point of view (Schank and Abelson 1977).

In an earlier but parallel theory, Lewin (1935) stated that any intention to reach a goal produces a tension system that is preserved until a goal is reached. It was this theory that led to the prediction of the Zeigarnik effect. The Zeigarnik effect is greater memory for incomplete than for complete cognitive tasks. Mandler (1964) suggested that in addition to the completion tendency of initiated plans, interruption may lead to a state of increased arousal that is distressing and is maintained until the plans have been completed. The organism thus favors completion in order to end this distress.

In his theoretical model of peremptory ideation, Klein (1967) further developed this concept of the completion tendency and the distress-reduction tendency of plans or programs. He added this concept of conscious and unconscious plans for processing thought and also the concept of defense as an interruption mechanism used when there is a threat of distress if the plan were to go forward unchecked. When inhibition is lessened or when motives increase, the cycle resumes operations and follows the interrupted plan. Thus the tendency toward cognitive completion is emphasized in various theoretical approaches.

The Completion Principle

The completion principle summarizes the human mind's intrinsic ability to continue to process new information in order to bring up to date inner schemas of the self and the world. This continual revision of relatively enduring structures of meaning is necessary to bring these inner models into accord with current reality so that they can guide decisions toward the next most effective possible actions. Persons in a healthy mental state maintain a variety of inner working models or "cognitive maps" of basic factors in their lives. These factors include their body image, various other self-concepts, role relationship models, scripts and agendas, spatial layouts of their repeated environmental circumstances, and other schemas that help them organize their perceptions and plan their next moves.

A stressful life event is, by definition, one that is not fully in accord with a person's usual inner working models. It contains either too much or too little of some familiar situation, but more often, it is not the familiar situation but something else that threatens equilibrium and the expectation that things will remain constant. When this happens, the news of the event must be reappraised so that it either conforms to inner models or is reappraised as unimportant, or else inner schemas must be revised so that they match the changed circumstances.

After deaths, personal injuries, and other serious life events, beliefs about and schemas of self, relationships, and other aspects of the personal world must be revised. Such processes require considerable cognitive change and extended time for the necessary information processing, and therefore, the point of completion cannot be achieved at once. In addition, every recognition of the discrepancy between the new state of affairs and the inner habitual model may bring emotional responses that are sufficiently painful so as to interrupt the information processing necessary to reach the completion point. Until completion, we assume that there is some type of memory that retains the important but incompletely assessed set of memories, ideas, and feelings. This type of memory re-presents this set whenever opportunity and inner choice permit.

Repetition as a Property of Active Memory Storage

A key assumption is a type of memory with motivational properties that tends to instigate a next step in processing. Because of this intrinsic property, it will be labeled as *active memory*. The assertion is that active memory storage has an intrinsic tendency to repeat the representation of contents. This repetition will cease when the contents held in active memory have been terminated by the completion of cognitive processing.

Active memory storage, with a tendency toward repeated representation in thought, is contrasted with inactive memory. *Active* and *inactive* memory can also correspond to current usage of the terms *short-term* and *long-term memory*, respectively. But the term active memory is preferable here to short-term memory because intrusive stress-event recollections may occur for a long time. This assumption of an active memory with special properties of recurrent representation is compatible with experimental findings in the fields of perception, attention, and memory. For example, Broadbent (1971) summarized this research and developed a model that has several forms of short-term memory that occur after sensory registration and before transformation of information into long-term memory.

Broadbent includes three kinds of short-term memory. One is a "buffer storage" that holds images for a while after the sensory registration ceases. The second is a "rehearsal buffer" that retains important images for longer periods than does the rapid decay of information in buffer storage. The third is "primary memory by slots" in which certain memories remain in a kind of active information bank. It is of greatest relevance to our formulation that information is retained in the primary memory slots until it is terminated by replacement with other, presumably more important, information. Stress-related information is, by definition, very important and hence is not terminated until it is assimilated. This concept of active memory is related to the concept of conditioned associations. Active memories include conditioned association between stimuli and threat response. They are also processed so they articulate with declarative as well as procedural knowledge. Extinction of conditioned threat responses would occur as completion was reached, that is, as articulations led to integrations. In that sense, working through a stressor event would involve many finer-unit linkages that were desensitized.

Processing Stressful and Nonstressful Events

The recurrence of a familiar nonstressful event is likely to be quickly and automatically assimilated. The cognitive processing will be completed, and the information in active memory storage will be rapidly terminated. The information in novel and stressful events, however, cannot be processed rapidly. Thus the point of relative completion is not achieved, and so the active memory retention is not terminated, with relevant codings of information remaining in active memory.

Assuming a limited capacity for processing, such codings will remain stored in active memory even when other programs (those used for processing other sets of information) have greater priority in the hierarchy of claims for channels. These actively stored contents, however, will generally be repeatedly represented. Each episode of representation will trigger a resumption of processing. Thus, whenever this set of information achieves a high enough priority, representation and processing will resume. If the contents are interrupted by controls that regulate priorities, they will remain in coded form in active memory.

Incongruity

Completion requires the resolution of differences between new information and enduring mental models. Thus, news of the death of a loved one is incongruent with an entire world picture that includes not only wishes and hopes but also habits and routine roles and self-images. Cognitive processing is reinitiated when representation occurs and may evoke unpleasant emotions such as fear or anxiety. Every repetition is a confrontation with a major difference between what is and what was and what was gratifying and may invoke various responsive emotional states such as fear, anxiety, rage, panic, or guilt. If these emotional responses are likely to increase beyond the limits of toleration, the result may be distraught, overwhelmed states of mind. To avoid entry into such states of mind, therefore, controls are activated that will modify the cognitive processes (Horowitz 1979a, 1998). For example, the path from active memory storage to representation and processing can be inhibited. This reduction in processing reduces anxiety and, in turn, reduces the motivation for controls. With the reduction in control, the tendency of active memory toward representation then reasserts itself. Other immediate programs may be interrupted with the repeated representation of the stress-related information. The processing of the stress-related information resumes; the anxiety increases, the control increases; and the cycle continues.

This simple model leads to states of high and low emotion, high and low degrees of representation, and continuation and cessation of processing. The oscillation continues because of the intrinsic tendency of active memory to repeat the representation until the point of completion. Only stable controls or absent controls lead to a steady state, a situation seldom encountered in human psychology.

With each "on" phase of information processing, more and more alterations of inner working models and plans for adaptive action are accomplished. This process continues until completion. With the relative completion of information processing, the cycle terminates, because the relevant contents are cleared from active memory storage. The "new" information has now been integrated with the inner mental models and organized memories. Inner models or schemas are now relatively congruent with the new information about the self and the world, and with the actual external situation to the extent that it is represented accurately in that new information.

Information Processing

One aspect of the processing of traumatic perceptions and memories can be conceptualized as a series of matchings of different types of representations. For example, new stimuli are matched with expectancies based on current needs or fears; new information about the world is matched with schematic representations of the world; current body sensations are related to body images, images are matched with relevant labels such as words; new demands are matched with available coping strategies; and so forth.

When there is not an immediate good fit between the new information and the existing schemas, further information processing is instigated. This then leads to progressive modifications of the meaning of the recently acquired information and/or to progressive modifications of the preexisting models. This processing for fit leads to a series of approximating representations of the stress event and the relevant schemas.

When there is a limited channel capacity for processing and when these channels are "claimed" by problems with greater priority, then the progressive series of representations that do not yet "fit" together is stored in active memory. This set mixes information from the life event with preliminary associations to it. It will be represented again when it has relatively high priority (e.g., when it is associatively triggered or primed or when more urgent business is finished, as when the driver of a car finds a place to stop after calmly driving through a nearly disastrous accident, then reconsiders the events and only then has a panic reaction).

A single traumatic event may set in motion several trains of thought and feeling. It may need to be associated with different constellations of memories, personal agendas, and varied schemas of self and relationships. The matching between inner sets of organized meaning and the traumatic event may lead to varied emotional states. A specific traumatic event may lead to an appraisal of the self as being too weak to cope; this might activate strong emotional responses of fear. The event might also be associatively linked to previous themes of personal blame, and activate usually latent schemas of the self as a bad person. The strong emotion of guilt might result if the information was processed along that route. To reduce the fear or the guilt, the processing of the given theme might be interrupted.

The activation of emotion begins as ideas are processed, and emotion is itself both represented and anticipated. These anticipations of emotional states are a part of both unconscious thinking and unconscious automatic processes. The person may have learned to interrupt processing of themes that lead to emotional states that feel particularly out of control, overwhelming, and unbearable. Although such interruption may prevent entry into intrusive, emotionally flooded states of mind, it also prevents completion of the work of integrating the stressful life event with that particular theme. Some themes may be worked through relatively completely at a given time; other themes may be warded off. In the latter case they have a "dynamic unconscious" property: preserved in active memory, they tend toward repeated representation and processing. When they are represented, it may be with an intrusive quality. When inhibited, a sense of numbing and avoidance may be present, or denial may be a totally unconscious mechanism without reflection in immediate consciousness.

CONSCIOUSNESS, UNCONSCIOUS PROCESSING, AND ADAPTIVE CHANGE

Encoded information about events, emotions, and defenses can become a conscious experience only when it is translated into representational form. Although only representations can become conscious experience, not all representations necessarily attract this special form of attention. Representational and prerepresentational thinking may proceed unconsciously, and many of the processes already mentioned proceed as unconscious computations. Even when representations become conscious, there are varieties and degrees of awareness, intensity, quality, duration, and memory for episodes of awareness. Their quality ranges from representation by action and sensory images to representation by word meanings (Horowitz 1970, 1998).

Theoreticians such as Hartmann (1939) and Kubie (1958) assumed a range of thought from automatic and relatively nonconscious forms of representational processing to conscious and nonautomatic processing. Roughly, the more conscious the thought is, the greater will be the probability of solving problems, but the slower will be the thought process. When information can be processed by habitual and automatic routes, then time is saved by doing so, and with a minimum of conscious awareness. This is what Lazarus meant by automatized coping. It thus follows that consciousness is most useful for working over representations that have high relevance and that do not fit well into habitual organizations of information. Suppose that consciousness is the experiential product of "recognizers" of representations that have high relevance but are not matched successfully with schemas. Stress events would then be more apt to reach conscious levels of awareness than would nonstress events because stress events are, by definition, of high relevance and out of the ordinary. Routine expectations and intentions are disrupted, and representations associated with stress events that are difficult to process to completion are also recognized. The recognizer function would be a kind of conceptual enlargement, as suggested by Tomkins (1962, 1978), or some method of reduplication, increased intensity, or spatial expansion of information. This enlargement then would produce a conscious experience of the representation.

The recurrent stress–event representations, often reported as intrusive and unusually vivid when compared with ordinary conscious experience, would be caused by the propulsion to consciousness by the recognition that the theme was important to the self and that its unconscious processing was stymied. The entry of these representations into conscious awareness may be experienced as intrusive for several reasons: the association of the thematic content with the threat and emotional pain of the states of mind during the traumatic events, the unusual vividness of representations derived from memories and traumatic perceptions, the intuitive knowledge that the representational process has been opposed by inhibitory controls, and the emergence of representations unconnected to the immediately previous and intended train of thought.

Despite the conscious experience of intrusiveness, however, the end result may be adaptational, because the conceptual processes initiated by the conscious representation may lead to revising the automatic processing of such information, to revising the relevant schemas, to inventing new solutions, and to completing the processing of the stressful information.

In the psychotherapy of stress response syndromes, the process of using conscious awareness for change is often of importance. The interventions of the therapist and the safe relationship established with the patient are aimed at altering the controls by which the stress-related ideas are warded off and the intolerable emotional states that threaten to emerge if the ideas are not warded off. Consciousness for the sake of awareness alone is not the goal; rather, conscious contemplation is used as a tool for unlearning automatic associations and resolving seemingly irreconcilable conflicts. Change is accomplished by a combination of conscious and unconscious processes, by the revisions, learning, and the creation of new solutions required by the altered situation. In other words, change can be explained as decisions, both conscious and unconscious, that revise inner schemas and plans for action. The goal is continuity of the traumatic experience with other life memories, and the reintegration of personal aims.

RECAPITULATION

The mind operates to maintain inner schemas that relate the self to others and the surrounding world. One interprets new information by means of those schemas and revises them to remain true to current reality. Serious life events such as a loss or injury present news that will eventually change the inner models. But the change is slow; time is essential to reviewing the implications of the news and the available options for response. The mind continues to process important new information consciously and unconsciously until the situation or the models change and the reality and the schemas of that reality reach an accord. This tendency can be called a *completion tendency*.

Until completion occurs, the new information and the reactions to it are stored in active memory. According to this theory, the active memory contents will be transformed into representations whenever that process is not actively inhibited. Only when the storage of those contents in active memory has been terminated will this repeated representation end. For very important contents, termination will not occur with decay but will occur only when the information processing is complete. At that point, the news will be part of the revised inner schemas.

As ideas related to the stress event are represented, there will be a natural comparison of the news with relevant and assorted enduring attitudes. Because a stress event is, by definition, an important change, there will be a discrepancy among the news, its implications, and the enduring, slowly changing schemas. This discrepancy between the new ideas and the schemas evokes emotion: serious life events are so different from one's inner models of oneself, one's attachment to others, and one's inner world view that very painful emotional responses result, threatening emotional states of such power that controls are activated to prevent their occurrence or continuation.

Perceptions and immediate responses to serious life events remain stored in active memory because on first encounter the meanings are recognized as having high personal importance. Because the contents are strongly coded in active memory, they tend to be represented intensely and frequently. With each recurrence of the information, the comparisons are made again, and the emotional activation increases. Emotional responses are also represented and so become part of the constellation stored in active memory. When other tasks are more immediately relevant or when emotional responses such as fear, guilt, rage, or sorrow are a threat, the controls are initiated. This feedback thus modulates the flow of information and reduces emotional response.

Excessive controls interrupt the process, change the state of the person, and may prevent completion. Failures of control lead to the excessive levels of emotional flooding and retraumatization. Optimal controls slow down recognition processes and so provide tolerable doses of new information and emotional responses. In this optimal condition, some intrusiveness will occur with repeated representation, and some denial will occur when the controls operate more pervasively, but the overall result will be adaptive in that the reaction to the stressful life event will eventually be mastered and completed. The schemas will also eventually conform to the new reality, as in the process of completing mourning.

At any given time, different sets of meanings of a stress event will be at different stages and levels of processing. The degree and effectiveness of controls of themes may vary. For example, fear of repetition or fear of merger with a victim may be a recurrent intrusive experience, whereas survivor guilt themes may be totally inhibited from conscious experience. Later, in situations of greater safety, the warded-off guilt theme may surface as an intrusive experience.

This model accounts for the phases of intrusion and denial and the eventual resolution of stress response syndromes. Although general stress response tendencies can be abstracted in this way, persons also respond in unique ways. This is due in part to how their developmental history colors their personal meanings of an event and in part to how their current life tasks and environment are affected by the event. Individual variations in response to the same kind of life event are also due in part to variations in their habitual style of controlling emotion.

CONTROL OF EMOTION

Control theory in psychodynamics has been historically discussed in terms of the defense mechanisms (A. Freud 1936). Yet the names of defense mechanisms indicate *what* is accomplished rather than *how* it is accomplished. Wallerstein (1967) pointed out this hiatus in the existing theory of defenses and defense mechanisms and defined *defense mechanism* as a theoretical construct used to denote a functioning of the mind, a way of warding off or modulating impulses, ideas, and feelings. *Defenses* are the actual thoughts, feelings, and acts that serve defensive purposes. Complex configurations of defense are called *defensive maneuvers*. Similarly, attempts have been made to detail coping strategies (Lazarus and Folkman

1984, Pearlin and Schooler 1978). Again, the available combinations of processes and actions complicate any limited or comprehensive categorization, although there are several coping styles (see also Coelho et al. 1974, Monat and Lazarus 1977, Moos 1976).

As Haan (1977) pointed out, a specific mental process may have various end results, including coping and defensive functions, as well as the failure to meet adaptive aims. It seems to me that a theory of defense, of coping, and of succumbing to stress (defensive or coping "failure") can be reformulated by considering the controls most used to modulate emotional reactions to serious life events. Understanding the inhibitions, facilitations, distortions, and deflections involved in the processing of information is useful also in formulating techniques of psychotherapeutic treatment of stress response syndromes. The aim is to help the person reverse a course of succumbing to stress, to use those operations that lead to coping, and to set aside those control operations that are so defensive as to impede adaptation.

Controls maintain a state of mind and determine the transition from one state of mind to another. The basic controls are inhibition and facilitation, but it is helpful to be more specific about what is inhibited or facilitated. To do so, we shall separate controls into the following three levels: (1) selecting the overall topic and mode of thinking about it; (2) selecting schemas such as the self-concepts, role relationship models, and agendas or scenarios that will organize the examination of this topic; and (3) selecting the information to be used and skirted in sequences of thought and feeling about the topic. Any phenomenon, such as a recurrent and intrusive image of a dead body weeks after seeing it during an automobile accident, will be a consequence of the operation of many controls at all three levels.

Mental Set: Selecting the Topic and Mode of Thought

Mental set is a broad level of abstraction that refers to the choice of topic, the mode of thinking on that topic and, in a general way, the activation or excitation level. Within this level of abstraction, the control operations most relevant to modulating responses to stress are summarized in Table 5–1. Listed first is the conceptual area selection, an operation that determines the next constellation of information for conceptual processing. While the person is working through serious news, the topic or an aspect of the event may be inhibited or facilitated, resulting in the experience of time on and time away from considering that constellation. This operation can lead to coping experiences, such as when a person doses the recognition of a threat with time off from facing unpleasant realities in order to regain composure. An end result called defensive rather than coping might be total inhibition with no time "on" any aspect of the topic. An inability to inhibit a stress event topic may lead to feelings of being flooded and dazed, a result that can be called succumbing to stress.

Another set of controls to format selects the mode of organizing information. One such operation is separating into long or short segments the time period to be considered. Extremes of such controls are common during responses to serious life events. One frequent end result is concentration on extremely short time intervals as a person handles a seemingly overwhelming situation by breaking it down into a series of steps, dealing with them one at a time, and describing only what should be done in the next minute or two, or by taking things "one day at a time." Another common response is to scan unusually long sweeps of time in order to place a bitter moment of suffering into a stretch of time that allows it to pale in significance or renders it meaningful in some larger, even cosmic, plan. Thoughts that suffering is a chance to "build character" or "expiate sin" are one result.

Another control over organizing stress-related information is selecting a sequential set. This sequential set determines the kind of flow from one bit of information to another. For example, problem solving is a mode in which bits of information are arranged by principles of logic and by fidelity to real probabilities. A quite different set is used in fantasy or experiential flows in which the next

Table 5–1. Controls of Mental Set

		SAMPLE OUTCOMES	
PROCESSES	Coping	Defense	Succumbing to Stress
Selection of next topics for thought	Dosing (periods of time on and off topic)	Denial of importance of an important topic	Amnestic states, intrusion of topics
Mode of organization: temporal set (viewing theme by short or long time orientation)	Looking at only one step at a time, relating the event to a life span	Denial of urgency of threat	Distraught states such as panic
Mode of organization: sequential set (problem solving versus reverie modes)	Thinking only about what to do next, restoring fantasies of lost situations	Workaholism, obsessive rumination and doubting, fantasy preoccupation, faith in unrealistic views	Confusion
Mode of organization: representational set (words, images, muscles, autonomic nervous system, hormones)	Solving problems in words because images evoke too many emotions (intellectual analysis)	Denial of emotional responses to threat, isolation of topics into one mode of representation (words without images, images without words, ideas without emotion)	Emotional flooding
Mode of organization: locus set (external or internal sources of information)	Making restorative changes of activity and contemplation	Compulsive action to avoid thought, fantasy to avoid action	Illusions, hallucinations, felt presences
Activation Level (excitation or dampening of various systems, regulating rate of information flow)	Creating cycles of working and resting	Hypervigilance, avoidant sleeping	Exhaustion

bits of information can be associatively linked to preceding bits by sensory similarities and to congruencies of wish or fear rather than probability or accuracy. This is sometimes called primary process.

Heightening such controls after a serious life event leads to common responses. For instance, after being raped, a woman may find herself thinking only of what to do next, whom to call, what to say, and where to shower and rigorously avoiding any experiential reliving in memory of the terrifying event or any similar past experience. Another result of such control is noted when after a rape, for example, the woman may only fantasize an unlikely revenge and avoid thinking about what she has to do next, such as telling someone who can help and support her. Similarly, after a death, the person may fantasize restoration of the lost object and avoid thinking of the implications of the event and the life functions that he must now assume. In such failures of control, the result may be an intrusion of fantasy during problem-solving thought or an intrusion into the awareness of real problems, either of which may lead to emotional flooding.

Control of representational set is another way to modulate expression of thought. These controls determine whether the flow of information will proceed in lexical, image, or enactive (motoric) forms. By using such controls, some persons think back on a serious life event, such as a car accident, only in words and block images to avoid emotional arousal from quasi-perceptual thought. Such operations help coping and also may provide defenses such as isolation and intellectualization. The episodes of intensive images of a bloodied body that may occur weeks after an accident are seen as a combination of the impetus of active memory, other motives, and the relative failure of the controls.

Likewise, other controls set the locus, as on the search for or relative acceptance of internal or external sources of information. The end results may be a successful search for relevant external information that also wards off the feelings that will emerge when personal implications are contemplated. The levels of activation of various systems can also be controlled, leading to various altered states of consciousness and also to physiological responses ranging from hyperarousal to hypoarousal (Fischer 1971).

CONTROLS THAT SELECT SCHEMAS OF SELF, OTHERS, AND RELATIONSHIPS

Controls that select schemas of self, others, and relationships choose how the self and others will be conceptualized. Every person has not just one self-schema or version of interaction between the self and others, but multiple inner models of roles and relationship sequences. The dominant model used to organize a train of thought influences the concepts and emotions that occur during the thought sequence. This will be discussed more in the next chapter. It helps to consider the control of such schemas here.

Controls select which of a person's several possible self-schemas will organize a series of ideas (Horowitz 1979a, Horowitz and Zilberg 1983). The results include the various progressions and regressions of identity that commonly occur after serious life events such as the death of a parent. The failure to select or stabilize a self-concept or the loss of a supraordinate self-schema may lead to experiences such as chaotic lapses in identity, as indicated in Table 5–2. Similarly, a person can decide whether to experience a given self-concept as a subject or an object, leading to a variety of common stress responses such as either unusually heightened states of self-actualization or depersonalization, or role reversals.

Another way to reduce emotional response levels while examining implications of a serious life event is to alter the governing model of role relationship between the self and others. A common coping response is to see oneself as more than usually in need and to seek help and support, or to become dependent on others. Common defensive responses are to adopt illusions of self-sufficiency, to split relationships into those that are all-good and all-bad, or to heighten introjective experiences in order to maintain an illusion

Table 5–2. Controls of Schemas as Organizers of Information

| | | SAMPLE OUTCOMES | |
PROCESSES	Coping	Defense	Succumbing to Stress
Altering which self-schema is an activated self-concept	Heightened sense of identity by using the most competent self-concept in the subject's repertoire of self-views	Omnipotent denial of personal vulnerability, "as-if" self-concepts, regressions to earlier self-concepts	Depersonalization, chaotic lapse of identity, annihilation anxiety
Altering dominance hierarchy of available role relationship models and scripts	Seeking help, sublimation	Dissociations and splitting, passive-dependent expectations	Sensation of helplessness, separation anxiety
Altering dominance hierarchy of available world views	Increased sense of unity or ideological commitment, altruism, increased sense of reality, sublimation	Altruistic surrender, increased self-centeredness	Sense of meaninglessness or derealization

of attachment. When these controls fail, a panicky state of mind with ideas of helplessness and emotions related to vulnerability and despair may result. All of these coping, defensive, and adaptive failure responses are well known to every psychotherapist. The point here is to indicate the need of going somewhat beyond managing the results of controls to recognizing the selection process itself, as a therapist's interventions can prevent inappropriate selections and maladaptive consequences.

INFORMATION FLOW SELECTION

The most familiar controls are those that govern the flow of ideas and responsive feelings because these controls accomplish the common defenses of denial, suppression or repression, undoing, and projection. The main controls of information flow are (1) facilitating; (2) inhibiting of representation; (3) switching among sets of information, a process of facilitation as well as inhibition; (4) sliding meaning; (5) shifting the locus of meaning, as from within the self to within another; (6) rearranging information, as in problem solving; (7) seeking new information; (8) revising preexistent goals and inner models; and (9) practicing to make revisions automatic rather than volitional efforts. The results of these controls are summarized in Table 5–3. The results are based on the interaction of many processes and are offered only to show emphasis. The most common impediments to working through the stress induced by a serious life event are inhibition, switching, and sliding meanings. These will be discussed in detail in later chapters on habitual personality styles.

BIOLOGICAL FACTORS

Activation of the neural systems into extremely high arousal or into special types of alarm and shock may interfere with the

Table 5–3. Controls of Ideas and Sequences

PROCESSES	SAMPLE OUTCOMES		
	Coping	Defense	Succumbing to Stress
Controlling Ideas by			
Facilitation	Contemplation of implications	Rumination	Inability to think clearly
Inhibition	Dosing, modulated arousal, selective inattention	Denial, repression, suppression, isolation, numbing, dissociations, use of drugs, flight, or suicide as avoidance	Intrusions and emotional flooding
Sequencing Ideas by			
Seeking information	Understanding, learning new skills	Intellectualization	Apathy
Switching among attitudes	Emotional balancing	Undoing	Indecision
Sliding meanings and valuations	Humor, wisdom	Reaction formation, exaggeration or minimization, displacement	Intrusions and emotional flooding
Arranging information into decision trees	Problem solving	Denial by rationalization	Inanition
Revising schemas	Adaptation, identifications, acceptance	Inappropriate role reversals by externalization or introjection	Giving up and hopeless states
Practicing new modes of thinking and acting	Deautomatization of outmoded linkages, automatization of new ways	Counterphobic rehearsals	Lack of preparedness for repetition of threat

consolidation of memory traces. This in turn may lead to memory impairments such as amnesias.

Christianson and Nilsson (1987) reported four experiments in which normal and horribly disfigured faces were presented to experimental subjects. Data from physiological measurements and post-experimental interviews indicated that negative emotions were aroused by the presentation of the disfigured faces. Each face was accompanied by four verbal descriptors, and amnesia was discovered for those items associated with the traumatic events. Various analyses of their data suggested that this amnesia was developed by limited encoding of the memory trace rather than by problems in retrieval or reconstruction. Such limitations on encoding traumatic perceptions probably have a biological basis.

Other biological factors found in post-traumatic amnesias may be due to head trauma. Even if there are no positive X-ray or electroencephalographic findings, the post-concussion syndrome may include general mental deterioration as well as particular memory disturbances and amnesias for a short period of time (Richardson 1979). These amnesias often include both retrograde and anterograde amnesia, lasting from minutes to months, in which the anterograde amnesia is usually more pronounced. Upon recovery, the retrograde amnesia gradually proceeds to cover the period of just a few seconds or minutes before the trauma and head injury (Whitty and Zangwill 1977). This phenomenon has been referred to as a recovery of "islands of memory." The entire issue of organic factors in the production of signs and symptoms of post-traumatic stress disorders pertaining to historical diagnostic issues, including the problem of malingering, was reviewed by Trimble (1981).

A third type of biological response may be the consequence of disruptions in attachment to another person, as is the case with bereavement. There may be several hormonal and immunological changes, and this psychological, neurological, and immunological circuit may lead to increased vulnerability to disease, though this has not yet been proved (see Osterweiss et al. 1984). Such changes in the biological systems, such as neurotransmitters, can also affect psychological capacities, such as feedback, and change a person's ability to exert regulatory operations, such as those pertaining to defense mechanisms.

These psychoneuroimmunological transactions are additions to the biology of how external threat stimuli activate the endocrine system's flight, fight, and conservation responses (e.g., Engel and Schmale 1967, Selye 1976). These involve not only the adrenal cortex and the noradrenergic system of neurotransmitters but other electrochemical messenger systems as well. Facilitations, inhibitions, and dysinhibitions may occur at synapses along particular pathways, and the mechanisms may change the configuration of protein molecules in different ways along neural pathways. Hormones may determine which genes in a neuron's nucleus will form the template for protein synthesis. This in turn will affect the vesicles near the synaptic cleft that contain neurotransmitters, and that may affect the synaptic potentials and information transfer (Kandel 1983). The brain under stress may also have an altered functional capacity, but the brain-to-mind connection of such factors is not completely understood. One may speculate that enduring psychological change, as in chronic fear arousal or extended despair, can set in motion a pathological brain state such as depression, which then secondarily impairs the kind of information processing emphasized here. Such factors would be in addition to the concomitant physical effects of certain traumas, such as head concussions during automobile or other accidents, or the malnutrition and sleep loss from some disasters.

Persons vary in their genetic inheritance and in how their basic neural systems are organized during development. Some persons may be predisposed to certain vulnerabilities that are then noted only in situations of stress. Biological predispositions—to a "short supply" of certain neurotransmitters, disruptive alarm reactions, or stabilization of a maladaptive state—may be different for those who can work through a stress response syndrome and those who may develop chronic symptoms.

SUMMARY

Everyone fears the inevitable loss of life and the trauma of capricious disaster. When these serious life events occur they can shatter a person's reality, and the inner models of the world that have sustained the person must now be changed to accord with the new situation. Such revisions take time. Recognition of the loss to oneself by accident or the loss of another by death evokes themes of guilt, fear, sadness, and rage. Avoiding recognizing these themes can numb the emotions, but that can create a discord between external reality and what the person believes. There is an interval of time before both the violent emotional pangs of recognition and the avoidance of recognition subside in favor of realistically accepting the new situation. During this interval, characteristic control processes help a person modulate her stress responses. This capacity for control is probably determined by biological as well as psychological factors.

6

RESCHEMATIZATION

Traumas can cause a shift from a competent to an incompetent self-attribution, with concomitant shifts in interpersonal behavior and internal working models of self–other roles. Such shifts are characterized by severely diminished self-esteem and self-confidence, irrational self-criticism, and heightened dependency or help-rejecting self-isolations. The self is experienced as unattractive, and contact with others is avoided to protect against *their* expected rejections. Disturbances in identity and relationships exacerbate symptoms such as intrusive memories, phobic avoidances, anxiety, dissociation, and depersonalization (Ursano et al. 1999).

Such disturbances are reduced as self and other views are reschematized to accommodate new stress-related facts. Such reschematizations can also lead to positive changes (Updegraff et al. in press). We know that in spite of stressors, some resilient children can grow to their full potential (Garmezy 1985, Rutter 1987). Stressful events in adulthood may be followed by a period of disequilibrium but can lead to a higher level of maturation than was present before the event (Calhoun and Tedeschi 1990, Pollock 1989, Taylor 1983).

Growth as a response to stress may occur when people are able to reach new levels of adaptation to the personal meanings of the dire events (Aldwin et al. 1996, Antonovsky 1987, Horowitz 1997b, Park et al. 1996, Tedeschi et al. 1998). This process involves giving up outmoded concepts, accepting the realities of the post-traumatic existence, and drawing upon strengths—both their own, and those within their social context or community (Epstein 1992, Horowitz et al. 1984a, Lazarus and Folkman 1984, Linville 1987).

In addition, some adult traumas reactivate childhood traumas. Adaptive change after the adult trauma can repair the prior damage and aid in self-reorganization (Horowitz 1998). This self-reorganization can result in an increase in self-esteem and a decrease in ambivalent attachments when compared with the pre-trauma personality.

The following two case histories illustrate post-traumatic shifts in identity. The case of Harold illustrates a mild shift, and the case of Sophia, a major one.

Harold

While traveling on business in another country, Harold and his wife escaped a hotel fire with minor smoke inhalation injuries. Their schedule was disrupted and Harold and his wife agreed that she would return home at once while Harold rescheduled local appointments.

Five days later, in the midst of work, he felt unreal and numb. He became too talkative and attention-seeking with the women he encountered in business. That night he awakened from a nightmare screaming "Mommy, mommy." During the next day he felt tense, anxious, and had a sense of chaos about his life roles. He canceled his business appointments, flew home, and sought professional help.

On evaluation, he had intrusive memories of the fire, of seeing his wife off at the airport, and of being embarrassed by his inappropriate encounters with businesswomen. He felt phobic and avoided planning future business travel even though his work depended on it. He had chronic tension and episodes of hyperventilation. In case formulation it was decided to focus brief therapy on how and why the fire and its sequelae led to an activation of maladaptive latent self-concepts. These included feeling like a needy, dependent boy requiring maternal attention, and feeling abandoned without it.

The task of restoring equilibrium was rapidly accomplished. Harold had fewer intrusive, avoidant, and hyperarousal symptoms but he still felt vulnerable and lacking in his usual verve and self-confidence. Additional therapy sessions then focused on his relationship with his wife. This work increased his sense of self-confidence and identity coherence and enabled him to engage more mutually with her than he was able to before the event. He recovered all of his pre-traumatic functional levels and felt even better about his capacity for intimate affiliation.

In the case of Harold, the trauma was minor as compared to the next example where a cascade of traumatic results was experienced due to an unfortunate accident.

Sophia

Sophia made an excellent living as a sought-after model until a sudden car accident resulted in severe injuries that caused permanent blindness and required amputation of one of her legs. She also emerged with severe facial scarring. Sophia spent weeks in the hospital and then months in a convalescent home.

Initially, she did not allow herself to be aware of her blindness; she would not discuss the topic. She did, however, think and talk about the loss of her leg. Her lack of recognition of blindness was astonishing to staff members since she had to be constantly assisted in many functions.

Sophia's sense of identity had not shifted to accommodate the terrible news of her altered body. She repeatedly asked staff members when she could schedule her modeling appointments. Only after weeks passed did she communicate about being blind;

the topic of her facial disfigurement and loss of a career was discussed even later. After three months passed, she was willing to have a psychiatric consultation and she then accepted a recommendation for psychotherapy.

In the context of this therapy, Sophia took two years to recover psychological equilibrium and develop an identity that was coherent with her altered bodily functions and social opportunities. She learned new self-concepts through a variety of means, including identification with the effective roles and positive attitudes she observed in various health professionals. She trained as a rehabilitation therapist specializing in music therapy. Later she married, and still later she became a teacher who trained music therapists. In order to comprehend the processes of such adaptive changes, we need to understand theories that explain both shock mastery and complex processes of reschematization.

SHOCK MASTERY AND RESCHEMATIZATION

Shock Mastery

As discussed in the prior chapter, traumatic memories have excessive associative linkages with stress-related ideas and systems that arouse alarm emotions (Epstein 1992, Horowitz 1976, Lazarus and Folkman 1984, Taylor 1983). If the person is exposed to stimuli similar to those of past traumatic perceptions, then the entire associative complex may be activated and lead to floods of intense emotion. Shock mastery is a shorthand term for the complex and multiple memory-cognition-emotion processes that reduce some of the strong associative connections. Habituation, extinction, and desensitization are outcomes of such processes.

Shock mastery leads to a decrease in the frequency and intensity of intrusive flashbacks and startle reactions. Reschematization is helped by shock mastery, but it involves even more extensive modifications in large and complex networks of associations. The remainder of this chapter provides theory for understanding such changes in person schemas.

Reschematization of Person Schemas

Person schemas store generalizations of knowledge in a cognitive map or model that contains views about self and others. The large networks of associational linkages that function as schemas include meanings that maintain bonds and can lead to a sense of attachment (Horowitz 1992b, 1998). An important aspect of person schemas is their multiplicity: each person has a repertoire of different possible selves, each leading to a different possible state of experiencing one's role in relation to others.

Post-traumatic responses often involve shifts in relationship roles. For example, Harold's altered behavioral pattern after the fire occurred with activation of a usually dormant role, that of a dependent self rather than his usual active sense of self as an autonomous adult. He experienced post-traumatic growth by integrating a latent and usually warded-off dependent-boy role with his realistic, desired, and usually competent and less needy adult role.

In the other, more severe example, Sophia defensively continued activation of her pre-trauma body image long after her accident. Concurrently she slowly and unconsciously formed a new body image that could accord with the drastic post-traumatic changes in her body. Her adaptation increased as her new body image gradually evoked less horror and self-disgust because she slowly forged new role concepts for herself.

A comparison between a desired and a dreaded body image can generate horrifying emotions. Control processes can attenuate such distress by inhibitions or distortions of meaning. Such control processes numb emotion at the cost of impairing the processes of reschematization if they are used persistently. Conversely, control processes that allow flexible appraisals of new realities can foster adaptive behavioral coping and can also promote gradual identity reschematization.

In adaptive coping, post-traumatic emotions are titrated by control processes to levels that are tolerable. A reduction of Sophia's defense against mental imagery (a function not impaired by her blindness) was approached gradually so that the fear, anger, and sorrow evoked in her by ideas of her bodily changes felt manageable. In the short term, she appeared worse because of the unavoidable arousal of distressing feelings. Over the long term, she improved because of the reschematization of her sense of how she appeared to others. She was less apprehensive about their possible responses to seeing her. She gradually revised her initial self-evaluation from an "I am disgustingly ugly" response to a later response of "This is how I look now, and both I and they can accept me as a worthwhile person."

Post-traumatic identity reschematization involves modification of schemas of attachment to others (Bowlby 1969, Parkes and Weiss 1983). Entire configurations of role-relationship models for the affected significant affiliations have to be revised. This slow change process can be complicated and prolonged in persons with prior personality deficits or conflicts that resonate with the meanings of stressor events (Horowitz et al. 1998, Horowitz, Siegal et al. 1997, McFarlane 1989, Prigerson et al. 1995, Resnick et al. 1992, True et al. 1993, Zaidi and Foy 1991, Zisook Schuchter 1991a,b, Zisook et al. 1990). For example, in one study of conjugal bereavement (in a mixed gender sample), we found that low levels of self-conceptualization six months after the loss were correlated with prolonged high symptoms of Complicated Grief Disorder and PTSD or Major Depressive Disorder (MDD) 14 months after the loss ($r = -0.47$, $n = 78$, $p < 0.001$) (Horowitz, Milbrath, Bonanno et al. 1998). Scores on self-report of "other as an essential support to identity" averaged 4.1 in the proportion of those subjects diagnosed by clinicians as having Complicated Grief Disorder and PTSD or MDD as compared to scores of 2.7 in the proportion of subjects diagnosed as having normal grief reactions ($p < .0005$) (Horowitz et al. 1996).

In other samples, when persons with Complicated Grief Disorders were treated in psychotherapy, issues of self-organization were among the most important but difficult topics to discuss. This was shown empirically by a statistically significant association of such topics with concurrent intensification of objectively scored verbal and nonverbal defensive maneuvers to control emotion (Horowitz et al. 1995). A successful therapeutic process required work on antithetical characteristics of self and ambivalent attachments to the deceased (Horowitz, Marmar et al. 1984a, 1996). As the patients learned to reconcile antithetical characteristics of self, some said they felt stronger than they had been before the loss. Person schemas theory helps us understand what changes can take place.

PERSON SCHEMAS THEORY

Traumas change the worldview of their victims, and identity has to be modified to accord with new realities. The substrates of identity experiences are conceptualized in terms of various self-schemas, their level of integration, and the way in which they are sustained in models of how the self relates with others.

Self-schemas

A sense of identity varies from state to state and trauma makes such shifts more pronounced. Each state of mind that is common and recurrent in a person is organized by an active or regnant schema of self. A self-schema is an organized compendium, a patterned aggregation of elements, and a package of usually unconscious associated meanings about the self. Each self-schema is a constellation of such subordinate elements as body image, role, scripts for relating to others, symbols, values, fears, desires, constraints, intentions, expectations, action plans, and styles of self-control.

The connectivity pattern of the elements is a nested hierarchy of beliefs: each element combines many subordinate bits of information that can be associatively combined and built into supraordinate patterns. The self-knowledge assembled in such schematizations can be simultaneously reality-based and fantasy-based, procedural and declarative, explicit and implicit, current and past, current and projected into the future.

The store of self-knowledge is primarily unconscious, its derivatives are represented for conscious self-observation. Trauma frequently activates usually dormant aspects of self-schematization, and alters usually active aspects of self-schematization. A change in the conscious sense of identity results.

A self-schema, one of several within the repertoire of a person, can be active or inactive in affecting current thought, emotion, perception, and action. An active self-schema leads to a style of thinking, communicating, and acting. Traumas alter the relative activity of self-schemas by a shift in the associations that are primed by implications of the event.

As mentioned, a conscious sense of identity, as in the shifting states of Harold and Sophia, is based on derivatives of self-schemas. Since multiple self-schemas are activated, different identity experiences may result. The more the person has coherent integrations of multiple self-schemas into supraordinate ones, the more continuous, coherent, and constant will be that person's memories about a sense of identity over time. The less the integration before the trauma, the greater the possibility for chaotic identity experiences in the post-traumatic period.

Several theorists propose that self-schemas are associated with other person schemas in various internal models of attachment bonds (Bowlby 1969, Epstein 1992, Horowitz 1992b, 1998, Parkes and Weiss 1983). In the clinical situation, these associations of self with other can be inferred in the process of case formulation as role-relationship models. Such models form a cognitive map of self and other attributes, characteristics, and scripts of potential transactions.

Scripts include future plans of the self intending to move toward desired possible future identities and away from dreaded ones.

As a person forms fantasies of dreaded and desired future identities, and these fantasies are retained in memory, these possible future identities become motivational. Some people employ identity compromises in self-view and self-presentation to others to defend against dreaded future states. When these encapsulated, defensive ways of relating become chronic, they are akin to Reich's (1949) "character armor."

If a desired future self is too idealistic for realistic attainment, as occurred in the case of Sophia's continued post-trauma desire to continue to be a famous model, a catastrophic mismatch occurs, leading to a self-state of feeling ugly, unwanted, and worthless. A compromise role as a completely isolated loner might have been used to avoid these dreaded humiliating experiences of self. Therapeutic intervention enabled her to construct a more adaptive, desirable sense of a future self which could be projected as a possible future for relationships. Such a future self-concept motivated Sophia to attain new skills to achieve a new ambition. She was then able to work on forming new types of relationships rather than withdrawing from society.

Supraordinate Person Schemas

One reason that we have more observations and theories on shock mastery than on post-traumatic identity reschematization is that the latter rests on more complex theories of associated meanings, a more complex physiology of neural networks, or both. Part of this complexity, at the psychological level of cognition of meaning, has to do with how supraordinate schemas might combine multiple self-schemas into an associative organization. Larger structures of meaning foster a conscious sense of harmony, coherence, and continuity in a sense of identity. Of importance here is how a supraordinate schema combines several self-schemas (or several role-relationship models) into an even more complex network of associational patterns.

People differ in the degree to which they have learned to integrate multiple self-schemas into a supraordinate schema. An experience of identity is simple when it is derived from information in just one self-schema; it is complex when it derives declarative beliefs from a supraordinate schema combining several possible selves. Research reported elsewhere (Horowitz 1998) supports the hypothesis that people who have formed more integrated supraordinate self-schemas are more likely to have harmony of character and are less likely to dissociate, depersonalize, or explosively shift their state of mind.

Some people have many contradictions across schemas, while others have fewer antithetical intentions and expectations. Those with major contradictions and without supraordinate schemas are vulnerable to sudden and even dissociative variations in their states of mind. That tendency may be exacerbated after traumas that have event qualities associated to their preexisting and contradictory identity elements. Under stress, such people are vulnerable to a sense of identity chaos, leading to heightened impulsivity and use of pathogenic reality-distorting defenses (Vaillant 1977).

Associative processing compares the possible meanings of a trauma to each organized schematization of self. Some dreaded self-schemas that are usually latent may be activated because of strong associative linkages. If these dreaded self-schemas have not been previously attenuated by supraordinate schemas that can contain and diminish them, then a regressive decompensation of overall self-organization may occur. For example, an adult who has had a current traumatic experience that seems similar in its roles to a childhood trauma, may become especially distressed if the roles of the childhood experience have never been mastered. Conversely, that adult may adapt resiliently if the roles have been previously mastered. This is why some people believe their character has been strengthened by prior traumas, and others believe they have an impairment and vulnerability of character.

To recapitulate, any traumatic event may be subsequently associated to multiple self- and relationship concepts as a part of cognitive processing. Some meanings of the trauma may have implications that conflict with existing schemas and their intrinsic expectations and intentions. The more discordant the elements are in schemas before the trauma, the harder it is to reorganize meanings after the trauma. In such instances, attention to self and relationship conflicts are important for accomplishing reschematization in psychotherapy.

Reschematization takes time. Mourning, for example, extends over many months for most people after the loss of an important relationship. Mourning itself is a part of many stress response syndromes, as in Sophia's grief work over loss of body parts and capacities.

7

MOURNING

By passing through the phases of grief, the bereaved person prepares to make new commitments to others and to accept new personal roles. This passage involves an unconscious change in mental structures of meanings about the self and other people. This chapter examines mourning in terms of such person schemas.

Unconscious processes lead to extremes of conscious experience during grief. Some time after a loved one dies, a preoccupation with the deceased may dominate the mourner's conscious experience. Visual or auditory images of the deceased may occur unexpectedly. The bereaved person may experience unwelcome and intrusive emotions: not just sadness, as expected, but also fear, rage, and guilt. An opposite extreme in conscious experience may also occur. The bereaved person may consciously attempt to recall a memory about the deceased and fail. Or the mourner may try to cry but cannot. The following case excerpt illustrates both intrusive and omissive types of deflection from voluntary control of conscious representation.

Mary's elderly mother died when Mary was middle-aged. Mary felt sorrowful, cried at the funeral, took a week away from her work and usual social activities, and then went through her mother's belongings, quietly contemplating her memories. She then resumed her life as usual, until, weeks later, she found herself preoccupied with unbidden images of hostile exchanges with her mother. These malevolent and dominating images were based on memories and fantasies of the past. When Mary tried deliberately to recall her mother in the context of pleasant, loving memories, she could not conjure up any image at all of her mother's face.

Unconscious mental processes dictate much of the experience of mourning. The person in mourning can seldom accurately predict *when* she might enter a particular mood, *what* memories of the deceased would then be recalled, *when or if* strong emotions would be triggered by some reminder of the loss, or *why* a new behavior emerged that exhibited traits of the deceased. Few persons ever predict the quality of anniversary reactions accurately, yet most persons have them. The unconscious mind is tracking time and recording dates in ways not reported to consciousness, even after a psychoanalysis. The next two vignettes illustrate such phenomena.

A clinical psychologist attended a talk on the relation of unconscious factors to the phenomenology of grief experiences. At the coffee break, she said that just that morning she had finally put on the earrings left her by her mother upon her death two years before. Up until the day of the seminar, the psychologist had left them untouched in her jewelry box. She had attached no significance to the act that morning, but during the talk she realized she had decided—unconsciously—to symbolically complete her mourning by taking the earrings as her own. She thought she had also probably signed up for the conference for the same purpose.

A more detailed vignette indicates a series of unpredicted anniversary reactions following the death of a loved one.

The noted psychiatrist and psychoanalyst Engel (1975) wrote of his anniversary reactions after his twin brother died suddenly from a heart attack, like their father before him. His brother died at age 49; the father had died at age 58. When Engel heard of the death, at first he felt stunned disbelief, and then began crying, twenty minutes later. Within a few hours he was experiencing chest pains. On later examination it was discovered that Engel, too, showed evidence of coronary heart disease, although not an infarction. During the next months, Engel worried that he would have a heart attack. Eleven months after his twin brother died, he did have a coronary occlusion. Afterward, Engel felt relief: he no longer had to fear a heart attack would fell him at any moment.

As the years passed, he became less concerned by anniversaries, and so did not anticipate he would have any reaction on the five-year anniversary of his brother's death when Engel himself was 54 years old. When the date arrived, however, he had a dream on a theme of guilt at surviving a heart attack when his brother had died from one.

On the five-year anniversary of Engel's own heart attack, he had another dream wherein he remembered that a friend had died suddenly. In the dream, he felt sad and agitated and tried to tell a colleague about the death. He awakened in a depressed mood. This friend, in many associations, had the characteristics of Engel's twin brother. He then realized that he had been looking forward to the anniversary as a cause for celebration that he had survived for five years. Yet during the actual day, he blocked out any conscious memory of its significance. That significance was represented in the dream thoughts.

When Engel reached 58, the age his father had been when he died, Engel made a number of errors in conscious thought. He remembered his father as dying at age 59 instead of age 58, although for many years Engel had feared that he, too, would die at 58. In this way he passed his fifty-eighth year without conscious anxiety, since the threat of death was projected into the future. After the threat had passed and he had survived his fifty-ninth birthday, Engel recalled that his father had died at age 58.

Such anniversary phenomena indicate how unconscious defensive control processes can serve to reduce levels of felt anxiety and guilt. The balance between impulsive aims at mastery by repetition in thought and unconscious defensive aims at avoidance of emotional pain varies over time, leading to phasic variation in what a person consciously experiences.

PHASES OF RESPONSE DURING MOURNING

Pollock (1978) described variations in affect as the mourning process progresses. The degree of conscious experience of affect provides an index of change. Parkes (1964, 1972) and Parkes and Weiss (1983) reviewed Freud's (1917), Lindemann's (1944), and subsequent models of the bereavement process, and differentiated specific phases of grief: (1) initial denial and avoidance of the loss; (2) subsequent alarm reactions, such as anxiety, with restlessness and physiological complaints; (3) searching to find the lost person; (4) anger and guilt; (5) feelings of internal loss, (6) adoption of traits or mannerisms of the deceased; and (7) acceptance and resolution, including appropriate changes in identity. To these seven phases Pollock (1972, 1978) added the importance of revived mourning on anniversaries and of phases of creativity during mourning. One can condense the phases of mourning into the phases already described.

NORMAL AND PATHOLOGICAL GRIEF

Grief has normal forms and pathological variations. Pathological grief is often a highly intense and out-of-control experience of the kind of ideas and feelings normally found during mourning (Bowlby 1980, Deutsch 1937, Freud 1917, Glick et al. 1975, Lindemann 1944, Pollock 1978, Raphael 1983). Sometimes, however, it is a failure to mourn (Clayton 1974, Horowitz et al. 1980b, Osterweiss et al. 1984, Windholz et al. 1985). And at other times it is a set of signs and symptoms atypical of normal grief (Abraham 1924). In one of his most important theoretical papers, "Mourning and Melancholia," Freud (1917) presented the decisive effects of the nature of the previous relationship with the deceased in predicting whether normal or pathological grief would occur. Preexisting ambivalence in this relationship predisposes the person to both more intense and turbulent affects and more extensive and regressive defenses.

Normal grief reactions, as already mentioned, may change in the quality of subjective experience during various phases of mourning. So, too, pathological grief reactions may have signs and symptoms with a phasic change pattern, as shown in Table 7–1.

The phases shown in Table 7–1 are generalizations. While the phases are often sequential as tabulated, no one person must necessarily follow the order presented, or even experience all of the phases. Personality style, current conflicts, and developmental level of the personality all affect the experience and length of the phases. Persons with compulsive personalities often remain longer in a low emotion denial phase, while those with histrionic personalities are often more prone to extended intrusive phases. Sometimes persons with narcissistic personalities show few direct manifestations of grief after a brief outcry phase. They may be too developmentally immature to have an adult type of relationship and so cannot exhibit an adult type of mourning at its loss.

THE PHASE OF OUTCRY

Outcry contains a rapid, unconscious assessment of the implications to the self of the loss. The sudden confrontation with bad news leads to a sharp rise in the experience and expression of such raw emotions as fear, sadness, and anger, and to physiological changes in sympathetic, parasympathetic, histaminic, and immunological systems. The result may range from hyperarousal to shock. Because

Table 7–1. Common Experiences during Grief and Their Pathological Intensification

Phase	Normal Response	Pathological Intensification
Dying	Emotional expression and immediate coping with the dying process	Avoidant, overwhelmed, dazed, confused, self-punitive, inappropriately hostile
Death and Outcry	Outcry of emotions with news of the death and turning for help to others or isolating self with self-succoring	Panic, dissociative reactions, reactive psychoses
Warding Off (Denial)	Avoidance of reminders, social withdrawal, focusing elsewhere, emotional numbing, not thinking of implications to self or certain themes	Maladaptive avoidances of confronting the implications of the death, drug or alcohol abuse, counterphobic frenzy, promiscuity, fugue states, phobic avoidance, feeling dead or unreal
Reexperience (Intrusion)	Intrusive experiences including recollections of negative relationship experiences with the deceased, bad dreams, reduced concentration, compulsive enactments	Flooding with negative images and emotions, uncontrolled ideation, self-impairing compulsive reenactments, night terrors, recurrent nightmares, distraught feelings from intrusion of anger, anxiety, despair, shame or guilt themes, physiological exhaustion from hyperarousal
Working Through	Recollections of the deceased and contemplations of self with reduced intrusiveness of memories and fantasies, increased rational acceptance, reduced numbness and avoidance, more "dosing" of recollections and a sense of working it through	Sense that one cannot integrate the death with a sense of self and continued life, persistent warded-off themes may manifest as anxious, depressed, enraged, shame-filled, or guilty moods, and psychophysiological syndromes
Completion	Reduction in emotional swings with a sense of self-coherence and readiness for new relationships, ability to experience positive states of mind	Failure to complete mourning may be associated with inability to work, create, or feel emotion or positive states of mind

unconscious thought proceeds further and more swiftly than conscious thought, intrusive emotions can take subjective awareness by surprise. A cascade of emotional experiences occurs during this phase, as different implications of the death are touched upon. A deeper review of these topics will take place during subsequent phases of response, but the first emotional indicators of their importance are now present.

I found an insightful illustration of this power of emotion during the outcry phase in James Agee's *A Death in the Family* (1957). The following excerpt illustrates the outcry phase of a woman whose husband died in a car accident only a few days earlier. She dons her mourning veil for his funeral, thinking as she does so that she has grown up almost overnight, for she realizes her loss and knows that terrible pain lies ahead. As she leaves the bedroom shared with her husband, she is stunned by grief.

> The realization came without shape or definability, save as it was focused in the pure physical acts of leaving the room, but came with such force, such monstrous piercing weight, in all her heart and soul and mind and body but above all in the womb, where it arrived and dwelt like a cold and prodigious, spreading stone, that groaned almost inaudibly, almost a mere silent breath, an *Ohhhhhh,* and doubled deeply over, hands to her belly, and her knee joints melted. [pp. 305–306]

If a death is unexpected, emotional expression may be more intense than if the death was long anticipated. In anticipatory grief, a working model develops showing the deceased as dying. After confrontation with an unexpected death, a person may form a working model in which the deceased is viewed as seriously harmed and critically in need of help. This working model sharply arouses emotional systems. Because the deceased is modeled as harmed, the self is aroused to act to reduce threat. The alarm emotions prepare the body for action and motivate the conscious mind to interrupt other activities in order to plan this action. As a result, the person may undertake frantic but hopeless activity to repair the hazardous condition of the deceased. Some funeral rituals serve this obligation to "do something!" The working model can be a bit irrational in regard to the reality of permanent loss, since it depicts the other as harmed but not completely beyond help.

The nature of the working model will determine the contents of the crying out of alarming emotional ideas. The emotional expression of an outcry phase may come as actions and images, as well as words. There may be appeals for divine help ("Oh God!") or expressions of rage ("God damn it!") or remorse ("I'm so sorry!"). Rapid, unconscious appraisals of the repercussions of the death may lead to defensive opposition to alarming ideas and emotions. Some form of denial can occur in the emotional exclamations that characterize this phase ("Oh no! It can't be! Say it isn't so!"). A rapid appraisal of the self during the outcry phase leads to conscious vows like "I'll survive this," or "I'll never enjoy life again—ever!" These inner assertions become an important part of the memory of receiving the bad news.

The term *working model* applies to a transient schema derived from both perception and enduring schemas (Bowlby 1980, Bretherton and Waters 1985). It is based heavily on immediate perceptions of external reality, although schemas organize (and potentially distort) that perception. An enduring schema of a role relationship model is less situationally dependent. It is activated by inner wishes. Thus we may infer that the mind unconsciously compares the working role relationship model and the enduring role relationship model. If they do not match, intense emotions may arise, serving to motivate either plans for correcting the mismatch or defensive avoidances to reduce recognition of it. This mismatch, which is illustrated in Figure 7–1, is the usual state of affairs in the outcry phase. The sharp expression of emotional alarms itself may serve an evolutionary adaptive purpose. Sobbing may summon aid; shock and fear may elicit protection; remorse may cause renewed support; and rage may alert others to treat the subject with tact and caution.

EVENTS:	Ordinary Relations With Other	News of Death of Other
CURRENT WORKING MODEL OF RELATIONSHIP	(Self) Mutality ↕ [Other]	(Self) Need ↑↓ Help [Other]
ENDURING SCHEMA OF RELATIONSHIP	(Self) Mutality ↕ [Other]	(Self) Mutality ↕ [Other]
ACCORD OF WORKING AND ENDURING SCHEMAS	Match	Mismatch
EMOTIONAL SYSTEMS	Equilibrium	Alarming Rate of Arousal
STATES OF MIND	Calm	Fearful Outcry

Figure 7–1. Modeling a State Shift from Calm to Alarm

THE PHASE OF DENIAL

As a result of the initial defensive inhibitions of some emotional themes, the alarm reactions characteristic of the outcry phase
are reduced. One is often aware that denial is operating, and one is
conscious of feeling numb or insulated. The seventeenth-century
poet John Dryden, in "Threnodia Augustalis" (quoted in Moffatt
1982) spoke of this when he wrote "Tears stand congealed and
cannot flow/And the sad soul retires into her inmost room." Emily
Dickinson (c. 1862) wrote, "After great pain, a formal feeling comes.
The nerves sit ceremonious, like tombs."

During the denial phase of mourning, the active memory of
some themes about the loss is avoided by an inhibition of topics
for conscious representation that is unconsciously decided upon.

The outcome is repression of topics, omission of recollection, avoidance of recognizing personal implications of the death, and often a conscious but vague sense of being frozen, insulated, derealized, or depersonalized. But, unlike certain other post-traumatic reactions, in bereavement total suppression or repression of the theme of loss is seldom observed. Some recognition of short-range consequences of the death to the self occurs, while many other long-range effects are not contemplated. The continued use of schemas that contain beliefs that model the deceased as alive is what is most prominent during this phase. The preserved role-relationship model of the self with the deceased as alive contributes to such phenomena as the use of the present tense in describing the relationship with the deceased, as in *"We* like to travel during vacations."* In other words, there is some dissociation of role relationship models during the denial phase. The person preserves a role-relationship model of the self as related to the living other, while separately developing a recognition of the self as alive and the deceased as dead when situational reminders force that recognition. The latter role-relationship model is inhibited from organizing ideas and feelings in many states of mind during the denial phase.

THE PHASE OF INTRUSION

The denial phase may last for days, weeks, or even months. During this time, the mourner may have returned to many of the customary forms of his life. A sense of safety may be returning. It may be just then, surprisingly, that intrusive experiences increase in frequency and intensity. In the fourth century, the poet and courtier P'An Yueh (Rexroth 1970) wrote "In Mourning For His Dead Wife." The poem indicates that a year has passed since her death, and yet:

. . . Her perfume
Still haunts the bedroom. Her clothes
Still hang there in the closet.
She is always alive in
My dreams. I wake with a start.
She vanishes. And I
Am overwhelmed with sorrow. . . .

Conscious recognition of the significance of a loss to the self becomes prominent during the phase of intrusive reexperiencing of memories about the stressful event and the previous relationship to the person lost. There is less use of repression as an unconscious defensive operation. Conscious efforts at suppression, however, may continue to curb the sharp pangs of emotion associated with this phase. This conscious, suppressive, defensive avoidance paradoxically contributes to the intrusiveness of recollections at this time because the conscious representations of ideas and feelings are a kind of breakthrough phenomenon.

During this phase one may become preoccupied with an aspect of identification with the deceased in which one views oneself as vulnerable to death. One may experience the physical symptoms of the disease that killed the other, or in fantasy reveries strike mental bargains with the gods to reduce fear and protect the self. One may feel guilty for worrying about dying when it is the other who is actually dead. This type of survivor guilt is just one of many motifs signaling development of new schemas of the self as alive and the deceased as dead.

Existing schemas still organize an expectation that the deceased will be alive and present in certain situations. Therefore, these situations feel particularly empty. Cooking a meal, going out with friends, or going to the movies painfully emphasizes the absence of the habitual companion. Emotional reactions to such empty situations are heightened during this intrusive phase of bereavement because the working schema of being alone still differs from the enduring schemas of being together. This discrepancy between the role-relationship models leads to alarm affects as shown in Figure 7–2. The person may be motivated to renew efforts to bring back the dead loved one, with an increase in pining and searching, use of magical offerings, and efforts to undo the incidents that led to the death.

Wishes for restoration of the deceased are long unsatisfied, obviously, and frustration mounts. In the face of death, the survivor mounts a last-ditch effort to fulfill his wish that the deceased be alive. Memories of prior satisfaction with the deceased are dramatically different from the emptiness of the current situation, and this has sharp emotional consequences. For example, great joy during a dream of wish fulfillment is replaced by a great pang of sorrow upon awakening to the realization that the dream is not real. The same

EVENTS:	Empty Situations	Empty Situations
CURRENT WORKING MODEL OF RELATIONSHIP	(Self) Need ↓ Absent Other	(Self) Need ↓ Absent Other
ENDURING SCHEMA OF RELATIONSHIP	(Self) Mutality ↑↓ Other	(Self) Need ↓ Absent Other
ACCORD OF WORKING AND ENDURING SCHEMAS	Mismatch	Match
EMOTIONAL SYSTEMS	Alarming Rate of Arousal	Equilibrium
STATES OF MIND	Agitated Sadness	Poignant Sadness or Resignation

Figure 7–2. Reduction of Alarm States, with Development of Schema of Other as Lost

dream of being with the beloved deceased may be remembered with pleasure, not sorrow, in some later phase of mourning, when more grief work has been accomplished.

At the same time, ideation proceeds with lessened inhibition. Unanswered questions during the outcry phase of initial realization, such as, "Who is to blame [for the death]?" and "Why did this [loss] happen to me?" reemerge during the intrusive phase. These themes may be organized during this phase by usually dormant schemas, such as those wherein the self is viewed as bad and harmful to the other, or defective and abandoned by the other. Survivor guilt, guilt over anger with the deceased, shame over helplessness, and fear of future repetitive suffering may recur as intrusive preoccupations.

THE PHASE OF WORKING THROUGH

During the working-through phase, there are recurrences of avoidant and intrusive phenomena. These omissions and preoccupations oscillate, taking the edge off either extreme and helping to promote equilibrium. Periods of relaxation occur in which neither defensive numbness nor emotional flooding is prominent.

Intrusive memories of the deceased begin to change in form. Current concerns and relationships with living people blend with scenes involving the deceased. These blends occur prominently in dreams. Not infrequently in such dreams, the bereaved occupies the role of the deceased, and vice versa.

Between the initial unconscious view of the deceased as alive, yet lost to contact with the self, and the eventual, full, unconscious acceptance of the death, unconscious beliefs undergo many changes. These lead to varied conscious experiences during the working-through phase, as the following case example illustrates.

A young husband suffered the death of his wife in a scuba diving accident. Six months later, during his waking hours and in dreams, he had intrusive, intolerably sad and frightening images of her blue face when the body was recovered. These unbidden images gradually subsided in frequency during a brief psychodynamic psychotherapy.

Before his wife's death, he never experienced a sharp elevation in heart rate when he saw her or a woman who resembled her. After her death, during the earlier denial and intrusive phases of his grief experience, he still did not have these sensations. The everyday situation of being with his wife, his earlier phase of grief after her death, and his later recognitions of his loss were very different contexts.

During the working-through period of the mourning process, however, he did develop this intrusive bodily sensation in a specific context. He worked as a trainer of personnel for a large corporation, and began a new class every two weeks. During this period, when he saw a woman in the class who resembled his wife, at first glance he would feel his pulse surge in his chest, wrists, and throat.

The everyday situation *before her death* was mainly one of calm belief in their continuing commitment to each other. The *intrusive phase of his grief* was characterized by visions of her as dead, primary-process beliefs in her continued life, and alarming pangs of sadness mixed with fear. The later phase of *working through* contained a growing recognition of loss, but still a pining for her return. With this phase near relative *completion,* the intrusion of physiologic arousal subsided.

During the phase in which he felt the sudden surges of pulse, he had no conscious ideas about the women who resembled his wife; his cardiac reaction felt instantaneous. Yet from our vantage point as observers, we may infer that there was some type of unconscious construction of meaning about the women that led to his excitation. He was hoping his wife had returned from death (primary process) while knowing that she was dead (secondary process). The primary process was rapid and unconscious, using ideas incorporated in a schema of finding and being reunited with his harmed, living wife. Fluctuation of that schema led to the emotional responses that would occur in such a reunion.

Changes in schemas occur most prominently in the working-through phase. Many repetitions of intrusive ideas and feelings will have occurred, and trains of thought will have been set in motion. These thoughts and the repetition of new situations and their working models will gradually build new, enduring role-relationship models.

During the grief work, one reviews the relationship with the deceased in terms of all the varied self-concepts that have participated in working models of the attachment. This may include weak, dependent, childlike self-concepts in relation to the other as a parental figure, even when the real relationship was between peers. It may include strong, dominating, or rivalrous views of self and other. The good and bad, clean and dirty, selfish and caring, and loving and hating themes will all have their time on the stage of reminiscence and decision—I say "decision" because this review is not just a searching, inner magical, primary-process restoration of things now gone. As mentioned above, the process serves an evolutionary, survival-of-the-species function in that it prepares the person to make new commitments after a loss and to accept the self with a true view of the present situation. Before this adaptive end of mourning is reached, the schemas and memories of the relationship require review in order to decide what is now true, what is now fantasy, and to discriminate the present from the past.

Sometimes it is a relief when a frustrating, hated, significant other dies. Even so, *the more ambivalence and conflict found in the themes for review, the harder it will be to reach the conclusions that complete the mourning process* (Bowlby 1980, Freud 1920, Lindemann 1944, Raphael 1983). The reasons for this are these: the thinking process will be complex and contradictory, the negative emotional experience will be intense and threatening, and the avoidant defensive maneuvers will tend to disrupt thinking. Most especially, consciousness as a tool for decision making will likely be obscured by repression, suppression, dissociation, denial, disavowal, isolation, and reaction formation.

Preexisting ambivalence will, all things being equal, intensify and lengthen or delay and derail the working-through process. These are two of the most common forms of pathological grief reactions. But all things are not equal, and a great deal depends on the integrity and resilience of self-organization.

Preexisting neurotic character makes ambivalence and conflict more likely, and will also impair one's ability to use others for emotional support during the extended crises of mourning. Preexisting narcissistic and borderline character pathology will make more difficult the review and change of person schemas (Horowitz 1988, Kernberg 1967, Kohut 1972). Reactive decompensation may result, as the absence of the bolstering functions of the deceased damages the bereaved's sense of self-organization. As a defense, mourning may be totally interrupted and the deceased replaced by imagined and distorted relationships with whomever or whatever is available for support.

Part of the task is to decide at the level of person schemas that the deceased is permanently, irrevocably dead. For example, with repetition of the current working model developed in the empty situations, a new, enduring role-relationship model develops in which self is related to the person in the past, but not in the present or future except through memories. Empty situations lose their threatening surprise; the person no longer dreads abandonment or losing contact; rather, the person is simply alone. Yearning remains but loses its component of alarm. The resulting state of mind may be *poignant sadness* rather than the more emotional *agitated sadness.*

The progressive changes in expected role-relationship models during working through can be reversed by a process of regression. Anniversary dates may trigger this, as in the case of Engel, but then progression is easier because developmental schemas for it have been forged by the working-through phase.

With the reduction in frequency of distraught states of mind during this phase, the person may attempt a new relationship of the sort that was lost. Another person is found to care for, relate to sexually, or serve as a companion. Commonly the new relationship is then colored by efforts to restore within it some aspects of the lost relationship. The discrepancy between the preexisting role-relationship model with the deceased and the patterns occurring with the new person may lead to emotional responses like alarm. In effect, an illusion of restoration occurs until it is suddenly seen as an error. This illusion is a form of transference reaction.

The new companion may react to inappropriate transference-based expectations. This contributes to distress, confusion, and disruptions of poise. After spending time with the new person, and with the mourning process closer to completion, the bereaved is capable of separating the relationship with the new companion from the previous relationship with the deceased. A more committed and realistic attachment with the new person is now possible because a schema of the new person as different from the deceased has been established, as illustrated in Figure 7–3.

EVENTS:	New Interpersonal Situation	New Interpersonal Situation
CURRENT WORKING MODEL OF RELATIONSHIP	(Self) ↓↑ (Companion B)	(Self) ↓↑ (Companion B)
ENDURING SCHEMA OF RELATIONSHIP	(Self) ↑↓ (Companion A)	(Self) ↑↓ (Companion B)
ACCORD OF WORKING AND ENDURING SCHEMAS	Mismatch	Match
EMOTIONAL SYSTEMS	Alerting Arousal to Strangeness	Equilibrium
STATES OF MIND	Perplexed and Awkward	Poised

Figure 7–3. Reduction of Uneasiness in Reestablishing Relationships of the Types Lost (Companion A = Deceased; Companion B = the New Person).

COMPLETION

Although listed as such in Table 7–1, completion is not actually a phase so much as it is a milestone. It marks the relative end of mourning. It is "relative" because some mourning for a major loss persists throughout the lifetime, and may be reactivated by reminders such as anniversaries (Pollock 1972, 1978). It is listed as a phase because it contains the sense of self-coherence and readiness for new relationships. In pathological grief this sense may never be achieved. There may be continuing impairment in work, creativity, or intimacy that can go on distorting the person's character for years. In contrast, in some states of completed mourning, the person feels an enhancement of competence and a freeing from the work of grief as well as from its symptoms.

SCHEMATIC CHANGE THROUGH PHASES OF GRIEF

The overall progression of schematic change discussed in the preceding text is outlined in Figure 7–4.

The course of transference reactions in the psychoanalysis of an adult who suffered a traumatic bereavement during early adolescence reveals the readiness with which role-relationship models can be tried out, one after the other, during the resumption of a mourning process interrupted for years by defensive inhibitions. Only when self-organization and relationship capacities develop may a warded-off mourning process be tolerable. This case followed shifting transference phenomena previously observed and reported by Fleming and Altschul (1963), Wolfenstein (1966), and Zients (1986).

The 27–year-old patient presented character problems involving phobic withdrawal from love and work, and avoidance of developing career-related skills. During the course of psychoanalysis, it gradually

EVENTS	BEFORE LOSS	LOSS OF [A]	AFTER LOSS OF [A]		NEW RELATIONSHIP WITH [B]	
			Intrusion			
PHASES:	Equilibrium	Outcry	Denial	Alarms, search	Pining	Illusions and mis-expectations in new affiliation	Completion
COGNITIVE AND EMOTIONAL PROCESSES:	Sense of affiliation	Recognition of threat	Knows of but denies implications of loss				Committed in a new affiliation
SCHEMAS SELF: OTHER: (⚡= threats)				fracture			

Figure 7–4. Schematic Change through Phases of Grief

became apparent that he had never mourned his mother, who died when he was 13.

During the first two years of treatment he remained indifferent to the analyst's vacations or work-related trips. Weekends apart meant nothing. Then he threatened to leave analysis on a variety of pretexts, citing the analyst's inadequacy. With each challenge, he observed the analyst's reactions carefully. Because the analyst did not appear anxious and did not act firmly to urge him to stay in treatment, he decided—unconsciously, I believe—that the analyst could tolerate his own fear of losing the patient.

The patient identified with the analyst's ability to tolerate sadness and anxiety at impending separation and loss. For the first time, he began to feel the analyst's departure on vacations as painful. He mourned each weekend as a loss. Earlier childhood fears of abandonment surfaced in conscious memories. Missing the analyst, and being pleased at reunions then awakened more positive memories of his mother. Only then, gradually, did he begin to grieve. He entered an intrusive phase, with sobbing, over vivid visual memories of his mother's funeral. He spent an extended period working through these reactions.

CONCLUSION

The human species has evolved with a capacity for mourning that reaches expression in the adult. During the outcry phase of mourning, alarming pangs of emotion may occur as the mind reacts to the serious mismatch between working models of the new situation and enduring schemas. The deceased may be modeled as harmed rather than dead. By the time of entry into a denial phase, the person has reconstituted defensive inhibitions. During this phase dissociations are prominent, with operative schemas of the deceased as both dead and alive. With entry into an intrusive phase, both usual and warded-off role-relationship models involving self and the deceased emerge, organizing not only conscious reviews, but unbidden ideas, hard-to-dispel images, and intrusive emotions.

In the working-through phase, the mourning person may more easily contemplate more themes. The new working models are repeated and so they begin to be established as enduring schemas. This work reduces alarm, emotion, and signal affects as it diminishes the discrepancy, or mismatch, between working models and enduring person schemas. As the bereaved person slowly develops schemas that match the reality of permanent separation, the work of grief gradually enters the completion phase.

It takes a long time to reach such a point of relative completion and the work of mourning cannot be rushed. Mourning is not heartbreak; it prevents the heart from being broken.

8

TREATMENT

As has been discussed in detail, stress response syndromes include emotional flooding with intrusive images and ideas. To avoid dreaded states of mind, people automatically inhibit information processing. That leads to denial, numbing, and avoidance. Because of avoidance behavior, attention to defensive coping and resistances to treatment is important. Hence, this cognitive-dynamic approach addresses patterns of defensive coping, efforts to counteract dysfunctional beliefs, and disturbances in roles of self and others.

Themes related to the traumatic circumstances may overflow to incorporate ensuing and preexisting topics. The result is an apparent contamination of other themes and a phenomenon such as phobic reactions due to *overgeneralization*. In normal reactions there is then a diminution of such wide-ranging associational linkages, a process called *extinction*. Overgeneralization is the antithesis of symptomatic disavowal of the meanings of the event or constriction of associational width, often prominent during denial phases. Sometimes a contrived continuation of "life as usual" contains an altered subjective quality; the person feels like an automaton, carrying out habitual patterns in a devitalized and joyless manner.

The goal of treatment is to help the person work through the linkage between self and the stressor events so that all such symptoms can be attenuated or terminated. The aim is to help the patient so he is neither blunted nor emotionally flooded, and is restored to a pre-event level of functioning. Sometimes additional efforts at personality development are indicated. In such instances, character may be developed to levels that are better than before the trauma.

In general, therapists plan how to help people achieve the following:

- A sense of safety,
- Optimum skills in decision making and adaptive coping,
- A realistic sense of self as stable, coherent, competent, and worthwhile,
- Competence in community, family, and personal functions,
- Rational preparation and resilience for future stressors.

These goals include plans for how to protect the patient from dangers, for example: accidents (from inattention and slowed reaction time); inappropriate decisions (made on the basis of erroneous beliefs or compulsive repetitions); social stigmatization (as the consequences of loss, injury, culpability, or victimization); demoralization or suicide (due to impaired sense of identity and meaning); disruption of chemo-physiology (from prolonged fatigue, stress hormones, substance abuse, or excessive use of medications).

STAGES OF TREATMENT

Real evaluation and treatment may be seamless; however, a didactic division of it into stages helps indicate how techniques may usefully change over time. The following stages will be discussed in sequence; these stages overlap.

1. Evaluation: diagnosis, formulation, and initial treatment planning
2. Support
3. Exploration of meanings
4. Improving coping
5. Working through
6. Terminating

This theory of therapy is an integration of approaches described by many, including Basch (1980), Beck (1976), Foa and Kozak (1988), Horowitz (1973, 1976, 1998), Klerman and Weissman (1993), Luborsky (1984), Malan (1963, 1976, 1979), Mann (1973), Sifneos (1972), Strupp and Binder (1984), and may also use special imagery techniques as described by Singer and Pope (1978) and Horowitz (1995).

Evaluation: Diagnosis, Formulation, and Initial Treatment Planning

Evaluation includes diagnosis, formulation, and initial treatment planning. When done well it establishes hope and an alliance as well as a plan for treatment. During treatment, formulations and plans are further revised.

Diagnosis

As already discussed, several descriptive diagnoses (*DSM–IV*) relate to the etiological category of Stress Response Syndromes. These diagnoses include Complicated Grief Disorder, Post traumatic Stress Disorder, Major Depressive Disorder precipitated by stressor life events, Anxiety Disorder precipitated by stressor events, and Adjustment Disorder. Flare-ups of personality problems also may be precipitated by stressor events. Diagnosis is important but individual case formulation is equally important. Treatment should be oriented by inferences about what has caused the disturbances in each individual patient. This will often involve a bio–psycho–social formulation that includes understanding of contexts before and after the cascade of stressor events.

Formulation and Initial Treatment Planning

Formulation is a vital part of treatment planning. It helps clinicians see what topics should be addressed. One system is Configurational Analysis (Horowitz 1997c), summarized in Table 8–1. This approach first looks at the *phenomena* and selects the key symptoms and problems to be explained. The second step is to describe *states* in which both unwelcome and avoidant phenomena occur. This may include *dreaded* states of intrusive images and horror, and less distressing and more *defensive* states of denial and numbing. These dreaded and defensive states can also be contrasted with *desired* states of restored equilibrium.

In the third step, the clinician notes the *key unresolved topics and defenses*. The fourth step adds *self–other beliefs that lead to identity and relationships*. Pathogenic stress-induced shifts into such roles as degraded, incompetent, abandoned, shamed, scorned, abused, and unworthy are identified. The fifth step, integration and treatment plan, takes inferences and explanations and develops an integration that includes a linkage among states, unresolved topics, and core role-relationship models. It also includes inferences about how defenses may shift schemas of self and other to alter emotionality. The treatment plan considers how to stabilize more adaptive states, when and how to address unresolved topics, and whether to interpret dreaded role-relationship models.

An important aspect of formulation is consideration of the organizational level of patients in terms of their ability to schematize

Table 8–1. Steps of Formulation for Stress Response Syndromes: Configurational Analysis Method (Horowitz 1997c)

1. PHENOMENA
Select the symptoms and problems that need to be explained, and describe the stressor events that precipitated them.

2. STATES OF MIND
Describe states in which the symptoms and problems do and do not occur. Indicate triggers to problematic or dreaded states. Include states of avoidance and impairments to achieving positive states of mind. Describe any maladaptive cycles of states.

3. TOPICS OF CONCERN AND DEFENSIVE CONTROL PROCESSES
Describe unresolved stress-related topics and how they evolve to problematic states. Indicate persisting dysfunctional beliefs. Infer how enduring beliefs mismatch with the news from the stressors. Describe how expression and contemplation of these unresolved topics is obscured. Infer how avoidant operations are used to ward off dreaded states.

4. IDENTITY AND RELATIONSHIPS
For each recurrent state, infer roles of self and others and schematized transactions between self and others. Describe desired and dreaded role relationship models. Infer how compromise role relationship models ward off danger. Describe repetitive dysfunctional beliefs about roles and cause–effect sequences.

5. INTEGRATION AND THERAPY PLANNING
Consider problematic bio–psycho–social interactions and how to ameliorate situations. Explain how schemas of self and other lead to problematic states, and how any pathogenic defenses prevent resolution of topics of concern. Examine factors that operate to prolong symptoms and state how to counteract them. From this formulation predict how to facilitate change. Plan how to stabilize working states and prevent pathologically impulsive actions. Consider how and when to modify beliefs and behaviors, alter social supports, and design treatments for biological impairments.

concepts about self and others. Patients who have more vulnerability to loss of identity coherence, who use reality-distorting defenses, and who have explosive shifts in their relationships usually require slower, more supportive explorations of their problems. One is less likely to interpret early the dreaded role-relationship models that lead to undermotiviated states.

The first stage of the work with a patient is summarized and related to the other stages in Table 8–2.

Support

Patients often seek professional help weeks or months after a traumatic event, when they still have symptoms and an intuitive sense that they are not recovering. Usually these symptoms occur in an undermodulated state of mind characterized by intrusive experiences, dangerous impulses, or a sense of loss of control. If so, state stabilization through initial supportive measures is indicated. At the biological level, this may include prescription of medications, restored nutrition, and more rest. At the social level, supportive measures include time structuring, advising other people who have contact with the patient, and other contextual interventions. At the psychological level, supportive measures involve the establishment of a therapeutic relationship and a plan for treatment. The patient gains hope for recovery after perceiving empathy, expertise, and a readiness to provide care from the clinician.

Biological Support

Many biological systems shift under stress. One system involves catecholamine chemistry. Changes affect neural networks that connect the limbic, frontal cortical, basal ganglia, and hypothalamic structures. Disturbances in electrochemical physiology of these networks can affect arousal control and alter capacity to regulate emotional responses (as in increased frequency of fright and rage). The amygdala may alter its danger recognition set points, the hippocampus may alter its memory encoding properties, and the medial prefrontal cortex may alter its abilities to establish or reduce (desensitize) associational connections.

A prominent catecholamine in the physiologic reaction to stress may be dopamine, which is concentrated in the norepinephrine-

APPROXIMATE PHASES	THERAPEUTIC ALLIANCE	PATIENT ACTIVITY	THERAPIST ACTIVITY
1. Evaluation: Diagnosis, Formulation, and Treatment Planning	Agreement on initial treatment, with hope fostered by expertise and empathy.	Patient reports events and personal contexts as well as symptoms.	Therapist obtains history, makes diagnoses and early formulations. Provides educative information if needed. Discusses treatment indications and options.
2. Initial Support	Roles of a therapeutic partnership are defined.	Patient expands story and focuses on how to cope with current stress.	Therapist acts to stabilize states if indicated, and establishes a preliminary focus (the traumatic event and its meaning to self).
3. Exploration of Meanings	Therapeutic alliance deepened by experience of safety. Patient may test therapist to see if fears of what may happen are justified, e.g., fear of emotional overload.	Patient expands on meaning to the self of the trauma and its sequelae.	Therapist realigns focus when arriving at later formulations. If avoidance is maladaptive, therapist counteracts or interprets defensive and warded-off contents. Therapist clarifies how intrusive and warded-off emotions and ideas are linked to stressor events and the patient's appraisals of them.
4. Improving Coping	Deeper expression of usually private thoughts and emotions.	Patient works on themes previously avoided.	Therapist acts to encourage desensitization of triggers to emotional reactions and helps patient modify dysfunctional beliefs.
5. Working Through	Projections and transference reactions are confronted and clarified in relation to the actualities.	Patient reschematizes current inner cognitive maps.	Therapist helps patient modify structure of beliefs (reschematization).
6. Terminating	Emphasis on safe separation.	Patient considers gains and unfinished issues as well as how to cope with loss of the therapy.	Therapist clarifies gains and any unfinished issues for the future. Interprets and differentiates any links between termination experiences and stressor event experiences.

rich areas of the brain such as the locus ceruleous and frontal cortex. These brain regions are connected to the emotional arousal-regulating functions of the amygdala. These chemicals may be involved in heightening biological propensities for hyperarousal, hypervigilance, and sudden alarm reactions to trigger stimuli. Repeated alarms can lead to fatigue and further dysregulation of cognitive-emotional functioning (Southwick et al. 1993). Stress can affect many neurotransmitters, the autonomic nervous system, and hormonal functions, as well as their interactive processes. For example, serotonin subtypes, and their receptors, probably regulate complex brain activities and are also involved in the production of stress hormones. Trauma-induced alterations in this chemistry could also lead to fight–flight arousals of the autonomic nervous system or even to hibernating withdrawals.

If and when assays or tests of dysfunction specified neurotransmitter systems become possible, then a rational prescription system will become possible. Until then *antianxiety* and *affect-dampening medications* are sometimes used to prevent extremes suggestive of excessive sympathetic nervous system arousal. The signs include excessive vigilance, tension, startle reactions, fatigue, emotional flooding, agitation, and racing thoughts. These sedating and possibly addicting agents can often be used in a single dose or as a night-by-night sedation. Transient use of benzodiazepines has sometimes been effective as a way of reducing explosive entry into extremely undermodulated states. Regular, extended use is inadvisable. Medications that reduce autonomic nervous system arousal, such as the beta-adrenergic blockers, have also been tried. In the main, however, antidepressive agents have been more useful in prolonged use than have antianxiety and arousal-blocking medications (Frank et al. 1988, van der Kolk et al. 1994).

A variety of *antidepressant medications* have been used for depressive disorders exacerbated or precipitated by stressor events, and also for PTSD (or for panic attacks exacerbated by traumatic events) (Davidson et al. 1990, Shetatsky et al. 1984). Selective serotonin reuptake inhibitors, tricyclics, and monoamine oxidase inhibitors have all been tried with some reported successes. The most widely prescribed are the SSRI agents. New research has also shown that some recurrent schizophrenic episodes may be precipitated by life events. At such times, prescriptions of antipsychotic medications (or adjustments in dosage) may be indicated.

Medications are best selected according to the symptoms and biological formulation of each individual patient. Prescriptions should be carefully considered in terms of the length of trial for each agent used. Addictive use of alcohol, prescription drugs, and street or over-the-counter drugs should be avoided.

Social Support

Persons who are exposed to traumatic events often experience themselves as overwhelmed. Interventions may consist of advice given to social companions who are less overwhelmed. This general advice is listed as follows:

1. The victim may need to be transiently protected from excessive stimulation. Structuring time following a disaster should emphasize short-range activities that affect reality.
2. The patient should be provided with opportunities for communication and a sense of positive connection to others. Discussion of events with others may be useful because it clarifies differences between realistic and unrealistic interpretations.
3. Giving time lines for dose-by-dose coping can restore a sense of personal efficacy to a bewildered or overwhelmed victim. The Scarlett O'Hara approach of "I'll think of that tomorrow" can be adaptive if not prolonged.
4. Activities should include time for respite. It is important for the person to feel that it is all right to rest, use humor, or change to non-coping activities for a period of restoration.

5. Give the person something active to do in the role of helping self or others. Sometimes membership in a mutual support group can serve this purpose.

6. Remember that the more the person has been traumatized, the longer it will take for symptoms to subside. This may contrast with the expectation in some work environments that the traumatized person return to her usual functional level within a week. The work place provides sustaining interest and social support; the victim should not be isolated from it, but neither should she have to meet excessive expectations.

7. Children may see repetitious film clips of a disaster on TV and believe that the depicted event is really happening over and over again. They need adult explanations to reassure them that they are safe.

8. Because sleep disruption is common, the victim may associate efforts to sleep with episodes of unpleasant imagery. It is helpful to increase a sense of safety. This can include leaving lights on or sleeping with a pet. Children may be allowed to sleep with a parent although that is not the usual domestic arrangement. In extreme cases, telling the victim that a companion will stay awake and watch over him during sleep can encourage rest.

9. The person may be more at risk for having an accident while driving or operating machinery. For these reasons, keeping the victim from driving unnecessarily or doing hazardous work tasks may be advisable for a time. It must be done tactfully so as to avoid incompetent self-concepts.

10. Right after a traumatic event, the victim's relatives and friends cluster around and want to know all about it. The victim recounts the story again and again. Later, companions may become tired of hearing about it but the victim may still feel the need to review what happened. At these

later stages, listening is still useful. The therapist may advise family and friends that "being there" and listening fulfills a useful function, and that they do not have to offer solutions, directives, or unsolicited interpretation to be helpful.

Psychological Support

Nearly all people experience a need for closer social support. Under strain, some regress to desperate or excessively anxious attachment patterns. Unfortunately, those prone to the more desperate forms of seeking it alienate those who might otherwise help them. The therapist can provide some of that needed relationship support, as discussed under social interventions.

Establishing appointments, a diagnosis, and a formulation can be quite reassuring. Conveying facts can reduce secondary anxieties. Some people may, for example, presume that intrusive symptoms represent such a high degree of lowered control over mental contents and interpersonal emotional expressions that they are losing their mind. The therapist can reduce patients' fears by giving them accurate information about the prevalence of such post-traumatic responses as well as the usual course of improvement (rather than deterioration) in such symptoms.

Patients may be told that they do not have to focus attention on intrusive memories, ideas, and feelings. Putting such topics out of mind can restore equilibrium and it does not mean they will be either forgotten or avoided forever. It may also help to identify a theme that occurs in some patients: they feel less attractive to others in their post-traumatic states of mind. They cringe because they believe others see them as cowards, weaklings, malingers, bores, or ugly companions. Realistic reassurance can be given; telling the patient that this is a common response can partially restore a rational perspective.

Establishing a commitment to care by giving a plan for what will be done provides both empathy for the patient's level of current distress and hope for change. Such initial support can lead to a sharp reduction in symptoms. The patient can then move rapidly toward exploring meanings, improving coping, and working through in the ensuing phases of psychotherapy.

There are a variety of systems for relaxation that may be useful to people who do not already know how to use such procedures. They may range from deep breathing exercises to systematic muscular relaxation or other somatic slow-down practices. In addition, other stress management techniques such as periods of socialization and relaxation, regular diet, and frequent naps if sleep is disturbed, should be utilized.

Exploration of Meanings

Once the patient is capable of working states in which intense, unpleasant emotions can be tolerated, the stressor event's meanings to self can be examined. That is why intense feelings are sanctioned within a therapeutic alliance and overwhelming feelings are divided into dose-by-dose experiences. The goal is a process of explanation aimed at reaching conclusions about the stressor event.

When the clinician discovers a block to working through reactions, he may help the patient by clarifying differences between realistic and fantasy-based beliefs. In doing so, the clinician allows the patient to learn by identification. The clinician is a person who is not overwhelmed by thinking about the implications of illness, injury, or loss. The presence of the clinician as a compassionate and empathic person, thinking logically, is reassuring.

To maintain a safe situation, patients may be urged to take a one-dose-at-a-time approach, contemplating the most immediate consequences of what has happened and putting off long-range considerations for a period of time. This reassurance indicates to patients how to tolerate what has seemed intolerable.

Improving Coping

After a reformulation based on explored meanings, the therapist can plan how to help a patient improve his future coping style. Attitudes that lead to unnecessary avoidances are interpreted. This usually entails explaining why a person is inhibiting thought. A dose-by-dose approach is again encouraged: this means the patient will be encouraged to think the unthinkable in tolerable amounts, using specific controls rather than global inhibitions. Reduced defenses will lead to negative emotions but these will be within tolerable limits. If not, additional desensitization procedures such as relaxation exercises, stretching, biofeedback, systematic body movement, guided imagery, or somatic patterning retraining (as in yoga, breathing, and meditation) might be considered. Various distraction procedures may also be helpful (Shapiro 1989).

The therapist may focus for a time in psychotherapy on reducing the shock of a surprising and terrifying mismatch that is carried into consciousness in the form of unbidden images. For example, a physically abused woman was surprised when her husband attacked her to see an expression of pure destructive hatred on his face. Her prior view of him had never included a concept of his wanting to annihilate her. The image of his face was an intrusive repetition of the shocking realization that he could enter into such an evil state. It would be important to acknowledge that she did feel shocked, and to explain that she might hope to gradually master this shock. Repeated discussions about her relationship with her husband would help her form realistic goals for making changes in the relationship, including whether or not to continue it. In this context, dysfunctional or catastrophic beliefs such as "I must be with him to be a worthwhile person," or " I must never express my anger or I'll be rejected," or "If I don't fill all his needs I am a total failure," would be clarified and confronted with alternative concepts about identity and relationships.

Coping can be improved by replacing pathogenic defensiveness with more adaptive conscious controls. To avoid dreaded states

of mind, some people develop habitual styles of warding off unresolved and highly emotional themes. Obstacles to working through
may stem from their automatic avoidance and unconscious distortions. Therapists may observe these defenses by noting how a patient minimizes, partially confronts and partially avoids, or dismisses
specific topics. These defensive controls should be tactfully counteracted.

Defensive operations are common. In a study of 66 cases of
Post Traumatic Stress Disorder (Horowitz and colleagues 1980a),
three of the most common were excessively inhibiting associational
connections (found in 69% of the cases), excessively switching attitudes to avoid emotion (64%), and unrealistically distorting reality
to avoid deflations of self-esteem (41%).

Because defensiveness is often excessive, it is useful to counteract some control processes by therapeutic interventions in order
to more fully explore meanings relating self to the stressor events.
Some techniques for use with people who habitually inhibit ideas
are presented in Chapter 10, for those who squash emotion in
Chapter 11, and for those who distort reality for self-enhancement
in Chapter 12.

Another defense is use of fantasy to disassociate from the reality of new, stress-induced situations. The avoidant fantasy may deny
the actual outcome. For example, a resident neurosurgeon had a
patient die in brain surgery. In therapy, he reported dreams of triumphant surgical successes. Interpretations that link a current experience to a past stressor event can reduce the dissociation. For
example, a therapist might say, "Your dream shows you would like
only great successes. You would rather have seen the operation come
out well than have had the brain tumor patient die." This sounds
obvious, but it is often experienced as a surprising and emotional
connection by an avoidant patient. It may help to add a future to
the time frame: in the real past, the surgery failed; in the imagined
present it succeeded; in the realistic future, the doctor can save other
patients.

During this stage of treatment it may be useful to introduce various types of exposure to the memory of the trauma or to situations associated with it (Foa et al. 1991, 1995, Marks 1981, Meichenbaum 1977, 1980). Many patients will worry that such repetitions will lead to a retraumatization. This fear is a legitimate one. For that reason a rationale for exposure to threatening stimuli needs to be provided to the patient. The effects should be evaluated. The desired outcome is not the re-experiencing of terror but a decrease in intensity and negativity of affective arousals. This will be more thoroughly discussed in a following chapter on inhibitory controls used prominently by persons with a histrionic personality style.

The rationale for exposure techniques involves a theory of habituation. Familiarity with the previously frightening stimuli can increase calm, especially if the repetition occurs in calm states. The goal is desensitization of the conditioned associational link between the stress stimulus and the alarm emotions. That is why it is important to assess whether or not a restoration of equilibrium occurs as a consequence of exposure techniques. Simple rating scales of distress can be used to indicate if reductions in alarm occur. A ten-point scale with "the most distress you could possibly experience" as ten, and "no distress whatsoever" as zero, can be helpful in obtaining patient reports of inner experiences during exposures.

In addition, exposure techniques can help the person reorganize her cognitive map of how the traumatic event relates to the self. The repetitions encourage emotional information processing. The therapist encourages the patient toward a differentiation of how the current stimuli are similar and different from traumas in the past, and also encourages a heightened sense of self-efficacy (Foa and Rothbaum, 1998).

The most common exposure technique is to retell the experience of the traumatic event. Another common technique uses imagery. During such *imaginal exposure*, gradations of imagery experience from mild to intense are used. The suggested images for review gradually move toward more painful and distressing experiences.

Another technique involves in vivo exposure, which is directly confronting fear situations. The patient returns, perhaps with a supportive companion, to the situation or place where the trauma occurred. Usually there is a hierarchy of avoided situations. The person first confronts those likely to induce only a mild level of anxiety. He then gradually confronts situations that might arouse more distress. This gives the person a learning experience that, with appropriate support, can make him calmer in previously avoided threatening situations.

It is sometimes helpful to teach the patient how to relax from tension during these imaginal or in vivo procedures. Muscle relaxation, breath control, and postural changes from guarded positions to more relaxed ones are useful techniques for this purpose.

After any recollection in in vivo exposure or imaginal exposure, it is important to review the experience. This includes assessing associations and clarifying any dysfunctional beliefs. The therapist may repeatedly contrast dysfunctional beliefs with more adaptive alternative ones.

Because exposure can lead to an increase rather than a decrease of intense negative emotion, it is important to again emphasize a dose-by-dose approach. That means the person can learn how she can stop paying attention to a threatening topic. At first, the therapist presents alternative topics for contemplation to encourage attentional shifts. The therapist may use role-playing techniques to show the patient how to both remember and how to change the topic of contemplation. Then methods for attention control without the presence of a therapist can be taught.

Working Through

If the person has contradictory schemas and emotional conflicts *before* a traumatic event it may be more difficult for him to reschematize identity and relationship beliefs *after* the event. Defensive avoidances may have become habitual ways to avoid negative emotions and dreaded, undermodulated states of mind. That may lead to overcontrol after the event. The effect may be such that an inhibition of information processing occurs and reschematization is not accomplished. The result is prolonged problems. The goal of therapy is then to work through the patient's dilemmas so that reschematization of identity and relationships can occur. The goal is to help a problematic response change to become an adaptive response. A review of what has been discussed in Chapters 8 and 9 on this topic is presented in Figures 8–1 and 8–2.

Working through usually involves exploration of prior personality-based beliefs and their association with the beliefs that were processed about the traumatic event. This often involves activation of the themes discussed in an earlier chapter that may lead to excessive fear of future victimization, enduring and irrational shame over vulnerability or incompetence, unusually intense anger and impulses for revenge, extreme sensitivity to guilt, and/or low threshold for despair with expectations of being abandoned.

The *fear of victimization* relates to the dread that either the self or loved ones will suffer torments and horrors. During a disaster, the person might have felt relief for having survived; that relief might later be remembered with shame or guilt because others suffered terribly. There may also be a fear of merger with victims, of being dead or maimed like them. A current trauma with self as victim can be associated with past traumas or fantasies of self as victim, intensifying emotional reactions, and making cognitive processing more complex.

Shame or vulnerability and incompetence during a disaster can be associated with childhood views of self as weak and lacking in sufficient skills or in courageous values. Anger, in which others are blamed, can be a defensive lid on such dreaded roles.

Anger at the source of a trauma and a thirst for revenge upon the aggressor persons (or displacement figures) is also a common but conflicted theme; it may serve as a self-strengthening defensive shift away from shame. Irrational attitudes may hold innocent others to

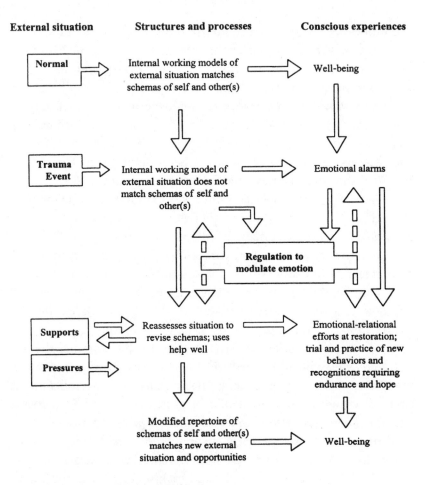

*dotted lines indicate inhibitions of processes

Figure 8–1. Normal and Adaptive Psychological Responses to Trauma

be aggressors. Such rage can activate latent role-relationship models with a scenario of other as aggressor or unreliable caretaker, followed by a sense of guilt at the self as having been too angry and vengeful. The conflict between expressing and stifling hostility is reactivated by rage at the loss, injury, or fright from the stressor event. The prior vulnerability schemas make normal rage more intense.

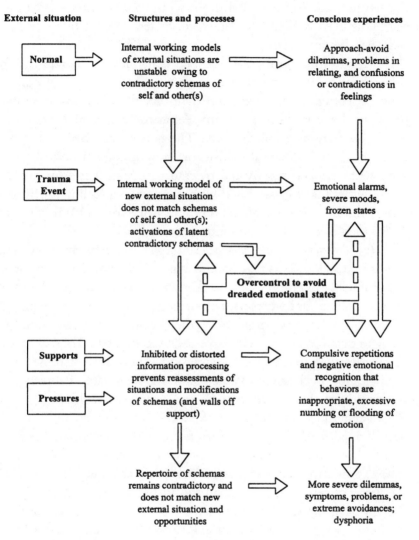

Figure 8–2. Problematic and Maladaptive Psychological Responses to Trauma

Sometimes rage is directed at those who did not suffer, as did the self. This may awaken previously conflicted, but relatively latent, personal themes of envy.

All stressors can increase general irritability. A therapist may suffer from or develop countertransference reactions to unjustified hostility from an easily angered patient. For these reasons, it is vital to avoid therapist overload from seeing too many such patients.

Guilt may be a vulnerability. The person may have self-concepts (bad, wicked, sinful, selfish, or irresponsible) that are latent, long-standing, and reactivated by traumas. After a stressor event, such themes may be associated with memories of feeling relief that others and not the self suffered the most (survivor guilt). Inhibiting guilty themes can prevent working through.

Low thresholds for states of despair and depression can be entered when events lead to loss. Loss may include loss of bodily functions and loss of comfort, as in chronic post-accident pain syndromes. In the case of loss of others, or body parts, a mourning process usually takes place, relatively resolving the grief. Nevertheless, unresolved grief is more likely to occur in people who have been too frightened of sadness to allow grief work to take place. Depression is more likely in those with biological or psychological vulnerabilities to such states. People with prior insecure attachments may be especially vulnerable.

Techniques for this phase often involve differentiation of beliefs derived from the past and from currently appropriated assessments. Both may also be contrasted with beliefs or plans about the future. Some meanings of the stressor event are linked to dreaded identity concepts and role-relationship patterns of the past. The therapist clarifies this link and then challenges the expectation that the beliefs will pervade the future. Reasons the person can now become capable of avoiding victimization, letting go of revenge plans, tolerating separations and losses, and expressing remorse without annihilation of self are emphasized. That is, for each conflicted theme in an individual patient, repeated attention is paid to how to envision and rehearse for a more adaptive future.

During the working-through phase, the therapist deepens the focus of the doctor–patient attention. This deepening involves interpretation of what has been warded off. Table 8–3 illustrates surface and deeper levels of interpretations. The therapist aims for the depth required to restore equilibrium. In most cases, attention is focused at levels 1–5; these can often be accomplished in a brief therapy to work through a trauma. Sometimes, however, focusing on the deeper levels of 6–8 is necessary. This enables more reschematization and may require a longer time in therapy. An example follows.

> Sally, a young woman in her early twenties, had a complex fracture of her femur, having fallen from a ladder while helping her father paint his house. A partial paralysis resulted from nerve damage. This complicated matters; it disrupted her plans to accept a teaching position after graduating from college. She came for therapy with a diagnosis of Major Depressive Disorder and Adjustment Disorder precipitated by her accident and its sequelae.
>
> One theme activated by her injury was hostility toward her father for not taking good care of her. The relevant ideas about the stress event were that her father had given her a rickety, second–class wooden ladder while he used his safer aluminum one. Awareness of her anger was partially warded off by defensive inhibitions of contemplating this theme at the time of treatment onset.
>
> During an early treatment hour, she expressed signs of anger at the therapist because he would not prescribe sleeping pills for her insomnia. Though the therapist was able to see the non–verbal signs of this emotion, it was not expressed clearly in verbal form by the patient. The therapist considered possible statements he might make. He could say, "I think you may be angry with me but are afraid to say so," or he could link the exploration of the transference anger to the father-ladder meanings of the recent stress event, worded as follows: "I think you may be getting angry with me right now because I am not meeting your need for a sleeping pill, just as you may be angry with your father because you feel he took poor care of you by giving you a rickety stepladder."

Table 8–3. Levels of Interpretation (from Horowitz 1997c)

LEVEL	TOPICAL FOCUS	TEMPORAL FOCUS		
		FUTURE	NOW IN THERAPY	PAST
1.	Stressor event and personal responses	Plans of how to prepare for future stressor events	Expectations of treatment	Relevant previous stress events
2.	Choices of how to cope with stress	Conflicting plans of how to cope with consequences of recent stressor event	Choice of therapy focus	Long-standing goals and dilemmas
3.	Avoidance of adaptive challenges	Defensive avoidances and distortions	Encouraging work on important topics	History of self-impairing avoidances
4.	Dreaded states of mind	Triggers to entry into symptomatic states	States of therapeutic work (and non-work)	Habitual dreaded states
5.	Irrational beliefs	Differentiation of realistic from fantastic appraisals	Reasonable expectations versus fantastic hopes	Origin of unrealistic expectations
6.	Maladaptive interpersonal patterns	Interpersonal problems and degradations of identity	Difference between transferences and therapeutic alliances	Relation of current problems to past patterns
7.	Life plans	Opportunities for adaptive change	Harmonizing conflicted beliefs	Development of intentions

This type of wording links transference reactions in the therapy situation to a relationship aspect of the current stressor situation. It maintains the focus of treatment on resolving reactions to recent events, but it also allows for a clarification of precursor themes. By raising unconscious sources of emotional arousal (her anger in therapy) to conscious recognition, contemplation can lead to revised views of the motives of others, and a clearer sense of one's own identity.

Terminating

During termination, the goals are to work through emotions about separating and to reinforce corrective beliefs and attitudes. Plans for repeating, rehearsing, and practicing adaptive cognitions and behaviors should be made and perhaps written down for later review. Termination of the treatment threatens reenactment of the patient's personal vulnerability as experienced during the recent stressor events. Therapists should introduce plans for terminating several sessions before the final one. This way, a loss can be faced gradually, actively rather than passively, and within a communicative relationship.

It may be helpful to inform the much-improved patient that internal work digesting the stress-inducing experiences will continue. Some alarm reactions that have subsided may reoccur. This should not lead to dismay. It will be one indication of the importance of patients' repeating on their own what they have learned in treatment.

Case Example: Frank

The following case illustrates a formulation for planning treatment using the Configurational Analysis Method.

Frank was a 25–year-old male lifeguard at a neighborhood pool. On one busy summer day, the pool was full of children and adolescents. There were many people in the water, and also unruly episodes were occurring on the deck. Frank was quite busy and realized that he was so overloaded with demands for his attention that he could not be sure that everyone was safe. He blew his whistle and ordered the pool cleared.

To his horror, there was an inert body at the bottom of the pool. He dived in at once and brought a small, limp, non-breathing figure to the deck. Frank began cardiopulmonary resuscitation. This failed to revive the small boy, who was later pronounced dead. Overcome with remorse, Frank went to the funeral of the deceased child. He was greeted with many angry scowls and became upset by the grief-stricken faces of the child's parents.

Phenomena to Explain

Frank went through turbulent periods of remorse, insomnia, attacks of anxiety, guilt, and shame, and developed a dread of dying. He quit his job, had difficulty concentrating, and avoided pools, children, and the neighborhood where he had worked as a lifeguard.

Six months after the event, Frank began having frightening nightmares, with visual images of a dead body in a pool, a blurred face of a child, and angry faces of adults. He was preoccupied with feelings of remorse, which disrupted his concentration at his new job. He had outbursts of anger with companions. These intrusions occurred despite his efforts to avoid them.

States of Mind

Frank could not sustain interest in his career or recreational activities. A desired lively state of productive working or focused concentration could seldom be stabilized. Instead, in a defensive problematic state, he felt that everything in his world was cloaked in fog. At times, he had a dreaded and undermodulated state that bordered on panic: he felt that he was about to die. These states were markedly different from his usual amiability and enthusiasm before the drowning.

Topics of Concern and Defensive Control Processes

Frank was remote and apathetic when pressed for details about his current feelings. It was hard to clarify those subjects that seemed to cause his most dreaded states. This was ameliorated as the therapist indicated empathic and compassionate recognition of his suffering. Frank was then able to move toward an exploration of the topic that seemed important: he had entangled realistic and fantastic aspects of his responsibility as a lifeguard for the safety of everyone in the pool. He felt terribly guilty; it was necessary to get beyond his surface statements that he had already worked through this issue. He used warding-off rationalizations, saying how it was the fault of others.

Identity and Relationships

Frank viewed himself in antithetical sets of self-concepts. His worst sense of identity was as an irresponsible, careless, self-centered caretaker. He wanted to regard himself as a truly caring person who was competent at protecting others. To shed guilt, he externalized blame onto pool directors who did not care enough to hire additional lifeguards or to control the number of people allowed to use the pool.

Integration and Treatment Planning

One topic was his rage at the pool managers for putting him in an overly demanding situation. As it happened, exploring this topic led to a negative reaction toward the therapist, including rage that the therapist was expecting too much of him. A warded-off but emergent feeling that recovery was too good for him was clarified. Frank brought up a past memory of how at age five, he had piled toys onto his unwanted 2-year-old brother in an effort to get rid of him. This past memory added intensity to his guilt.

In the stage of improving coping, the plan was to focus on the current stressor. Frank was asked to explore the question of how much remorse he needed to feel in order to reduce his sense of guilt. As Frank worked on this issue, he decided to volunteer his services in teaching drowning prevention to schoolchildren, even though it made him tense and anxious. He saw how he could be constructive; this differed from a need to be self-punitive as in seeking to fail in his current career efforts.

Frank was at an intrusive phase with many continuing avoidant responses. In the stage of initial support, the treatment plan was to empathically accept him as suffering and worthy of help, as well as needing a therapeutic process. Exploring meanings began in an initial treatment session. Several topics were designated, and working-through stages on these topics would follow.

In the termination stage, the plan was to help Frank feel less dependent on the therapist in order to shore up his sense of identity; he feared relapse after the treatment ended. By the next-to-last session, he felt that he could stop at the appointed time, provided booster visits could be available as needed. This plan was agreed upon.

EFFICACY: RESULTS OF THIS TYPE OF PSYCHOTHERAPY FOR STRESS RESPONSE SYNDROMES

Colleagues and I developed useful measures for assessing the levels of distress, subject predispositions, and therapist techniques and therapy outcomes. These measures include the Impact of Event Scale (self-report) (Horowitz et al. 1979, Zilberg et al. 1982); the Stress Response Rating Scale (clinician's assessment) (Horowitz 1976, Weiss et al. 1984); the Patterns of Individualized Change Scales, which assess work, intimacy, caretaking, and other life functions (DeWitt et al. 1983, Kaltreider et al. 1981, Weiss et al. 1985);

assessments of the therapeutic alliance (Marmar et al. 1987, Marziali et al. 1981), therapist-actions (Hoyt 1980, Hoyt et al. 1981); and patients' motivations (Rosenbaum and Horowitz 1983). The dispositions measure of most importance was the *organizational level of self and other* schematization (Horowitz 1979a, 1987, 1998, Horowitz, Marmar, Weiss et al. 1984).

Using all of these measures in the study of 52 cases of pathological grief reactions after the death of a family member, we examined the results of a 12-session, time-limited therapy (as reported in detail in Horowitz, Marmar, Weiss, et al. 1984). Before treatment, this sample had levels of symptoms comparable with those of other psychiatric outpatient samples studied in treatment research: intake on the Symptom Checklist-90 (SCL-90) (general psychiatric symptoms rated by self-report) (Derogatis et al. 1976) for the sample was 1.19 (SD, 0. 59). This level is almost identical with the figure of 1.25 (SD, 0.39) reported by Derogatis and colleagues for a sample of 209 symptomatic outpatients. The mean depression subscale score in our sample at intake was 1.81, and in the Derogatis study it was 1.87. The scores for anxiety were also comparable: 1.39 in our sample and 1.49 in the sample of Derogatis.

A significant improvement was seen in all symptomatic outcome variables when pretherapy scores were compared with follow-up levels. Our results can be expressed in terms of the standardized mean difference effect size coefficient recommended by Cohen (1979) for presenting before–after treatment data. He defined a large effect as 0.80 or greater. Our large effect sizes were in the domain of symptoms and ranged from 1.21 to 0.71. Changes in work, interpersonal functioning, and capacity for intimacy on the patterns of Individualized Change Scales indicated improvements that were more moderate (Horowitz, Marmar, Weiss et al. 1986).

This synthesized cognitive-psychodynamic approach was effective in studies by other investigators in other institutions. It did as well as behavioral therapy in treatment of PTSD in the Netherlands (Brom et al. 1989). It also did as well as behavioral-cognitive therapy in brief treatment of Major Depressive Disorders (Gallagher-Thompson et al. 1990, Thompson et al. 1987, 1991). In both studies, the psychotherapy groups did better than wait-list controls. As reviewed in meta-analyses of equivalent studies, this cognitive-psychodynamic approach is one of the effective treatments (Crits-Christoph et al. 1988). The synthesis of cognitive-psychodynamic theory is reported elsewhere (Horowitz 1998), as is a systematic method of formulation (Horowitz 1997c).

III

INDIVIDUAL VARIATIONS

9

INHIBITORY OPERATIONS: REACTIONS TO STRESS AND PSYCHOTHERAPY WITH HISTRIONIC PERSONALITIES

The next three chapters model the defensive maneuvers used to counter the tendency to intrusion and painful emotional response after trauma: these are inhibition, switching, and sliding to alter valuation. Inhibition has been frequently associated with histrionic styles, switching with compulsive styles, and sliding of meanings with narcissistic styles. We begin with the histrionic style.

The development, diagnosis, and treatment of histrionic personality disorders are described in more detail elsewhere (Horowitz 1977a,b, Horowitz et al. 1984a). Styles of thought, felt emotion, and subjective experience relevant to our discussion have been described by Shapiro (1965). Shapiro emphasized the importance of impressionism, that is, the prototypical histrionic character lacks a sharp focus of attention and arrives quickly at a global but superficial assumption of the meaning of perceptions, memories, fantasies, and felt emotions. There is a corresponding lack of factual detail and definition in perception, plus distractability and incapacity for persistent or intense concentration. The historical continuity of such perceptual and ideational styles leads to a relatively nonfactual world in which the guiding schemas of self, objects, and environment have a flat quality.

Dwelling conceptually in this nonfactual world promotes emphasis on fantasy meanings. For example, the person may react swiftly with an emotional outburst and yet remain unable to conceptualize what is happening and why such feelings occur. After the episode she may remember her own emotional experiences unclearly and will regard them as if they were visited upon her rather than self-instigated.

This general style of representation of perception, thought, and emotion leads to patterns observable in interpersonal relations, traits, and communicative styles. A tabular summary of what is meant by these components is presented under these headings in Table 9–1.

CONTROLLING THOUGHT AND EMOTION

We shall now consider Harry as if he responded to stress and treatment in this manner. One of his six conflictual themes, as described earlier, will be used to clarify the mode of controlling thought and emotion. This theme is Harry's relief that he was alive when someone had to die. Harry's perceptions of the dead woman's body and his own bodily sensations of being alive matched his fear of finding himself dead. The discrepancy between his perceptions and his fears led to feelings of relief.

In the context of the woman's death, his relief was incongruent with moral strictures. Harry believed that he should share the

Table 9–1. Patterns in the Histrionic Typology

INFORMATION-PROCESSING STYLE

- global deployment of attention.
- unclear or incomplete representations of ideas and feelings, possibly with lack of details or clear labels in communication; nonverbal communications not translated into words or conscious meanings.
- only partial or unidirectional associational lines.
- short circuit to apparent completion of problematic thoughts.

TRAITS

- attention-seeking behaviors, possibly including demands for attention, and/ or the use of charm, vivacity, sex appeal, childishness.
- fluid change in mood and emotion, possibly including breakthroughs of feeling.
- inconsistency of apparent attitudes.

INTERPERSONAL RELATIONS

- repetitive, impulsive, stereotyped interpersonal relationships often characterized by victim–aggressor, child–parent, and rescue or rape themes.
- "cardboard" fantasies and self-object attitudes.
- drifting but possibly dramatic lives with an existential sense that reality is not really real.

fate of others rather than have others absorb bad fate. This discrepancy between current and enduring concepts led to guilt. Harry had a low toleration for strong emotions, and the danger of experiencing guilt motivated his efforts to control the representations that generated the emotions.

Although controlling helped Harry escape unpleasant ideas and emotions, it impeded his information processing. Were it not for controlling efforts, Harry might think again of the woman's death, his relief, his feelings about surviving at her expense. He might realize that he was following unrealistic principles of thought and forgive himself for feeling relief. If thinking itself were not enough, he could undertake some act of penance and remorse. But inhibition prevented the thought or act that would change his attitude and reduce the discrepancy between his feelings and his sense of morality.

If inhibition of emotion is *what* Harry accomplished, one can go further to indicate *how* it was accomplished in terms of cognitive operations. These operations can be abstracted as if they were in a hierarchy. The maneuver to try first in the hierarchy is inhibition of conscious representation. The initial perceptual images of the woman's body were too powerful to ward off, and immediately after the accident, Harry might have flooded himself with undermodulated emotions. Later, when his defensive capacity was relatively stronger, the active memory images could be inhibited, counteracting the repeated representation. Similarly, the initial ideas and feelings of relief might be too powerful to avoid, but later, as components of active memory, their reproductive tendency could be inhibited.

Suppose this inhibition failed or was only partly successful. Warded-off ideas were expressed in some modality of representation. In a secondary maneuver, the ideas' extended meanings could still be avoided by inhibiting the translation from initial modes into other forms of representation. Harry could have only his visual images and avoid verbal concepts concerning death, relief, and causation.

A third maneuver is to prevent association to meanings that have been represented. This is again, hypothetically, an interruption of an automatic response tendency. Harry might conceptualize events in image and word forms but not continue to develop the obvious associational connections. The purpose would be avoiding a full conscious awareness of threatening meanings.

These controlling efforts are three typical forms of inhibition: avoidance of representation, avoidance of translation of threatening information from one mode of representation into another, and avoidance of automatic associational connections. If these efforts fail to ward off threatening concepts, there are additional methods. A fourth maneuver is to reverse from active to passive. Harry could avoid thinking about his own active thoughts by studying how other factors (fate, the woman, the listener to his story) are involved. He could then change his belief that he is alive because he actively wished to be alive even if another person died, by thinking of one's passivity with regard to fate, of the woman's activity in hitchhiking, and of how she got herself into the accident.

The fifth maneuver is altering the state of consciousness by changing the organization of thought and the sense of self. Harry used alcohol for this purpose, but no outside agents are necessary to enter a hypnoid state, with loss of reflective self-awareness. These five cognitive maneuvers can be listed as if they were a hierarchy of "rules" in the inhibitory style for avoiding unwanted ideas (Horowitz 1977a,b).

1. Avoid representation.
2. Avoid intermodal translation.
3. Avoid automatic associational connections (and avoid conscious problem-solving thought).
4. Change self-attitude from active to passive (and vice versa).
5. Alter state of consciousness in order to change hierarchies of wishes and fears, blur realities and fantasies, dissociate conflicting attitudes, and alter the sense of self as instigator of thought and action.

In addition, Harry could manipulate situations so that some external person could be held responsible for his survival. This would reduce the danger of a sense of guilty personal activity. In regard to very long-range maneuvers, Harry could characterologically avoid experiencing himself as ever fully real, aware, and responsible. He could identify himself with others, real or fantasied, which would make any act or thought of crime their responsibility and not his.

CLARITY IN THERAPEUTIC INTERVENTIONS

If the person with a histrionic personality style enters psychotherapy because of stress response symptoms, the therapist will try to terminate the state of stress by helping him complete the processing of the stress-related ideas and feelings. This activity will include thinking through ideas, including latent conflicts activated by the event, experiencing emotions, and revising concepts to reduce discrepancies. The interpretation of defense may help remove impediments to processing, but the main goal in this model is to end or reduce a state of stress rather than to alter the character style. Even with such limited goals, character style must be understood and the usual therapy techniques used with appropriate nuances.

The nuances are versions, variations, or accentuations of major techniques such as clarification. One example is simple repetition of what the patient has said. The therapist may, by repeating a phrase, exert a marked effect on the hysteric, who may respond with a startle reaction, surprise, laughter, or other emotional expressions. The same words uttered by the therapist mean something different from those thought or spoken by the patient himself; they are to be taken more seriously.

Additional meanings accrue, and some meanings are also stripped away. For example, a guilty statement by Harry, repeated by the therapist in a neutral or kind voice, may seem less heinous. More explicitly, to call this "repetition" is to be correct only in a phonemic sense. Actually, the patient hears the meanings more clearly and also hears new meanings. The previously warded-off contents and meanings may seem less dangerous when repeated by the therapist.

Simple repetition is, of course, not so simple. The therapist selects particular phrases and may recombine phrases to clarify them by connecting causal sequences. At first, when Harry was vague about survivorship but said, "I guess I'm lucky to still be around," the therapist might just say "yes" to accentuate the thought. A fuller repetition, in other words, such as "you feel fortunate to have survived" may also have progressive effects; it "forces" Harry closer to the potential next thought: "and she did not, so I feel bad about feeling relief."

Left to his own processes, Harry might have verbalized the various "ingredients" in the theme, might even have painfully experienced pangs of guilt and anxiety, and yet might still not have really listened to his ideas. In response to this vague style, the therapist may pull together scattered phrases: "You had the thought 'Gee, I'm glad to still be around, but isn't it awful to be glad when she's dead?'" Harry might listen to his own ideas through the vehicle of the therapist and work out his own reassurance or acceptance. This seems preferable to giving him permission by saying, "You feel guilty over a thought that anyone would have in such a situation," although this is, of course, sometimes necessary.

As we shall see, these simple everyday maneuvers are not so effective with persons with a compulsive style.

Other therapeutic maneuvers are equally commonplace. To avoid dwelling further on well-known aspects of psychotherapy, some maneuvers are listed that apply to specific facets of histrionic style (Table 9–2). Each maneuver listed has additional nuances. For example interpretations or clarifications should be very short and simple, delivered in a matter-of-fact tone that counters their vagueness, emotionality, and tendency to elaborate any therapist activity into a fantasy relationship.

NUANCES OF RELATIONSHIP

Histrionic persons have a low tolerance for emotion, although they are associated with emotionality. One emotion is often used as a defense against some other emotion, but even the substitute may get out of control. Because motivations are experienced as inexorable and potentially intolerable, the ideas that evoke emotion are inhibited. If toleration for the unpleasant emotions associated with a stressful event can be increased, then the cognitive processing of that event can be resumed. The therapeutic relationship protects the patient from the dangers of internal conflict

Table 9–2. Some Aspects of the Histrionic Style and Their Counteractants in Therapy

FUNCTION	STYLE AS "DEFECT"	THERAPEUTIC COUNTER
Perception	Global or selective inattention	Ask for details
Representation	Impressionistic rather than accurate	Selective reliving in memory plus conceptual reconstruction
Translation of images and enactions into words	Limited	Encourage talk Provide verbal labels
Associations	Limited by inhibitions Misinterpretations based on schematic stereotypes, deflected from reality to wishes and fears	Encourage production Repetition Clarification
Problem solving	Short circuit to rapid but often erroneous conclusions Avoidance of topic when emotions are unbearable	Keep subject open Interpretations Support

and potential loss of control and so operates to increase tolerance for warded-off ideas and feelings. The therapist effects the patient's sense of this relationship by his activities or restraint. How this is typically done is also a nuance of technique.

After a stress event, the histrionic patient often manifests swings from rigid overcontrol to uncontrolled intrusions and emotional repetition. During these swings, especially at the beginning and with a desperate patient, the therapist may oscillate between closeness and distance, always staying within the boundaries that characterize a therapeutic relationship.

The histrionic patient may consider it imperative to have care and attention. This imperative need has been called, at times, the "oral," "sick," or "bad" component of some hysterical styles (Easser and Lesser 1965, Lazare 1971, Marmor 1953). These are inappropriate terms. During the period of imperative need, especially after a devastating stress event, patients need sympathetic concern and support from the therapist. Without it, the therapeutic relationship will fall apart, and the patient may regress or develop additional psychopathology (Myerson 1969). During this phase the therapist moves, in effect, closer to the patient: just close enough to provide necessary support but not so close as the patient appears to wish. This is not an endorsement of transference gratification. It is simply a matter of the degree of support needed and extended.

As the patient becomes more comfortable, she may begin to feel anxious at the degree of intimacy in the therapeutic relationship because there may be a fear of being seduced or enthralled by her own dependency wishes regarding the therapist. The therapist then moves back to a cooler, more distant, or less supportive stance.

The therapist thus oscillates to keep the patient within a zone of safety by modifying his manner of relating to the patient. Safety allows the patient to move in the direction of greater conceptual clarity (Sandler 1960, Weiss 1971). Naturally, the therapist's manner includes his nonverbal and verbal cues, what the therapist allows himself to do in the context of his own real responses and qualities of being. This is not role playing; rather, the therapist allows or inhibits his own response tendencies as elicited by the patient.

If the therapist does not come in from a relatively distant position, and if the patient has urgent needs to stabilize his self-concept through relational support, then the discrepancy between need and supply will be so painful that the patient will be unable to expose problematic lines of thought. Inhibition will continue. If the therapist does not change from a relatively close position to a more distant one, then conceptual processing will begin, but transference issues will cloud working through the stress response syndrome.

10

SWITCHING
MANEUVERS:
REACTION TO STRESS
AND PSYCHOTHERAPY
WITH COMPULSIVE
PERSONALITIES

Inhibitory controls are a capacity. Some persons may have different predispositions or learning opportunities and, therefore, different abilities to inhibit emergent information. Even with a strong inhibitory capacity, other avoidance operations may be necessary to ward off a powerful theme. Another common defense is switching to alternative themes, which jam the representational systems and prevent painful recognition of the warded-off contents. This type of operation is commonly linked to a style that has been called compulsive, obsessional, and rigid (Salzman 1980, Shapiro 1965, 1981).

HISTORICAL BACKGROUND

The contemporary theory of obsessional style evolved from analysis of neurotic obsessions, compulsions, doubts, and irrational fears (Abraham 1924, Fenichel 1945, Freud 1909). The manifestations of the neurosis were seen as compromises between aggressive or sexual impulsive aims and defenses such as isolation, reaction formation, intellectualization, and undoing. Underneath a rational consciousness, ambivalence and magical thinking were prominent. Common conflicts were formed in the interaction of aggressive impulses and predispositions to rage, fears of assault, and rigid and harsh attitudes of morality and duty. These conflicts led to the co-existence and fluctuation of dominance and submission themes in interpersonal relationships and fantasies.

Salzman (1968, 1980) emphasized the compulsive's sense of being driven, strivings for omniscience and control, and concerns for the magical effects of hostile thoughts.

Vagueness seems less possible for compulsive personalities than for histrionic personalities. Because obsessionals are often more apt to have an acute awareness of ideas, their staying with one position threatens to lead to unpleasant emotions. Seeing the self as dominant is associated with sadism toward others and leads to guilt. And seeing the self as submissive is associated with weakness and leads to fear of assault; hence either position evokes anxiety. Alternation between opposing poles, as in alternation between dominance themes and submissive themes, serves to undo the danger of remaining at either pole (Sampson and Weiss 1972, Weiss 1967).

To avoid stabilizing at a single position and to accomplish the defense of undoing, obsessionals often use the cognitive operation of shifting from one aspect of a theme to an oppositional aspect and back again. The result is continuous change. At the expense of decision and decisiveness, obsessionals maintain a sense of control and avoid emotional threats (Barnett 1972, Schwartz 1972, Shapiro 1981, Silverman 1972).

Although some compulsives move so rapidly that their emotions do not gain full awareness, they cannot totally eliminate their feelings. Some obsessionals have intrusions of feelings either in minor, quasi-ideational form, as expressed in slips of the tongue or intrusive images, or in major forms, as expressed in attacks of rage. Even when this occurs, however, the event can be undone by what Salzman (1980) called "verbal juggling." This process includes alterations of meaning, use of formulas to arrive at attitudes or plans, shifts in valuation from over- to underestimation, and, sometimes, the attribution of magical properties to word labels.

Shapiro (1965, 1981) described how such persons' narrowed focus misses certain aspects of the world while engaging others in detail. The ideal flexibility of attention is smooth shifts between sharply directed attention and more impressionistic forms of cognition. But the compulsives lack such fluidity. Shapiro also explained how the thoughts, emotions, and behaviors are driven by "shoulds" and "oughts" dictated by a sense of duty, by their fear of loss of control, and by their need to inhibit recognition of their wants. Despite their usual capacity for hard work, productivity, and will power, such persons may experience difficulty and discomfort when they must make a decision. Instead of deciding on the basis of wishes and fears, obsessionals must maintain a sense of omnipotence and therefore must avoid the dangerous mistakes inherent in a trial-and-error world. The decision among possible choices is likely to rest either on a rule evoked to guarantee a "right" decision or else is made on impulse, to end the anxiety. The result of these cognitive styles is an experiential distance from felt emotion. The exception is feelings of anxious self-doubt, a mood instigated by the absence of true cognitive closure. These aspects of cognitive style are summarized with the common traits and patterns of behavior in Table 10–1.

COMPULSIVE TENDENCIES
OF RESPONSE TO STRESS

Stressful events may so compel interest that there may be little difference in the initial registration and experience of persons with histrionic or obsessional styles. But, short of extreme disasters, compulsive persons may remain behaviorally calm and emotionless, in contrast with the emotional explosions of hysterics. There are exceptions, of course, to such generalizations. During some events,

Table 10–1. Patterns in the Compulsive Typology

INFORMATION-PROCESSING STYLE

- sharp focus of attention on details.
- clear representation of ideas, meager representation of emotions.
- shifting organization and implications of ideas rather than following an associational line to conclusion as directed by original intent or intrinsic meanings.
- avoiding completion or decision of a given problem, instead switching back and forth between attitudes.

TRAITS

- doubt, worry, overly detailed productivity and/or procrastination.
- single-minded, unperturbable, intellectualizing.
- tense, deliberate, unenthusiastic.
- rigid, ritualistic.

INTERPERSONAL RELATIONS

- develops regimented, routine, and continuous interpersonal relationships low in "life," vividness, or pleasure. Often frustrating to be with.
- prone to dominance-submission themes or power and control struggles.
- duty filling, hardworking, seeks or makes strain and pressure, does what one should do rather than what one decides to do.
- experiences self as remote from emotional connection with others, although feels committed to operating with others because of role or principles.

compulsives may become quite emotional, and histrionics may remain calm. The difference is in the quality of the person's conscious experience. Histrionic persons can have a calm state of mind because it is based on the inhibition of some aspects of potential knowledge, and there is no emotion because the implications of the stressful event are not known. If and when compulsives behave emotionally, they may experience it as a loss of control, one to be "undone" by retrospective shifts of meaning, rituals, apologies, or self-recriminations.

Compulsives respond to threatened repetitions in thought with cognitive maneuvers such as shifting. By shifting to something else, obsessionals are able to jam their cognitive channels and prevent emergence or endurance of warded-off contents, or to shift meanings so as to stifle emotional arousal. That is, by shifting from topic to topic or from one meaning to another meaning of the same topic, they can avoid the emotion-arousing properties of one set of implications.

CONTROLLING THOUGHT AND EMOTION

To model Harry as using switching operations to avoid the hazard of strong emotions, a time in psychotherapy was considered when Harry began to talk of the unbidden images of the woman's body. At this period in therapy he began to associate to his memory of feeling relieved to be alive. The next conceptualization, following the idealized line of working through outlined earlier, would be association of his relieved feelings with ideas of survival at her expense. This cluster would be matched against moral strictures counter to such personal gain through damage to others, and Harry would go on to conceptualize his emotional experience of guilt or shame. Once this was clear, he could revise his schematic belief that someone had to die, accept his relief, feel remorse, even plan a penance, and reduce incongruity through one or more of these changes. But Harry did not follow this idealized route because he determined the potential of these emotional experiences as intolerable at a not-fully-conscious level of information processing. Thus he switched to another ideational cycle in order to avoid the first one. He also associatively related to the images of the woman's body.

A common element in both ideational cycles allowed a pivotal change and reduced Harry's awareness that the subtopic had changed. The pivot for the switch was the idea of bodily damage. In the second ideational cluster, Harry's concept was that bodily damage could happen to him, perhaps at any future time, as it had now happened to her. Through the comparison between his wishes for invulnerability and his dread of vulnerability, his fear was aroused.

Although fear is unpleasant and threatening as a potential experience, the switch allowed movement away from the potential
feelings of guilt (the prior theme). When the second theme becomes
too clear, fear might be consciously experienced. The procedure
can be reversed with return to the former guilt-provoking topic.
Harry could alternate conscious and communicative meanings between these topics without either set of dangerous ideas and emotions being fully experienced. But Harry did not need to limit his
switching operations to the two contexts for ideas about bodily
damage; he could switch between any permutations of any themes
and could transform, reverse, or undo guilt with fear or anger (Jones
1929). He could see himself as a victim, then as an aggressor, then
as a victim, and so forth. These shifts would dampen his emotional
responsivity but reduce his cognitive processing of themes.

This does not imply that inhibition of representation would
not be found in a compulsive version of Harry or shifts of theme
would be absent in a histrionic version of Harry. A compulsive Harry
might attempt inhibitions and use his shifts when inhibitory efforts
failed. A histrionic Harry might shift from active to passive, as noted
earlier, but the timing and quality of the shifts would differ. A compulsive Harry would shift more rapidly, with less vagueness at either pole. The shift could occur in mid-phrase, between an utter-
ance of his and a response from the therapist, or even as virtually
simultaneous trains of thought.

It is because of rapid shifts that therapists who attempt clarity
with compulsives may be thwarted in their task. Suppose the therapist makes a clarifying intervention about the survivor guilt theme.
The compulsive Harry might have already shifted to his fear of body
injury, and thus hear the remarks in a noncongruent state. The clarification procedure might not work well because Harry was clear in
the first place, was not listening from the earlier position, and un-
did the therapist's intervention by further shifts. An interpretation
to the effect that Harry feared bodily damage as a retribution for his

survivor relief and guilt would be premature at this point because he had not fully experienced either the fear or the guilt.

HOLDING TO CONTEXT: AN IMPORTANT NUANCE WITH PERSONS WHO HABITUALLY USE SWITCHING MANEUVERS

Holding a person who shifts to a topic or a given context within a topic is equivalent to clarifying for the person who typically inhibits ideas. Metaphorically, the switcher avoids conceptual time, whereas the inhibitor avoids conceptual space. The goal of holding is a reduction of shifting so that the patient can progress further along a given conceptual process. The patient must also be helped to tolerate the emotions that will be experienced when he cannot quickly divert ideas into and out of conscious awareness.

Holding to context is more complicated than clarification. One begins with at least two current problems. When the patient is not shifting with extreme rapidity, the therapist may simply hold the patient to either one or the other theme. But the patient will not comply with this maneuver, and the therapist must not confuse holding with forcing. Ferenczi (1926), in an effort to speed up analysis, experimented with various ways to make the obsessional stay on topic until intensely felt emotions occurred. For example, he insisted that his patient develop and maintain visual fantasies relevant to a specific theme. During this technical maneuver his obsessional patients did experience emotions, and they even had affective explosions, but the transference complications impeded rather than enhanced the therapy.

The therapist thus must shift, even though he attempts to hold the patient to a topic. That is, the therapist must shift at a slower rate than the patient does, like a dragging anchor that slows the process. This operation increases the patient's progress in both directions. That is, with each shift, he is able to go a bit further along the conceptual route of either theme, even though he soon becomes frightened and crowds the theme out of mind with an alternative.

The therapist may use repetitions, as with the histrionic, in order to hold or slow the shift of a compulsive patient. But this same maneuver is used with a different nuance. With the inhibitor, the repetition heightens the meaning of what the patient is now saying. With the switcher, the repetition goes back to what the patient was saying before the shift away from the context occurred. With the histrionic, the repetition may be short phrases. With the compulsive, greater length may be necessary in order to state the specific context that is being warded off. For example, if Harry were talking about bodily damage and shifts from a survivor guilt context to his fears of injury, then the therapist's repetition must link bodily damage specifically to the survivor guilt theme. With a histrionic, such wordy interventions may only diminish clarity.

At times, this more extensive repetition in the compulsive may include the technique of going back to the very beginning of an exchange, retracing the flow carefully, and indicating where the patient introduced extraneous or only vaguely relevant details. Reconstruction may add warded-off details. This technique has been suggested for long-term psychotherapy (Salzman 1968, Weiss 1971), during which defensive operations are interpreted so that the patient increases conscious control and diminishes unconscious restrictions on ideas and feelings. In shorter therapy, aimed at working through a stress, this extensive repetition is still useful, because during the review by the therapist, the patient attends to the uncomfortable aspects of the topic.

Increased time on the topic allows more opportunity for processing and hence moves the patient toward completion. Emotions aroused by the flow of ideas are more tolerable within the therapeutic relationship than for the patient alone. Also, time on the topic and with the therapist allows continued processing in a communicative state, emphasizing reality and problem solving rather than

fantasy and magical belief systems. Identification with and externalization onto the relatively neutral therapist also allows temporary
reduction in rigid and harsh introjects that might otherwise deflect
thought.

Focusing on details is sometimes a partial deterrent to shifting
in the compulsive, just as it may also aid clarity with the histrionic.
The nuances of focusing on details differ because the purposes differ. In general, the aim with the histrionic is to move from concrete, experiential information, such as images, toward more abstract or more extended meanings, such as word labels for activities
and things. The aim with the compulsive is to move from abstract
levels, at which shifts are facile, to a concrete context. Details act as
pegs of meaning in concrete contexts and make shifts of attitude
more difficult. This maneuver uses the compulsive's predisposition
to details but allows the therapist to select them. Again, the nuance
of asking for concrete details is part of the general aim of increasing
conceptualization time.

In states in which the shifts are so rapid as to preclude simple
repetition or questioning, the therapist may use a more complex
form of repetition. The therapist repeats the event, for example,
Harry's intrusive image of the woman's body, and then repeats the
disparate attitudes that the patient oscillates between in a single
package. For example, the therapist might tell Harry that the image of the woman's body led to two themes. One was the idea of
relief at being spared from death that made him feel frightened and
guilty. The other was the idea of bodily harm to himself. Were the
rate of oscillation less rapid, this form of "packaged" intervention
would not be as necessary, as simpler holding operations might be
sufficient and the therapist could focus on a single theme.

These efforts by the therapist encroach on the patient's habitual
style, and the patient may respond by minimizing or exaggerating
the meaning of the intervention. Compulsives are especially vulnerable to threats to their sense of omniscience, especially after traumatic events. If the therapist holds them on a topic, compulsives

will sense their warded-off ideas and feelings and develop uncertainties that cause their self-esteem to fall.

To protect the patient's self-esteem, the therapist uses questioning to accomplish clarification and topic deepening, even when he has an interpretation in mind. The questions aim the patient toward answers that contain the important warded-off but now-emerging ideas. Compulsive patients can then credit themselves with expressing these ideas and experiencing these feelings. With histrionic persons, the therapist might, in contrast, interpret at such a moment, using a firm, short delivery, as a question might be followed by vagueness.

To compulsives, incisive interpretations often mean that the therapist knows something that they do not know. A transference bind over dominance and submission arises as the patients rebel against the interpretation with stubborn denial, accept it meekly without thinking about it, or oscillate between both extremes.

Timing is also important. After experience with a given patient, the therapist intuitively knows when a shift is about to take place. At just that moment, or a bit before, the therapist asks the question. This interrupts the shift and increases the conceptual time and space on the topic about to be warded off. These technical nuances are shown in Table 10–2.

NUANCES OF RELATIONSHIP

Therapists should create a safe situation for the patients by remaining stable within their own clear boundaries (e.g., objectivity, compassion, understanding, concern for the truth, or whatever are their own personal and professional traits).

Patients learn the therapist's limits within this frame. It gives them faith that the therapist will react neither harshly nor seductively, and this trust will increase patients' breadth of oscillation. They can express more aggressive ideas if they know the therapist

Table 10–2. Some of the "Defects" of Compulsive Style and Their Counteractants in Therapy

FUNCTION	STYLE AS "DEFECT"	THERAPEUTIC COUNTER
Perception	Detailed and Factual	Ask for overall impressions and statements about emotional experiences
Representation	Isolation of ideas from emotions	Link emotional meanings to ideational meanings
Translation of images into words	Misses emotional meaning in a rapid transition to partial word meanings	Focus attention on images and felt reactions to them
Associations	Shifts sets of meanings back and forth	Holding operations Interpretation of defense and of warded-off meanings
Problem solving	Endless rumination without reaching decisions	Interpretation of reasons for warding off clear decisions

will not submit, be injured, compete for dominance, or accuse them of evil. Harry could express more of his bodily worries when he knew the therapist would not himself feel guilty or overresponsible.

If the therapist changes with compulsives' tests or needs, then they will worry that they may be too powerful, too weak, or too "sick" for the therapist to handle. Also, compulsives may use the situation to externalize warded-off ideas or even defensive maneuvers. The therapist shifts, not they. This is not to say that such patients do not, at times, need kindly support after disastrous external events. But their propensity for shifting makes changes in the degree of support more hazardous than does a consistent attitude, whether kindly supportive, neutrally tough, or otherwise.

Suppose the therapist became more kindly as Harry went through a turbulent period of emotional expression of guilt over survival. Harry might experience this as an increase in the therapist's concern or worry about him. Or he might shift from the "little" suffering position that elicited the therapist's reaction, to a "big" position from which he looked down with contempt at the "worried" therapist.

Similarly, if the therapist is not consistently tough-minded, in the ordinary sense of insisting on information and truth telling, but shifts to this stance only in response to the patient's stubborn evasiveness, then the patient can shift from strong stubbornness to weak, vulnerable self-concepts. Within the context of this shift, the patient experiences the therapist as hostile, demeaning, and demanding.

Transference resistance will occur despite the therapist's efforts to maintain a therapeutic relationship. Patients will exaggerate the therapist's stability into an omniscience that they will continually test. When negative transference reactions occur, the therapist will act to resolve those that interfere with the goals of therapy. But some transference reactions will not be negative, even though they act as resistances. Histrionics may demand attention and halt progress to get it. Compulsives may take an oppositional stance not so much out of hostility or stubbornness, although such factors will be present, as out of a need to avoid the dangerous intimacy of agreement and cooperation. Because the therapist is not aiming at analyzing the transference to effect character change, he need not interpret this process. Instead, with a compulsive patient in an oppositional stance, he may word the interventions to take advantage of the situation. That is, interventions can be worded, when necessary, in an oppositional manner. Suppose Harry were talking about picking up the woman and the therapist knew he was predisposed to feeling guilty but was warding it off. With a histrionic Harry, the therapist might say, "You feel bad about picking up the woman." With a compulsive and cooperative Harry, he might say, "Could you be blaming yourself for picking up the woman?" With an oppositional compulsive stance, the therapist might say, "So you don't feel at all bad about picking up the woman." This kind of Harry might disagree and talk of his guilt feelings.

To summarize, holding to a topic or subtopic is a nuance of technique used to help persons disposed to switching types of warding-off maneuvers to complete the processing of stress-related ideas. Clarity, though useful with those who inhibit, is not as directly helpful with the switcher, who may require both clarity and holding to a topic. Distortion of meanings, a third type of control maneuver, is used frequently to avoid conflicting ideas triggered by stress events and requires other nuances of technique, illustrated in the next chapter.

11

SLIDING MEANINGS: REACTION TO STRESS AND PSYCHOTHERAPY WITH NARCISSISTIC PERSONALITIES

Narcissism has been regarded as an important aspect of human character throughout recorded history, and it was summarized in Ecclesiastes: "Vanity of vanities, all is vanity." Freud's (1914a) explorations of the unconscious led him to emphasize the compensatory nature of such vanity, and Adler (1916) centered a psychology on inferiority and narcissistic compensations for deflated self-concepts. There has been a major resurgence of interest in the psychodynamics of the narcissistic character (Kernberg 1970, 1974, 1975, 1976, Kohut 1966, 1968, 1971, 1972, 1977). Pertinent to such interest is the question of how persons of narcissistic character respond to the inevitable stresses of life such as injury or loss. The typical narcissistic response of sliding meanings is contrasted with the classical typologies of the histrionic and compulsive, as are the nuances of therapy that help change this defensive avoidance.

BACKGROUND

Freud (1914a) used the concept of narcissism as a polarity between self-centeredness and relationships with others. Instead, the development of self-interest and self-concepts is now seen in two simultaneously related but partially independent series. In one series the self-representation and self-regard gradually become an independent function. In the other series there is an interdependence of one person with another, that is, self-representation and self-regard gradually develop object representations, object interests, and patterns of self- and object transaction (Kohut 1971). Increased narcissism can be motivated by either a need to compensate for a deflated self-concept, without the associated withdrawal of interest from objects, or by a problem in relationships with others that must be handled by increased self-interest (Kernberg 1970).

In the narcissistic character, damaged self-concept underlies a more superficial self-love, grandiosity, or idealization of others regarded as appendages to the self (self-objects). Dominance of narcissistic traits in either or both parents may predispose a child to difficulties in developing a flexible, accurate, and independent self-representation because the parents may treat the child as if she were a function of themselves rather than a separate entity.

Being an only child or having a real or "special endowment" projected by a parent may build a sense of unusual importance into the child, one that is doomed to a rude awakening when she moves socially beyond the nuclear family. That is, any atmosphere that encourages and gratifies inflated self-representations will also predispose a child to traumas when realistic limitations, inability to perform, or depreciating types of interpersonal treatment are encountered. Such encounters will also occur in the family when the child develops enough will and ability to contest parental superiority and power and to feel betrayed and let down when her own power is insufficient to achieve her own goals.

NARCISSISTIC RESPONSES TO STRESS

When the habitual narcissistic gratifications that come from being adored, given special treatment, and admiring the self are threatened, the results may be depression, hypochondriasis, anxiety, shame, self-destructiveness, or rage directed toward any other person who can be blamed for the troubled situation. The child can learn to avoid these painful emotional states by acquiring a narcissistic mode of information processing. Such learning may be by trial-and-error methods, or it may be internalized by identification with parental modes of dealing with stressful information. The central pillar of this narcissistic style is a polarization of good and bad, with externalization of bad attributes and internalization of good attributes in order to stabilize grandiose self-concepts and avoid entry into states of mind organized according to deflated self-concepts. These operations demand distortion of reality and imply either a willingness to corrupt fidelity to reality, a low capacity to appraise and reappraise reality and fantasy, or a high capacity to disguise the distortions. The disguises are accomplished by shifting meanings and using exaggeration and minimization of bits of reality as a nidus for fantasy elaboration.

The narcissistic personality is especially vulnerable to regression to damaged or defective self-concepts on the occasions of loss of those who have functioned as self-objects. When the individual is faced with such stress events as criticism, withdrawal of praise, or humiliation, the information involved may be denied, disavowed, negated, or shifted in meaning to prevent a reactive state of rage, depression, or shame. If such measures should fail, in addition to externalization of bad attributes and internalization of good qualities, there may be a shift not only in affect but also in global being. This change in state includes changes in demeanor and style. If the stress event—for example, criticism of the person—leads to a mild level of threat, then the behavioral response may be an increased effort to obtain external narcissistic supplies. That is, there may be a search for other persons to erase the criticism, supply praise, or provide, through idealized power, a useful umbrella that can be extended over the self. Much like the histrionic personality, the narcissistic personality will try to woo or win attention from sources that enhance self-esteem.

If the stress event is of greater magnitude or if the restorative efforts outlined above should fail, then narcissistic types of deviation from realistic information processing will be more prominent. The goal of these deflections from knowing reality is to prevent a potentially catastrophic state in which a cohesive sense of self is lost. The hazard is not simply guilt because ideals have not been met. Rather, any loss of a good and coherent self-feeling is associated with intensely experienced emotions such as shame and depression, plus an anguished sense of helplessness and disorientation. To prevent this state, the narcissistic personality slides the meanings of events in order to place the self in a better light (Horowitz 1975b). What is good is labeled as being of the self (internalization). Those qualities that are undesirable are excluded from the self by denial of their existence, disavowal of related attitudes, externalization, and negation of recent self-expressions. Persons who function as accessories to the self may also be idealized by exaggeration of their attributes. Those who counter the self are depreciated; ambiguous attributions of blame and a tendency to self-righteous rage states are a conspicuous aspect of this pattern (Horowitz 1981, Kohut 1968).

Such fluid shifts in meanings permit the narcissistic personality to maintain apparent logical consistency while minimizing evil or weakness and exaggerating innocence or control. As part of these maneuvers, the narcissistic personality may assume attitudes of contemptuous superiority toward others, emotional coldness, or even desperately charming approaches to idealized figures.

Reality testing and reality–fantasy differentiation are not as readily lost in the narcissistic personality as they are in borderline or psychotic personalities. But the distorted meanings force further

distortions as cover-ups. The resulting complications lend a sub-
jectively experienced shakiness or uncertainty to ideational structures. Lapses in these defensive arrangements of ideas may occur
during states of stress. Paranoid states and episodes of panic, shame,
or depersonalization may also occur. Self-destructive acts may be
motivated by wishes to end such pain, to achieve a "rebirth," to
harm the offending self, to feel something, and to achieve secondary gains such as obtaining sympathy or enacting a "wounded hero"
role. These and other attributes of the narcissistic personality are
summarized in Table 11–1.

CONTROLLING THOUGHT AND EMOTION

During Harry's psychotherapy, several conflictual themes activated by the accident became apparent. Prominent among these were
his feelings of fear that he might have been killed, guilt over his own
sexual ideas, guilt for "causing" the death of the hitchhiker, remorse
for feeling relieved upon realizing he was alive and she was dead, and
anger at her and the other driver for causing the accident.

Let us consider one of these various themes, worked through
in different phases of therapy. The presumed context, now, was the
time in psychotherapy when Harry was talking about the intrusive
images of the woman's body and the association between these
images and his ideas about his own vulnerability to death. Con-
ceiving his possible death was highly incongruous with Harry's
wishful attitude of invulnerability. The hazard of the incompatibil-
ity of these ideas is especially great for narcissistic personalities, as
they have to maintain a brittle, but inviolately ideal, self-concept.

Conceptually experienced, the incongruity tends to evoke
fear beyond a level of toleration. For two reasons controls are
instituted to prevent continuation or enlargement of such felt
emotion: to prevent the threatening levels of fear and to avoid
representation of fear because it would also be a narcissistic injury

Table 11–1. Patterns in the Narcissistic Typology

INFORMATION–PROCESSING STYLE

- Slides meanings of information that might damage self-concept. Also uses denial, disavowal, and negation for this purpose.
- Attention to sources of praise and criticism.
- Shifts subject-object focus of meanings, externalizes bad attributes, internalizes good attributes.
- Occasionally dissociates incompatible psychological attitudes into separate clusters.

TRAITS

- Self-centered.
- Overestimates or underestimates self and others.
- Self-enhancement in accomplishments real or fantasied, in garb or demeanor.
- Avoids self-deflating situations.
- Variable demeanors depending on state of self-esteem and context:
  - charm, "wooing-winning" quality, controlling efforts, or charisma.
  - superiority, contemptuousness, coldness, or withdrawal.
  - shame, panic, helplessness; hypochondriasis, depersonalization, or self-destructiveness.
  - envy, rage, paranoia, or demands.

INTERPERSONAL RELATIONS

- Often impoverished interpersonally or oriented to power over others or controlling use of others as accessories (self-objects).
- Absence of "I-thou" feelings.
- Social climbing or using others for positive reflection.
- Avoidance of self-criticism by goading others to unfair criticism.
- Discarding of persons no longer of use.
- Pseudo twinning relationship.

for Harry to admit that he was scared. This "double jeopardy" of the narcissistic personality makes insight treatment difficult, as will be discussed shortly.

The repetition of an image of the woman's dead body was an intrusive symptom Harry developed after the accident. The associated and responsive idea was that because she was dead he too might die. The concept of personal death vulnerability was grossly incongruous with an enduring concept of personal invulnerability, and this discrepancy evoked anxiety.

Defensive maneuvers are motivated by such signal anxiety. Subject designation is inhibited, leading to a more abstract idea: "someone dies," a less frightening concept than that the self may perish. Thus, by means of externalization and disavowal of the death construct, Harry slid the meaning of personal mortality into personal immortality, a version of undoing. Instead of anxiety, the shifts of meaning allowed a sense of triumphant excitement. The very image that evoked anxiety now led by a slight irrationality into a more positive emotional experience.

Meanwhile Harry disavowed any similarity between himself and the hitchhiker. Narcissistic Harry exempted himself from this group membership by thinking, in effect, "She is the kind who dies; I am not." To use an exaggerated version of this prototypical narcissistic defense, Harry classified himself as an exception, perhaps with an extension of the idea that someone had to die. If someone had to die, then someone had been chosen to die, and it was she and not he. This then meant he was saved by this selection, presumably because he was special. This membership in the chosen group is like a sign of immortality, and it is incongruent with the enduring concept of humans as vulnerable to death. This is a positive affect kind of incongruity: things are better than anticipated. Harry felt a kind of triumphant excitement in responding to this set of ideas. Thus a complete reversal of emotions was accomplished by shifting and undoing meanings and externalizing mortal contaminants such as death and vulnerability.

This sliding meaning maneuver is similar to the compulsive's control process that uses one train of thought to block out another. But unlike a prototypical compulsive, a narcissistic Harry experienced emotions, perhaps both fear and triumph. Also, the narcissistic Harry would not as readily go back and forth in endless undoing operations. In pure narcissistic form, he would not have to undo the triumph by feeling scared, even though he remained vulnerable to fear and might repeat the sliding of meanings whenever fear-related ideas reemerged.

TACTFUL RECONSTRUCTION OF EXPERIENCE

In cognitive-emotional processing, a useful counteractant in therapy is reconstruction, and for the nuance of relationship in therapy, tact is important (Goldberg 1978, 1980, Kohut 1971, Ornstein 1978). Narcissistic personalities present a double problem, as mentioned before. There is both the threat of warded-off ideas and experiences and the realization that they have been warding something off. Interpretations of defense and latent content are intolerable for narcissistic personalities unless they are tempered by the proper dosage, timing, nuance of delivery, and context in the therapeutic relationship. Otherwise the patients recognize that they have distorted the information in unrealistic ways and can have three traumas: (1) recognition of the self-threatening information previously avoided by distortions, (2) shame that they needed to be told and were "caught" distorting something, and (3) experiencing a reactive need to relinquish the unrealistic but sustaining gratification of seeing themselves as persons chosen by destiny for immortality.

Tact is also vital because, like histrionics, the narcissistic personalities may be more attentive to the therapist than to topical meanings. The therapist is an important current source of praise or criticism, and the real or fantasied observations of the therapist's degree of interest or lack of interest will affect the patient's general equilibrium.

In the psychotherapy of a narcissistic Harry, during his expression and avoidance of the death themes just discussed, it would be helpful to recover and reconstruct the sequence of his fear of dying, including his memories of conceptual experiences during the accident. This procedure should be done as slowly as necessary to help Harry avoid a threat sufficient to throw him into a state of self-fragmentation.

During the reconstruction the therapist should also be unusually careful to agree with Harry's self-experiences as an instigator and as an object. This is similar to the importance of scrutinizing activity and passivity in histrionic styles. Both therapist and patient would sort out ideas about how involved Harry was in every aspect of action and what happened for external reasons. This sorting out would include discriminations among realities, real probabilities, and fantasies about his personal vulnerability. In the sorting out and reconstruction, some particular externalizations would be reversed, although the general tendency to externalization might not necessarily be interpreted.

For example, suppose a narcissistic Harry expressed rage at the other driver who forced him off the road. This externalizing of blame would be an effort to symbolize to all that the fault lay with the other driver, not with Harry. Underlying this are not only threatening ideas of his realistic faults but also unrealistic potential accusations regarding his full culpability. The reconstruction contains every possible element of "blame": how responsible he was for picking her up, for the cars in near collision, for pulling off the road in the way that he did, for his actions after the crash. Some end point of realistic decision, reached for each topic, would relieve Harry of the unrealistic components of blame. In the narcissistic personality these blame components are not necessarily an unconscious or conscious sense of guilt but, rather, are criticisms that may come from any source and demolish self-esteem. The therapeutic action of review and reconstruction would allow Harry to come to a conscious decision about his degree of culpability and would offer him the experience of not being assaulted with criticism by the therapist (even when the therapist was goaded to make such assaults by the patient's flagrant externalizations).

Reconstructions and reviews include the fear-evoking theme used for illustration. Working through this vulnerability theme would be especially difficult for the narcissistic Harry. Realistic threats to the self-integrity were his Achilles' heel, probably already lacerated by earlier traumas that might be revived and reopened in this context. These recollections, when seen, would also require reconstruction in the light of the present. These reconstructions with narcissistic patients need special extended efforts clarifying self- and object distinctions among motives, beliefs, actions, and sensations.

During this process there will be shifts in topical meaning, and so holding to a given aspect of a topic, as with obsessional patients, may be indicated. The nuance common with narcissistic personalities is to arrive at more stable meanings by encouraging the one meaning that has implications of current importance. For example, the "someone dies" idea has multiple meanings such as "each may die" or the salvation of one through the "sacrificial death" of another. The grandiose idea of the sacrifical absolution is deflated by holding and discussing the more important fear themes around "each may die." If necessary, interpretation of the corruption in reality adherence, as implied by the sacrifice-exemption theme, may be necessary but can be possible only if the therapeutic situation in some way provides adequate support for the patient's self-esteem.

NUANCES OF RELATIONSHIPS

Treatment of narcissistic personalities is often difficult for the therapist because the relationship with the patient is less infused by the real therapeutic alliance than in less narcissistic patients. The narcissistic patient uses rather than relates to the therapist. Despite feeling unimportant as a real person, or distant, or bored, the therapist must understand what is going on and provide a closer relationship with the patient. The therapist may have to be supportive for a period. With the narcissistic patient, support and closeness may not be so much a matter of warmth as of accepting externalizations without interpretations. This will not be done without consequence, however, because later in therapy it may be necessary to interpret and discourage such externalizations.

Narcissistic personalities achieve the sense of safety necessary to experience and express usually warded-off ideas and feelings through three types of quasi-relationships. One form is characterized by personal grandiosity with the expectation of admiration, another by idealizing the therapist with the expectations of being all right because she is related to by an ideal figure. The third is to regard the therapist as a twin who restores the self by simply being there, in the here and now, together (Kohut 1971, 1977).

The grandiose quasi-relationship usually occurs either at the beginning of treatment or during recovery from an initially defeated state of mind precipitated by the stress event. Bragging and self-endorsements come in subtle or gross forms and take away conceptual time from stress-relevant topics. Tact, as emphasized earlier, takes the form of allowing these efforts to restore self-esteem, rather than insisting on staying with core conflicts or interpreting the grandiose effort as compensatory.

This tact and forbearance may be unusually difficult for therapists who are used to relying on the therapeutic alliance or positive transference to tide the patient over periods of hard work on threatening ideas. It is difficult to remember that the relationship with narcissistic patients is not stable and that their need is imperative but not coordinated with the usual concerns, however ambivalent, for the person toward whom they direct their needs.

In idealizing the therapist, the second most common form of quasi-relationship, the damage is repaired as the patient imagines that she is once again protected and given value by a powerful or attractive parent. The stress response syndrome becomes a ticket of admission for this kind of self-supplementation. Again, tactful tolerance is necessary early in the treatment when the person is still partially overwhelmed by the stress response syndrome. It would be an error to see behavior such as giving exaggerated testimonials about the therapist's unique ability as equivalent to the transference-motivated seduction gambits of some histrionic patients or to the undoing of negative feelings by compulsive patients. The testimo-

Table 11–2. Some "Defects" of Narcissistic Style and Their
Counteractants in Therapy

FUNCTION	STYLE AS "DEFECT"	THERAPEUTIC COUNTERACTION
Perception	Focuses on praise and blame	Avoids being provoked into either praising or blaming but is realistically supportive
	Denies "wounding" information	Uses tactful timing and wording to counteract denials by selective confrontation
Representation	Dislocates bad traits from self to other	Repeatedly reviews in order to clarify who is who in terms of the sequence of acts and intentions in a recalled interpersonal transaction
Translation of images into words	Slides meanings	Consistently defines meanings; encourages decisions as to most relevant meanings and how much to weight them
Associations	Overbalances when finding routes to self-enhancement	Holds to other meanings: cautiously deflates grandiose beliefs
Problem solving	Distorts reality to maintain self-esteem	Points out distortion while (tactfully) encouraging and supporting reality fidelity
	Obtains illusory gratifications	Supports patient's self-esteem during period of surrender of illusory gratification (helped by the real interest of the therapist, by identification with the therapist, and by identification with the therapist as a noncorrupt person). Finds out about and gradually discourages unrealistic gratifications from therapy
	Forgives self too easily	Helps develop appropriate sense of responsibility

nials simply indicate idealization that provides a momentary repair of damage to the self, a safer time during which there may be some work on processing and integrating stress events.

Even externalizations can help patients gain sufficient emotional distance from loaded topics so that they can tolerate thinking about them. For example, if a patient projects a feeling of disgust about death onto the therapist, the relevant nuance would be to ask the patient to talk further about how the therapist feels. This allows the patient to work along the ideational route as if it were the therapist's route. A direct interpretation, such as "you are disgusted by death," should come only later.

Narcissistic considerations are present in every character type, not just narcissistic personality, and some of these nuances of treatment might be pertinent at any time. The "defects" commonly found in the typical narcissistic personality and comparable therapeutic counters are summarized in Table 11–2.

IV

CLINICAL
EXAMPLES

12

LOSS OF A LIMB
With Robert Nadol

A single external event can trigger divergent reactions. These separable yet interconnected responses may occur in different phases at any given moment in time. One set of ideas and feelings may be warded off, resulting in a period of relative denial; another set may be intrusive in terms of conscious experience. Xalia's story is presented here to illustrate such phasic differences and to show how these differences can orient a therapist in his intervention strategy.

Xalia is a 19–year–old woman. Her left leg and knee joint were mangled in a car accident. The injury was severe, but the doctors at her local hospital attempted immediate restorative surgery. Gangrene set in after the emergency operation; consultation with specialists led to a hospital transfer and an amputation. She was then discharged to recuperate at home.

Six weeks later, Xalia reentered the hospital so that the stump could be fitted with an artificial leg. She received intensive physical therapy, to strengthen the stump and learn how to use a prosthesis. During this hospitalization, she asked for a psychiatric consultation.

Initially, the surgical staff resisted her request because she seemed to be doing well. But they decided to comply with it when she persisted. Xalia was seen by a resident psychiatrist. She told him she had requested the consultation because she had become aware of a lack of appropriate emotional response to the loss of her leg. In the physical therapy exercise room and on the ward she met other persons with amputations. She recognized their losses often as less severe than her own. They grieved for the loss of part of their body, whereas she remained cheerful. She felt that she had not faced her situation and was going on as if nothing had happened.

The psychiatric consultant agreed that she was avoiding the implications of the amputation and explored some of the circumstances of the accident. He recognized the defensive operations of thought stopping and inhibition of communication but did not know what thoughts and feelings she might be warding off. Moreover, he felt uncertain about disrupting her denial at this time. She was in the midst of active physical treatment and cooperating well with it. True, for a young, attractive, unmarried, and unattached woman to lose a leg would necessitate psychological work in reorganizing her body image, self-concept, and future plans. But should this work be done now or after she learned to use her prosthesis successfully? When is denial useful, and when does it impede adaptation? After talking with her and with the staff, the resident psychiatrist referred the patient to a stress unit therapist for further exploration and formulation.

This therapist then interviewed Xalia on the orthopedic ward. She was pleasant but urgent in her self-presentation. She communicated a feeling of pressure that could be verbally described as, "You really must help me right now."

Following is a transcript of that interview and the one that followed, interspersed with commentaries on meanings and implications of what is being communicated. The psychiatrist has already introduced himself and obtained consent to tape the interviews.

FIRST SESSION

T *(Therapist)*: Why don't we start with you telling me why you asked for a psychiatric consultation?

X *(Xalia)*: What I asked for a psychiatrist for?

T: Yes.

X: Because, um, I think that I need somebody to help me.

T: Uh-huh.

X: Um, because uh *(pause)* well, since the accident and my stepbrother was driving, I start hating him later *(pause)*, and I don't want to hate him.

Note that almost at once, Xalia presents a new topic that was not mentioned to the consultant. This hatred of her stepbrother is a complex of ideas and feelings that intrude upon her: "I start hating him later, and I don't want to hate him." She had told the first consultant about a complex of ideas in a denial phase, that is, her intellectual observation of the absence of appropriate reactions to missing a limb. This psychiatrist had, of course, not heard about the hatred theme from the first consultant. He listens attentively to her further development of this theme.

T: Yes.

X: I don't want him to think that, um, it was his fault, but *(pause)* or, um, something 'cause, um, well, I don't want him to. And, ah, sometimes, well, I feel like yelling it to him and telling him it was his fault and, uh, that he can get out of that game *(pause)*, so, um, so I just don't want to tell him never.

T: Yes.

X: Not even to my family 'cause I'm the only one who knows.

T: That's something we might be able to talk about. Anything else?

X: Mm mm.

T: Well, tell me what happened. I know you've had an accident, but I don't know anything else.

X: Well, um, we went to a dance (*pause*); I was, um, two of my stepsisters and me, we went with my stepmother and father. It was a dance for Andy, my stepbrother. So, after the dance, my parents were going to go somewhere else, so they told us to go with Andy in the car, and, um (*pause*) oh, yeah, and then when we were, we were going just to (*pause*) go in a street, it was a blind intersection. It was like this.

T: Yes.

X: And, uh, and, uh, he, he was, um, my, I think he was drunk, and um, I was, I was talking with my stepsisters in the back, I was in the front seat, and, um, and then I saw that, that he didn't put no brakes on and we were going to, getting to the corner. So, um, I saw him, I was thinking that was really strange. We were almost at the corner. He didn't put the brakes on, and we were going to crash. He didn't; he was just smiling; that's all I remember, and then I, I woke up in the hospital (*long pause*). Well, they were trying to save my leg for two weeks. And Dr. Smith told me that he was going to amputate it, and, uh (*long pause*) well, my parents didn't tell me nothing, you know, about Andy. After, only when I was over here, about a month and a half later since the accident, she told me that (*pause*) he was very, very, um, very bad, that he was (*pause*) um, crying all day in his room (*pause*), that he wasn't eating or nothing, that he thought it was his fault. And she told me it wasn't his fault, it was the brakes' fault (*pause*). But I knew it wasn't the brakes. I mean, I told, I told the police, I told the (*pause*) the, um, insurance man, everybody, that it was, uh, it was the brakes. 'Cause I didn't realize before; I still don't realize that I, I don't have my leg. And um, more, I guess I feel funny about it.

T: Yes.

X: See, I don't realize, I don't care. Right now I don't care about it, 'cause I don't realize that I need it.

T: Yes.

X: But when I was at home last month for a couple of weeks, and, uh, Andy was going out (*pause*), he was going to take the car, and, uh, and then I was thinking that, uh, how could, how could my parents let him drive again. How? And how was he going out and I was staying, it was his fault. And I felt like yelling and telling him it was his fault, but I don't want him to blame himself.

T: Yes. But you're one of the only people that realizes how much he was at fault.

X: Yeah. I'm the only one who knows that it was his fault.

T: Yes.

X: See, 'cause I told the other people that it was the brakes' fault too.

T: Yes.

X: 'Cause I didn't want him, you know, if I'm, if I'm like this right now, I don't want another person to get (*pause*) hurt, or losing his feelings.

T: So, then, there are two things that you recognize might be helpful to talk out. One would be that you don't quite realize all the implications of what's happened.

X: Mm.

T: And then, you have this load about your stepbrother. You want him to be punished, but you don't want him to be punished. When did all this happen?

X: September 12th.

T: Uh-huh. And how long were you in the hospital the first time?

X: I was in the hospital there three weeks. Then I came (*pause*) for about, for about a month, then I was home for a month, then I came here.

T: And you've been here for 15 days now. Does Dr. Smith see you here?

X: Yeah. He's my doctor.

T: I'll give him a telephone call and see if it's all right with him that I talk with you. Would that be all right with you?

X: Oh, he's on vacation.

T: Well, I'll do it when he comes back, and we'll just talk anyway.

X: Yeah.

T: Now, what's your mood been like all that time?

X: My, um, what do you mean?

T: Oh, what has it been like for you day in and day out when you go home? Have you been cheerful or sad or numb or waiting, or . . . ?

X: No. That's strange. I live with my father and stepmother.

T: Uh-huh.

X: I lived in Canada, but I came two years ago here to study. And, uh, I don't know, I feel like, a little like, right now, I don't want to go home.

T: Yes.

X: My real mom was here since the accident. But right now, I don't want to go home. I would prefer to stay over here and, now, not to go away. I don't know why, and, well, sometimes I start to get angry at my father and my step-mother, even my stepsisters, and I feel guilty for it.

T: Just since the accident?

X: Mm-hm.

T: You get angry at them and irritated?

X: Yeah, it's funny because they think that, that Andy's very innocent and he's a very good boy and like he is some-times, but (*pause*), I don't know.

T: Yes. You know something they don't know.

X: Mm-hm.

T: Okay. Well, you get around pretty well in a wheelchair and on crutches too?

X: Yeah.

T: I can't stay too long now. I just came up to see you. But could you come next door to my office? Would you mind coming over there? I think we'd have a quieter room. We could just set up a time, and then we can just have a little longer to sit and talk this over.

X: Yeah.

SECOND SESSION

T: I'd like to know more about what you've been thinking about.

X: (*Pause*) Well (*pause*), I already told you, well, (*pause*) mm (*pause*), I think that I love my father and stepmother, but at the same time I don't. I don't know.

T: Uh-huh. You get angry with them.

The therapist has already noted that instead of saying she is hostile and instead of describing family members as bad, she will inhibit her communications and presumably her thoughts by trailing off and saying "I don't know." She has, of course, made critical remarks about her stepbrother, but she regards such revelations as lapses in control. Knowing that she has such feelings is experienced as a threat to her sense of well-being. The therapist wants her to discuss her conflicted feelings so that they can examine them together in the therapeutic situation. He knows hostile ideas are at the surface because they intrude into her awareness. He refrains from questioning her about her warded-off ideas and feelings. If he were to say here, "I wonder if you are possibly angry at your father and stepmother?" it would be her style to answer either "I don't know" or "Yeah, I guess so" in a passive manner. Instead, the therapist labels her thoughts in a brief, firm, and direct way. He does this in order to clarify the thoughts and to establish a ground rule that in this situation there is to be open communication of those ideas and emotions that are usually suppressed in social situations.

X: A lot, yeah. (*pause*)
T: And yesterday we talked about your stepbrother and you.
X: Yeah.
T: How old is he?
X: Eighteen.
T: So he's a little younger than you are.
X: Mm-hm.
T: And what's he like?
X: (*Pause*) He's a very tall, strong, very nice guy. Kinda crazy, mm.
T: Kind of crazy? How?
X: Well, you know, always drinking and, uh, with me, I mean, he was my favorite.
T: Uh-huh.
X: And I was his favorite too.
T: Uh huh.
X: So, we were always going together; well you know, when I first came from Canada, then, uh, well, he was, uh, the first one, that, um, if one of my stepsisters came and started fighting with me or something, he came and told them to leave me alone, that, you know. And then, uh, he taught me how to drive, he taught me how to get around.
T: Mm.
X: The city and all that, uh, well he was—(trails off).
T: He was very close to you.
X: Yeah (*pause*). Sometimes.
T: Right. So maybe right now we could talk about the busi-

ness with your stepbrother not pressing the brakes and then telling the police and everyone else that he did press the brakes. Maybe we can just see where we can get with that right now. That seemed to be a problem that you had coming back into your mind.

The therapist seeks to explore the more intrusive theme. He watches her facial expression as he talks. He slowly adds each new phrase until he sees that she is ready to take up the topic.

X: Yeah, I just remember that, um, that I, um, I thought that it was kind of strange when we were going to turn around the corner, he didn't put the brakes on (*pause*). And then, I suddenly saw he was smiling, and, uh, well, at the dance, I don't (*pause*), or I was sitting with some friends, so I saw that he was drinking. But, well, he always, he always drinks, but he never got, gets drunk; you know what I mean?

T: Yes.

X: So, then we get—got out, then some friends were outside, and, and they told him to, you know, how 'bout a race? He goes, "Oh, okay."

T: Mm–hm.

X: So, we left from the dance, and the car was working pretty good. So then, we left them, and we were going to go home and (*pause*), well, he didn't put the brakes on.

T: Uh–huh.

X: And he was going very fast.

T: Was there a race going on, a play race?

X: No, yeah, well it's kinda, it's kinda a park and, uh, it's named Boyle Park.

T: Uh–huh.

X: And, um (*pause*), they have a big place where they have bands some and they have a space to drive there (*laughs*) and, uh (*pause*), well, when we were coming back home, um, he was going kind of fast. Well, he, he admitted, he told everybody he was going very fast (*pause*). He was going over 80 miles, close to 85. So, I didn't get scared or nothing; nobody did and, 'cause he always goes that fast (*pause*). But then my stepmother told me, um, later that, and, uh, asked them when the car was there and then a lot of, you know, uh, the police and fireman, doctors came to take me out of the car and then, that he went out running into the car kind of crazy and that he was crying and all that, that it was his fault. So, partly because of that, I didn't tell them nothing 'cause I felt, I don't know, that, like, um, I was going to blame myself forever if I, I tell them the truth or something.

T: Yes.

X: So, uh, I didn't say nothing, and, uh, oh, when I went home, he was very nice with me. He didn't tell me nothing, though. One time when I was here in the hospital, I called home and he answered the phone, so he knew it was me and he started crying, telling me that it was his fault, to forgive him, and all that. And, uh, I told him it wasn't his fault and (*pause*), you know, to realize that it was an accident. But I, I wasn't thinking that.

T: Yes.

X: I would think that it was his fault, but I shouldn't tell him. And then when I'm home, I feel like yelling at him, telling him, you know? And I'm always in a bad humor sometimes, and I, I never was like that.

T: But you haven't told him?

X: Mm-mm.

T: Now there's something there, because, you see, while everyone else may not know, he knows. He knows what happened. And you've been very close with him.

X: Yeah.

T: So, you must be the kind of people who talk to each other. And you know something, and he knows something, but you don't tell him.

X: Yeah, but he knows this, but I think that right now he thinks that it wasn't his fault.

T: Ah!

X: Because, you know, everybody was telling him that it was the brakes. But it wasn't.

T: Yes.

X: The brakes were okay, and he didn't even put the brakes on.

T: Yes.

X: So, it wasn't the brakes. Now he probably doesn't remember because, oh, yeah, he said that, uh, well, yeah, it sounded like he was drinking, so he's probably been remembering.

T: Yes.

X: And, uh (*pause*), well, everybody's saying, you know, nobody mentions it anymore.

T: Well, do you have the feeling that maybe they're trying to protect him?

X: Yeah.

T: And you want to protect him too. . . .

X: Mm-hm.

T: But, there are different levels of protecting. He's actually feeling very bad.

X: It doesn't sound like it (*angry outburst*).

T: It doesn't? He's not feeling very badly now?

X: Mm-mm.

T: You told me that he was crying?

X: That was at first.

T: That was at first, so he's forgetting about it now?

X: He forgot all, all of it.

T: Uh-huh.

X: That was about two weeks, three, a month. About a month. But now, well, he doesn't remember or nothing. That time, that time when we, we go out, I told them, well, everybody was kind of afraid that if they told him to take me out that I was going to say no, or tell him I wasn't going to go with him because I was afraid and all that. So my parents and, um, everybody, every time that I had to go out, they took me, and they didn't tell him. Even though I told them I was—that I want to go with him.

T: Driving in the car?

X: Yeah.

T: So you don't get to have as much time with him.

X: Yeah. And then one time when we were alone, then I told him, "Why don't we go over there, you know?" And he goes, "Okay, you want to; you want to, okay." So we left. He was very happy, I mean probably because he knew that I was trusting him again.

T: Yes.

X: And then, he started asking me when I was going back to Canada, what I was planning to do, and, uh, how I felt. But he didn't say nothing about the accident or anything; he didn't mention it.

T: Yes. Well, the accident is kind of like a taboo subject right now, isn't it?

X: Yeah.

T: No one's supposed to mention it.

X: Nobody (*laughs*).

T: But I guess what I'm wondering is if your father and step-mother don't want you to talk about it, if they want it to be all over and done with.

X: Mm-hm.

T: But I wonder if that's the way your stepbrother feels. I'm just wondering about the idea of you and him having a very private kind of conversation about this.

In what may be too rapid an approach, the therapist is trying to suggest a move toward completion by interpersonal working through. He believes she is torn between her anger at the stepbrother and guilt if she expresses her resentment.

He has not picked up the clues, at this point, that she is also feeling that the local family wants to get rid of her, as in "he started asking me when I was going back. . . ."

One problem will be that she is conscious only of resentment based on her limitation of activity, being forced to tell a lie, and being no longer rewarded for going along with the story. She is not yet in touch with her rage at her stepbrother as the cause of her loss of a limb. The loss complex is still being warded off by inhibitory processes.

X: (*Long pause, voice very soft*) Be very painful. I mean he was— (*pause*).

T: I'm not sure you should either, but I'm just entertaining the idea. We'll just think about it; you don't have to do it or anything. What do you think would happen if you were to, in some very private way, have an opportunity to just talk it over with each other?

X: He'll probably tell my stepmother that I was thinking it was his fault. And then that was going to be a big problem because they were going to, um, going to tell me that it wasn't his fault, then I was going to get mad. I was going to tell him the truth (*voice intense*), and then, my mom was going to come and tell them, and then there was going to be a big ton of trouble.

T: Yes. You've already thought about what would happen.

X: Yeah (*pause*). So I don't want it to; I don't want it to happen (*laughs*).

T: But let's just see what that would be like if it were like a script, you know, written out for a television program. You would have this talk with your stepbrother. He'd get mad, I guess, and he'd go tell his mother that you were blaming him for the accident, and then they'd make life miserable for you?

X: Mm–hm.

T: And then what would happen? Would you have to go home to Canada? They'd kick you out? Or they'd be mean to you?

The earlier clues have now registered in the therapist's mind.

X: (*Laughs*). No, well, they're not mean with me. We only don't, um, you know have a good relationship; well, we do, but (*trails off*).

T: You do and you don't.

X: Yeah, we do and we don't. Well, I was always, I was always thinking that they prefer, well, it does (*pause*) that's, um, logical, that she prefers her sons and daughters, well, yeah. I was the stepdaughter only. And, uh, well (*pause*), they didn't let me do nothing, not even to go someplace, because they said that they were responsible for me and that if something happened to me, they were, it was going to be their fault, their responsibility. That's, that's right; they don't like it.

T: Yes.

X: So, mm (*pause*), you know, they wouldn't tell me to go back to Canada, but I would (*laughs*). I would feel—

T: You would feel you had to go back?

X: Yeah, 'cause I, if I, I won't feel good staying there.

T: Well, what would going back feel like? What would you go back to?

X: My real mother.

T: Yes, well, I don't know what that's like.

A sign of this patient's immaturity and dependency is seen in her talking to the therapist as if he knew her history. The telling of her story to many persons in a university hospital contributes to this effect, but she reveals in many other ways a psychological developmental level of less than her chronological age. Her deportment, posture, and mannerisms are those of an early adolescent. The therapist believes that this is not merely a regression due to stress and hospitalization but, rather, a continuation of a pre-event character structure. Other thoughts strike him: that she probably has an incompletely developed feminine self-concept and body image, is sexually conflicted, may use the injury as an excuse to avoid sexuality, and may have unusual problems in working through the sexual and other implications of the body loss. The stress, were this substantiated by later material, would be a complex of the new event, earlier conflicts, and impeded psychosexual development.

The patient gives her background history at this point, which indicates that she feels like a second-rate child with both her real mother, who remarried and had more children, and with her stepmother and real father. She left Canada when she had difficulty in high school and felt excluded from her family there. She hoped to make a better home with her father and to form an attachment with her stepmother and stepsiblings.

The accident disrupts the refuge she found, and she is frightened that they will exclude her because she "knows too much." She must stifle her rage to avoid this threat. She reveals this story but is not actively aware of the psychological meanings, a relatively histrionic style of "not knowing." Nonetheless, this material is at the surface and is clarified by the telling process.

The therapist then summarizes, as the transcript continues:

T: There are kind of two things that are problems for you now, that you wanted to talk over. One is the business with your stepbrother, you know, your anger where you can't win, no matter what you do.

X: Mm-hm.

T: And the other was your feeling that you don't quite real- ize what it means that you were in the accident and that you lost your leg. And that's probably going to be a pretty gradual thing as you get used to using your new leg. It may feel artificial and funny at first before you get used to it. Do you want to talk at all about that today?

X: Well, you know, lots of people, they lost their leg too, and they were very sad and, uh (*pause*), even, because I saw a man down in physical therapy who lost his finger. He was crying (*pause*).

T: Yes.

X: And he was very sad, and I lost my leg and I didn't realize it. I was very happy. Well, I always have been happy; I never get mad or anything and, um, well, I was thinking that probably I'm not normal (*slight laugh*).

T: Uh-huh.

X: Simply 'cause I don't realize it.

T: Well, you know, I've seen people who've lost differ- ent parts of their body, and everyone doesn't get sad about it. It's not necessarily abnormal or crazy or anything like that. Some people just take it and go on with their life.

The therapist has made a quick decision to support her denial of the limb loss complex for the time being and focus on the family support system, establish a therapeutic alliance, and then see what happens.

X: Yeah, but I mean, not even crying? Not even that?

The therapist realizes that by her response he may have erred: supporting the denial sets up a therapeutic misalliance that will perhaps disrupt the therapeutic possibilities. He thus tries to reverse himself.

T: Well, let's find out more about it, though. Do you find yourself having any dreams about yourself?
X: Yeah (*as if disappointed*).

The therapist persists in his error by asking too peripheral a question. Dreams are important to the self-concepts contained, but the timing of this question is poor and based more on the therapist's discomfort than on the need for this information at this point. It would have been better to have ended the remark with, "Well, let's find out more about it."

T: What are you like in your dreams?
X: (*Long pause*) Like I was before.
T: Uh-huh.
X: Dancing again, and then, uh, I see myself in a place and all my friends over there.
T: Uh-huh.
X: And then, they don't go over there to ask me for a dance 'cause they know that I have an artificial leg or something like that.

The therapist obtains useful information. Despite his procedural error, the patient goes ahead.

T: Yes.
X: And then, I see my stepbrother dancing (*pause*), and I don't know, I feel something against him. It's not, it's not only 'cause I don't have my leg. It's because I don't like the way it looks either.
T: Yes.

X: To say to me they had to do two, some operations and I didn't li———. I don't like the way it does.

This is a typical avoidance of words to clarify her repugnance at how her leg looks. The therapist decides to ask for details to see how deep seated this defense is.

T: Would you describe it to me? Of course, I haven't seen your leg.

X: Well, it's kind of, um, well, they took skin from here to go over here.

T: Yes.

X: So, it's kind of, uh, looks black and all that.

T: Mm.

X: And, uh, well, I thought I was going to be, you know, there was, they were just going to amputate my leg and that's all.

T: Yes.

X: It wasn't going to look like that, but it does. And every time that I, I w———, I just saw it last month. The doctors wanted me to see it, but I didn't want to, and I said well, if they're going to do another operation, plastic surgery, it's not gonna look the same; it's not necessary for me to see it right now. So, I wait. And I thought I was going to look better.

T: So you didn't look at it then?

X: Only one time, and I, I didn't want to, but I did. And I didn't, I didn't like it.

T: Yes.

X: That's the only time that I cried for it and then, uh—

T: You did cry, though?

X: Yeah (*pause*). Only because it looked like that (*voice tone insistent*).

T: Yes, but that's part of the sadness. It's partly there. These things come in doses. But tell me more about it.

The therapist means the sadness is partly there and will occur in doses, but as often happens, his own primary process echoes the patient. "It's partly there" is what is wrong with the leg. These slips are not uncommon when treating persons with stress response syndromes. The therapist unconsciously sides with the patient's avoidances, feeling that the loss is so real that reminders will hurt the patient. He also, at a primary process level, explores his own reactions to the universal threat of body injury. The conflict in the therapist to express and to avoid expressing the loss leads to parapraxes.

> *X:* I will cry, too, because, uh, well, I am (*pause*), all the time, you know, when I saw people in the streets on crutches and things, I felt (*voice very soft*) ashamed.
> *T:* Yes (*empathically*).
> *X:* You know that? And, uh (*pause*), when I was, when I was over, I didn't want to go to the store or something like they were going to bring me, just that I don't want to, people to feel ashamed of me; something.
> *T:* Yes.
> *X:* That's why I didn't go to graduation, either.
> *T:* Oh, you didn't?
> *X:* Mm-mm. Well, I wasn't, I didn't have to.
> *T:* Yes, but you didn't want to go because you thought—
> *X:* No (*Interrupts*).

The patient gets the incipient thought and wants to prevent the clear statement, but the therapist persists.

> *T:* —people would look at you and—
> *X:* Well.
> *T:* —think you didn't look nice?
> *X:* Y-y-y-eah, but (*pause*) I didn't like myself, you know, people staring at me 'cause I only had one (*pause*) leg.

Possibly identifying with the therapist, the patient does add the descriptive word *leg*, after a pause. Previously she had used the label *it*.

T: Yes.

X: So, um (*pause*), well, I didn't want to go.

T: Yes (*pause*). So this is something that's still tender emotionally for you (*pause*). And you don't like to look at it, don't like how it looks.

X: I do now.

T: A little better now?

X: (*Laughs*). Yeah, I guess.

The interview ended with their agreeing on a brief therapy to extend beyond the point of discharge from the hospital. During the therapy, the discussions were similar to the above material in that more time was spent on working through Xalia's rage and only a little time was devoted to the sadness and shame over her loss of the limb. In other words, Xalia's accident and amputation set in motion at least two main cycles of thought and feeling, both incomplete when the treatment began. One was more intrusive, and the other was still in a phase of denial and numbing.

All such statements are relative. For example, Xalia did have thoughts about looking different after the amputation or finding the stump ugly. But many more reactions lie ahead before she can adapt to an altered body. In comparison, the impulses to castigate her stepbrother are urgent and conscious, as is the opposing desire to maintain family harmony at the price of silence and thereby avoid both guilt over harming her stepbrother and fear that she would be sent back to her real mother and stepfather in Canada. The discussion and working through of this conflict thus meant recognizing the implications of losing a leg.

One explanation for the inhibition of personal loss and the emergence of interpersonal anger is the association of personal loss with a more profound threat. There was a brief emergence of this theme during the therapy when Xalia told of intrusive ideas that came very briefly into her awareness, of wanting to be dead, and of persons on TV who killed themselves. The implication was that if she were to realize fully her personal losses (of her leg and her family closeness), she was afraid she might commit suicide. The profoundness of this threat is one reason that techniques that would thwart or skirt her defensive denial would not be advised. The time to master these issues will come later, when her rehabilitation is more advanced, her social support system is stabilized, and she has a well-established relationship with a therapist.

The rage at her stepbrother, a theme dealt with immediately in therapy, was not instigated solely by the accident. Though very close to him, Xalia also resented his being the complete child of her stepmother and the prize male in a family that prized sons. In addition, ambivalence and competition among the siblings was a major theme in the extended family, going back three generations. Work in this area meant recognizing the major themes of conflict present before the stress event.

SUMMARY

The case of Xalia illustrates both intrusive thoughts and denial. Two complexes activated by the accident were described, and at a given moment in time one was more emergent and one was more successfully inhibited. The inhibited complex, revolving around sadness and shame over bodily loss, was not purely denied but was partly recognized and contributed some intrusive thoughts. Nonetheless, therapy focused mainly on the more emergent themes, which involved preexistent conflicts, and followed the patient's leads.

13

VISUAL SHOCK AND THE COMPULSION TO LOOK

With Erik Gann

A young man walks down a Chicago street. A woman jumps to her death from a window high above him. Her body smashes into the pavement just behind him. He turns to find her mangled corpse in full view, her brains spattered on the cement and on him. Stunned, he has a compelling impulse to stare at the woman's remains. Simultaneously, as he continues looking at the body, he feels an equally disturbing sense of transgression.

Experience of this event did not result in a stress response syndrome of sufficient intensity to motivate this man to seek consultation. Instead, other events led to an interview two years later and provided an opportunity to see what happens to such a memory, independent of treatment issues. The result is an illustration of (1) the enduring intrusion of images from traumatic perceptions; (2) the interaction of the repetition tendency with aims to inhibit such intrusions and pangs of emotion; and (3) the compulsion to look at stressful scenes, even though it conflicts with social taboos against doing so.

Daniel, the young man, had been interviewed by a physician as part of the admission procedures for a medical school in Chicago. During the interview, he described the incident as it had occurred two years earlier in Chicago. A young Latin-American secretary working for the same firm as he did threw herself from a window in the building, landing very close to him as he passed on foot below her. The memory of this event was still vivid in his mind. He often found himself talking about it or thinking about it. He had not sought psychiatric help, however, for the recurrent disturbing memories or for any other problems. The physician was impressed with the intensity and peremptory emergence of this memory during the entrance interview. She suggested, and he agreed to, an interview with a psychiatrist who had a research interest in this type of situation.

During the interview, it became apparent that this event had had several ramifications for Daniel. First, he had been immediately thrust into the midst of several universal responses and conflicts. He had found it imperative to look, to discover what was going on, and to attempt to comprehend the meaning of what were highly unusual and disturbing visual perceptions. There seems to be a quasi-instinctual need to look at such things; for example, the uncanny fascination of observing accident victims, looking at executions, watching horror films. In addition, he became aware of his concern about the woman who was essentially unknown to him. This appears to have been connected to a common response of identifying with the victim. Finally, another conflict was aroused: the survivor's guilt. These universal conflicts became enmeshed with his own personal conflicts.

After an initial agreement concerning the exploratory and investigative nature of the interview, Daniel was asked to tell the incident in any way he wished. He responded as follows:

> I've talked about this a lot (*pause*). I was very upset when it happened (*pause*). A woman jumped out of a ten-story building; she landed next to me. I don't really remember. I didn't see her. She landed

about ten feet away from me. I don't remember any sounds except the blood rushing in my ears, which I guess didn't happen 'til I turned around and saw what happened. She was lying on the ground with her head facing me. There was a large hole in the top of her head (*pause*). My first reaction was that she had fallen down, that she had tripped on the sidewalk or had a heart attack. My first reaction was, what could I do to help her? You know, what's the smartest thing to do—cover her up with a blanket, give her artificial respiration? That was my immediate thought, even though I saw that there was nothing in her head . . . just a big, empty hole (*pause*). I stood and stared for quite a long time. I remember one of my thoughts was that I shouldn't be looking at that, but for some morbid reason, I wanted to look at it and kept staring at it. Then I noticed her brains were all over the sidewalk. Some was on me too, and that upset me. Initially, people just walked by . . . (*pause*) that really upset me too. Nobody stopped, and I started crying. I walked closer and looked more (*long pause*). I noticed her right leg was split open. She was wearing big black boots about up to here, and her right leg was split open through the boot, and the next thing I remember was that people started to gather around. I walked off quite a good distance and then stared again, again for a while; I don't know how long. It seemed that what happened was that everything stopped, and I couldn't hear anything except the blood in my ears. I wasn't aware of anything going on except this one scene with nothing moving, and then I turned around and stared again, and the same thing happened, and then I left. I got on the bus and kind of looked at people; I'd been in Chicago about eight months then. It was starting to bother me because people were so unfriendly there. And I looked at them (on the bus) like, well, at least now, be friendly; at least now, open up, but I didn't say anything to anybody.

He then added that all this did not hit him at that time, and at first, talking about it did not affect him very much; he just forgot about it. However, not long after the incident, talking about it made him nervous, and in fact, the phone conversation to set the appointment had also left him feeling nervous.

One aspect of the scene that still bothered him was an image of a passerby stepping on a piece of her brains. He stated, "That still bothers me. I don't think I've accepted that. It upsets me when it comes into my head; I immediately shove that out of my mind. I say, 'How could that have happened' and then say, 'Okay, that happened; forget about it.'"

At this point, still early in the interview, Daniel spontaneously reported a dream he had had approximately two weeks before (between the medical school interview and this one). He was reminded of it in this context only because his girlfriend, an aspiring psychologist, told him that it was related to the suicide incident.

> I saw a man get killed in a car accident in the dream. Something that I flash on when I see, picture what happened, was that hole in her head (the woman in the stress event). That was empty, and in this accident, the man had his legs cut off, but I could see all the way up into his body cavity and it was all scooped out. I could see all his bones and everything; it was as if the legs were part of the actual body cavity.

At this point, he paused and remained silent for a minute or two. The psychiatrist asked if that was the whole dream and he replied, "Yeah; there's more detail, but I don't know if you want to hear the whole thing." When interest was indicated, he proceeded.

> I was walking over an overpass; there had been an accident. There were police around and I saw the man lying there, and he looked kind of plastic, like he had black, plastic hair, very smooth olive skin but looked like he was android or plastic. He had a shaft in his chest; it looked like a metal shaft had gone into his chest and had broken off about there, (gesturing). And blood, kind of, on his chest. And when I walked by, I noticed that his legs were cut open; of course, I just saw a cross section of his legs, the muscles and the bone, and then it turned into the part where it was all hollow. And I could see his spinal—his backbone and his rib cage, but it was covered with—you ever see the inside of a fish? It's kind of silvery,

a silvery coating? Well, it (the man's backbone) was all covered with that kind of silvery coating. And then the man started squirming and blood started gushing out of his mouth and would kind of cover his face and run off very smoothly, and I could kind of put myself in his position, and I knew he was in a great deal of pain, and I knew he was saying to himself, "I just wish this would be over." And I knew he knew it would be over very soon.

He continued immediately by reporting that his girlfriend had said that the dream was probably related to his having observed a similar occurrence. When asked for his thoughts about this comment, he replied, "It (his girlfriend's statement) didn't click with me; I don't think it (the dream) had anything to do with it (the stress event), but it might. I've never had a dream like that before, where I've seen somebody actually in the process of dying. And when I saw the woman jump out of the window, it was about two years ago—so I think that was a pretty long time ago. The dream doesn't bother me, though when I had it, I just said, 'Okay, you've had this dream."

The remainder of the interview focused on the immediate and long-range impact of the event. Daniel reported that the time spent in Chicago came during a period in his life when he was somewhat depressed and lonely, and he was struck by the city and its inhabitants as being indifferent, cold, and uncaring. The woman's suicide was "the last straw" for him, and he decided to leave for the West after that.

Immediately after observing the body and the ensuing scene, Daniel had gone home. While on the bus, he caught himself staring intently at a young woman across the aisle and became "self-conscious" and felt he "shouldn't have been staring" at her. For the next several days, he felt numb and somewhat withdrawn and then began noticing a need to tell people about it. There followed a period of intrusive thoughts about the accident, which he kept trying to push out of his mind. After approximately a month, he would not think about the event unless something brought it to mind.

Daniel became essentially free from intrusive images of the scene, unless he heard specific topics mentioned that triggered a series of images. He would then feel compelled to review this set of images in his mind and would often feel the need to describe the whole memory to someone. He was aware that hearing of an incident in which someone was hurt or mutilated or hearing anything concerning Chicago would initiate this conscious and compulsive repetition of the imagery. However, hearing about death, suicide, or accidents in general would not have the same effect.

When his memory was triggered by one of these cues, Daniel would envision the following sequence: first, an image of the woman lying on the ground with the hole in her head; then he would see "her face, which was flattened because she landed on the back of her head." This was followed by an image of the leg, "split, with no blood in there either, and white"; and finally he would see "a piece of brain on the sidewalk, and I remember thinking, it must be a part of her medulla because of the convolutions." The images would make him "nervous" and "depressed" because they were "close" to him and occasionally evoked his own vague thoughts of suicide.* Over the two-year period, Daniel felt that he had achieved some conscious control over reexperiencing the imagery at any given moment. That is, he could choose either to push the thought out of his mind or to think about it, and, inevitably, to re-create the above cycle of images.

In general, Daniel had not noticed the onset of any other symptomatology since the event. He was not aware of any other intrusive imagery or any difficulties with sleeping, eating, or sexual functions. The only behavioral disturbance he remarked upon was his reactions after talking about the incident, when he would invariably feel "spaced out . . . my mind just goes out of focus . . . feel emotionally like being

* Although Daniel experienced episodes of mild depression, he never seriously entertained suicidal notions, nor did this depression ever interfere with his functioning.

about to faint; conscious, but as if there are no stimuli coming in." This feeling would persist for about 30 minutes after having described the scene and the unbidden images, and he reported having felt this sense of dissociation during this interview.

In addition, he reported two other significant consequences of his experience. The first involved driving past an automobile accident about six weeks after the stress event. He saw a man on the side of the road holding his bleeding head in his hands. He then noticed that the top of the car was smashed in and that there was a baby crib in the back seat. Upon observing the crib, he suddenly became upset and began to fantasize about the baby or the man's wife being trapped in the car. Then he was struck by the thought that "it was unnecessarily morbid to fantasize about it and I should stop." Whereupon, he consciously and with difficulty, forced himself to cease thinking about this episode.

The second consequence was an extended fantasy, a story that he had evolved over time about the suicide victim and her reasons for killing herself. She had many children and was working hard to support them. The children were too much to handle, and her husband had left her. She felt alone, alienated from her children, and as if she were fighting the whole world alone. This was too much for her, and so she killed herself.

In fact, Daniel did not know her and knew none of this to be necessarily true, but he told me, "I had to give myself an understandable reason why she'd do that."

In the final minutes of the hour, Daniel spoke of his fears about this interview. He found that he was more nervous discussing the incident in this instance than at any time in over a year. He was worried that the psychiatrist would notice something that was bothering him but that he was unaware of and would not care to admit, such as the idea that the incident had affected him more than he thought it had.

The psychiatrist observed aloud that Daniel had been able to continue his life with a minimum of disturbance, despite the occasionally troubling thoughts. He offered him a chance to return to talk about it and to be treated briefly for help with the recurrent distressing visual images. Daniel thanked the psychiatrist and said he would call if the need arose.

DISCUSSION

From his own subjective memory report, one can reconstruct the behavioral and ideational contents of Daniel's immediate response to this terrible scene. Perhaps it would be best to begin by placing the whole stress event in the context of this lonely period in his life when he was mildly depressed. A manifestation of that mood was his thought that one is not cared for in Chicago. In this frame of mind, he had an incredible experience.

Suddenly "something" made him turn around as he walked along the street. He reports not remembering any sounds except "the blood rushing in my ears." One must surmise that he heard the awful sound of the impact of the body, which probably would have resulted in an explosive noise. But Daniel either repressed this entirely or else did not record the initial impressions in memory. He was then presented with an awful sight—a dead, mutilated, female body with a gaping, empty hole in her cranium. The shock of this visual perception may have eroded preliminary codings of the auditory percepts. Next he was aware of a thought—"she has fallen down (perhaps), has tripped on the sidewalk, or has had a heart attack." He wondered what he should do to help her and yet was aware of the irrationality of these thoughts while observing simultaneously "that nothing was in her head." His mind rapidly appraised alternatives along multiple lines of associations. He tried to disavow the terrible finality of bodily destruction but concluded by recognizing its reality.

He was frozen into a state of staring. Then after a moment, he became acutely uncomfortable with his awareness that he was staring, and he thought, "I shouldn't be looking at that." Then he found himself caught in a conflict; he "shouldn't" look, "but for some morbid reason, I wanted to look at it and kept staring at it." A large part of what followed, according to Daniel's description, involved both his looking and what he saw.

One source of disturbance stemmed from the incongruity between Daniel's ordinary schema of how bodies should look and the way this particular body looked. Bodies are supposed to be intact, shaped in an ordinary manner, and the insides invisible. But this body was misshapen, and the insides were visible. In order to resolve this incongruity, he instinctively needed more information, and his eyes were glued to the body by an automatic tendency to obtain that information. In addition to this automatic tendency, there may have been psychodynamic factors such as a body schema developed around fearsome but unconscious castration fantasies.

The compulsion to look is thus an adaptational function based on a need to find out about any possible danger in novel situations. But self-awareness gives new meanings to automatically instigated staring. Daniel felt that looking was socially taboo. Customarily, eyes are averted from dead bodies, corpses are covered up as rapidly as possible, and children are protected from them. He thus felt guilty for having looked and wanted social confirmation of his act. Since the event, he relived the horror of looking, the compulsion to look, the aim never to look at such things again, and the wish for social sanctions.

Another facet of the scene was his observation that other potential onlookers were not looking, an aspect of the general tendency to deny threat. People walked by, stepping on pieces of the brain, and, incredibly enough, disregarding the body. These other people, then, represented the opposite, or mirror, response: the need to not look. For Daniel, cognitive and emotional processing of the event included not only appraisal of the meaning of the woman's body but also understanding, integrating, and accepting his own immediate responses and those of other persons who, in a sense, socialized his reactions.

While riding the bus, he caught himself reenacting what had just occurred as he stared with tears in his eyes at the young woman opposite him. Perhaps he was identifying with the dead woman as he thought, "Well, at least, now, be friendly" (to him). He was also asking, nonverbally, if looking was all right.

Despite his identifying with the dead woman's plight as being depressed in Chicago, there was probably a countertheme of relief that it was she who died and not he, that she was mutilated and he was intact. This thought could only serve to reinforce his sense of guilt.

By this time, Daniel was already manifesting a stress response syndrome. Over the next several days, he forgot about it but felt vaguely depressed. This represented an initial period of denial and numbing, which soon began to alternate with a need to tell what happened. He also began to experience intrusive imagery and was most aware of this when exposed to one of the trigger stimuli, like hearing one of a set of words or seeing events such as the automobile accident. In general, he was preoccupied with the presence of the memory of the event and with his efforts to prevent it from coming to mind. He was also trying to ward off the guilt, fear, and depression associated with this memory, and one would imagine it was the discomfort of these potential emotions that prompted him to try actively to suppress the images. But two years later, he still had intrusive images of the event after certain specific triggers, such as the word *Chicago*.

THE MEANING OF THE INTERVIEW
AND THE DREAM

Daniel's dream occurred some time after the medical school interview, at which he had somewhat impulsively told his story and while he was anticipating the interview reported here. It occurred probably as these stimuli activated unworked-through aspects of the memories and represented a continued ideational cycle responsive to the stress event. His decision to follow the medical interviewer's suggestion and to come for the interview with a psychiatrist may also have included a covert wish to continue with and complete the cycle of thought initiated by the stressful perceptions. He continued to deny, however, that he was bothered very much at this point by the memory of the event. Accordingly, he did not view the dream as connected to this memory or to the recurrent, disturbing, intrusive imagery he still experienced. Instead, his girlfriend suggested it, and he found that the suggestion "didn't click." He maintained his denial despite his report of an association in the initial part of the dream presentation that confirmed his feeling that the dream was related to the stress memory. He associated the man's exposed body cavity with the hole in the woman's head. However, after adding more detail in the second part of the dream, he told of his disagreeing with his girlfriend's interpretation.

It will be helpful to examine briefly the form and content of the interview in this context. Daniel began with a description of the stress event. He emphasized the impact on him of the woman's empty cranium, the brains splattered about, and his own behavior, looking and staring—first at the body and then later at people on the bus. He immediately presented the disturbing conflict as his desire to look and his guilt about doing so.

Soon afterwards he mentioned having had the dream and offered a description, concentrating on the part concerning the body cavity that was "all scooped out" and the association to the woman's empty cranium. Then he stopped and was silent. The interviewer asked whether that was the whole dream, and he replied, "There's more detail in it, but I don't know if you want to hear the whole thing."

Interactionally, he was asking if the interviewer could stand hearing more detail, as the interview process was a reliving of some aspects of the stress situation with the externalization of some of his quandaries to the therapist. He presented the distressing images to the interviewer in a forceful way and watched his response. If the interviewer preserved his equanimity, then, by identification, Daniel too could remain unperturbed. If the interviewer did not criticize or reprimand him for staring, then the compulsive looking would be made socially acceptable. If the interviewer expressed his own wish to see and know more, then Daniel could feel less guilty about looking.

Several references have been made linking his dream to the stressful event. What is the evidence for this? A connection between the man's body cavity in the dream and the woman's cranial cavity in the perception has already been mentioned. The view is reversed, from above and downwards to below and upwards. Daniel said the man in the dream had been in an accident, a term he used during the interview to refer to the woman's fall. The man's legs had been severed, and the bones could be seen, an image similar to what he had received when looking at the woman with her leg split open.

After learning that the interviewer wanted to hear the details, Daniel reported the second part of the dream: "The man looked kind of plastic, like he had black, plastic hair . . . looked android or plastic." The woman had worn black (patent leather or plastic) boots, probably had dark hair, and her face, flattened from the impact of the fall, may have looked "android" or unreal and plastic. The man had "very smooth olive skin"; the woman was Latin American. In this second telling, Daniel again described the man's legs as "cut open . . . I saw a cross section of his legs, the muscles and bone." This is an even stronger suggestion of his image of the woman's leg "split open." He saw the man's "spinal—his backbone." He had described a part of the woman's brain as being quite identifiable as her "medulla." The "silvery coating . . . like the inside of a fish" in the dream is probably associated with the luminescent quality of the meninges, which he might have observed on the brain parts. Finally, in the dream, he spoke of putting "myself in his position." The woman has become a man in the dream, as her suicide was "very close to home" for him. The dream's manifest content contained images derived from the original stress event and occurred in expectation of reliving the event in the forthcoming interview.

To recapitulate, two years after a frightening experience, images of that experience continued to have an intrusive quality, emerging despite suppressive efforts when there were certain associational triggers. In addition, there was a continued need to retell the story while both awake and asleep. Even the process of the interview itself had aspects of reenactment. This is by no means an unusual story and illustrates the endurance and intensity of a response to stressful events in a normal person.

14

AN AUTOMOBILE ACCIDENT

With Richard Olsen, M.D.

J ane is a 23-year-old woman who developed a relatively severe reaction to an automobile accident. Her therapy was completed in five interviews which will be reported in detail here to illustrate the process of treating stress response syndromes. The relevant issues are the succession of intrusive and denial signs and symptoms, a technique of focal working-through, and the interaction of the external stress event with Jane's current tasks in personal development.

Six weeks after her automobile accident, Jane called asking for immediate help because she was tense, nauseated, and unable to eat or sleep. She had been seeing a physician for neck and back pain and had been placed on several medications for pain, muscle spasms, nausea, and insomnia.

Nothing helped, and her physician referred her to the stress research clinic for evaluation. When she telephoned, she sounded tearful and desperate and complained of extreme nervousness and preoccupation with the accident. An appointment was made for later that same day. After discussing the research and teaching aspects of the clinic service, Jane gave an informed consent for participation. The following interviews then took place.

FIRST SESSION

Jane appeared for the first session looking pale, tense, and wearing a protective collar around her neck. A slender and moderately attractive person who dressed modestly, her face was rigid, and she moved in a guarded and halting manner.

> *T (Therapist)*: What's up?
>
> *J (Jane)*: I'd rather you didn't ask me that leading question (she appears to be very tense).
>
> *T*: Well, you called this morning.
>
> *J*: My doctor thought I'd better call because I was getting more and more anxious and I couldn't eat. He knows—he's treating me for a whiplash . . . (*long pause*).
>
> *T*: Yes.
>
> *J*: . . . and it brings on the pain . . . (*long pause*).
>
> *T*: What does the not eating . . .
>
> *J*: What does it do?
>
> *T*: Well, how does it come upon you?
>
> *J*: Well, whenever I get upset, I slow down on whatever I'm eating. I never have had an appetite too much. And when I got upset this week, I just began to vomit in the morning and couldn't keep anything in my stomach.
>
> *T*: Well, that was just this week that you got upset?
>
> *J*: Well, yeah, but this is like I've been upset before.

T: When did it seem to start, being upset?

J: I've never calmed down since the accident, not completely. I've been on the medication ever since.

T: What medication is that?

Ordinarily, at the very beginning of a contact, the therapist would not focus on a detail such as medications but would instead encourage reports of more central material. This focus is made in order to help the patient establish a therapeutic alliance as well as to evaluate the current situation. She is quite tense, resistant to the idea of communicating with the therapist, and focuses on somatic issues. She has not presented psychological reasons for coming. At the same time, she is indicating nonverbally that she is in great need and wants to be taken care of. A somewhat tangential discussion thus may establish a model of successful communication, provide a calming effect to counteract the extra stress of a first therapeutic contact, and pave the way for freer communication of the more central details.

J: It depends on what week you're talking about. He's been changing it as I change.

T: Uh-huh. Have you been taking antianxiety, antidepressant, or sedative medications?

Her remark, "it depends on what week," is sarcastic, and the therapist knows that the state of her relationship with her doctor may be important. Her dependence on and her irritation toward her physician already impress the therapist. He expects that there may be a potential for this sort of transference in the therapy and considers the possibility of its being related to her reactions to the stress event. He chooses to persist in finding out the answer to his earlier question "What medication?" in order to establish the model for the therapeutic communication mentioned above.

J: Antianxiety, pain killers, and a joint deflamatory medication 'cause I messed up my hips as well. I have to wear a lift on my shoe now.

T: Who is your doctor?

J: Doctor Smith.

T: What kind of a doctor is he?

J: He's an M.D., internist.

T: Uh-huh. Are you seeing him privately, or are you a clinic patient?

J: Privately. He is the one who I went to after the accident 'cause he was my doctor.

T: And he suggested you come here?

J: Yeah.

T: When was that?

J: I went to him Tuesday because I had missed work. I just started substituting as a nurse's aide, and I was really upset with some nurse, and I had to have a head nurse find another substitute at the last minute because I got all the way down to Zone City where I'm working and I couldn't stay. And I went to his office and I slept there for three hours while I was waiting for him to come. The receptionist let me sleep there. And then he changed my medication, and by Thursday, I was in the same state all over again. I got through Wednesday somehow, but by Thursday I couldn't so I didn't even leave and go to Zone City. And I called him, and he started making arrangements, so he contacted the clinic.

T: Yes, right. So here you are. Well, this is what we'll do now. I'll just try and find out what I can about you this time and maybe another time. Then, we'll try and assign you for appropriate treatment. It already sounds like something is indicated.

J: What?

T: I don't know, but something.

J: Something?

Her rejoinder is subdued sarcasm and is provocative. The therapist again has the impression that Jane will set up a passive-dependent or passive-dependent-aggressive type of transference situation. She is challenging him to do something before he knows what is going on. She has not said clearly that she is in psychological distress but has presented only physical complaints. He is comparatively certain that she is in psychological distress and chooses to focus on this issue. His next remark will, therefore, be made as a statement. This again points toward developing a therapeutic contract. The therapist illustrates his intentions here; he will clarify and interpret but not assume responsibility for her life. He already has a hunch that her physical complaints are both real and used as a defensive denial of emotional responses to the accident. He is, in a mild way, undercutting that defense by focusing attention on the area of warded-off experiences. These early choices are often quite important, but unfortunately, they have to be made on very few data.

> *T:* It sounds like you're in psychological difficulty.
> *J:* Yeah, I know, it has to be psychological. There is no other reason to have all these problems at once (*long pause*).
> *T:* Well, I'd like to know much more. Where do you think would be a good place to start; would it be to tell me about the accident, or—? (*trails off*).

The patient is still resistant to telling the therapist what kind of difficulty she is experiencing. The therapist now senses that this is not simply a high level of anxiety or inarticulateness but that there is also an element of defiance. Perhaps he is being equated with the referring physician. She may be covertly communicating an accusation that would go something like this were it to have been expressed verbally rather than nonverbally: "You see, you won't help me enough: I still hurt, and so I won't cooperate with you. Let's have you make me do what you think will help. Then we'll see that it won't help either. That will prove that if anyone is to blame,

it's you, and not me." To avoid this type of transference, the therapist backs off a little from the firmness of his earlier remark, "It sounds
like psychological difficulty" and places the responsibility for choos-
ing their next topic partially with her.

> J: Well, the accident stopped me from doing all kinds of things.
> On the day of the accident, I was on my way to an assign-
> ment to substitute in Zone City. And I took Banning Road
> because the school was near Banning. I never take it unless
> I have to, and in the fog, someone rear-ended me at a stop
> light. And after that, after I gave out flares and told every-
> body that my neck hurt, we moved the cars because other
> cars were bearing down and nearly hitting them again. And
> a policeman came and passed out flares and put them out on
> the highway, and another car came and smashed into my
> car and I went into shock. And I was just like a robot from
> there until a few hours later when I came down again.
>
> T: Uh-huh. You were driving alone?
>
> J: Yeah, I was on the way to work. I have to be alone to get
> there because substitute nurse's aides never know where
> they're going to be. But the doctor kept me off work for a
> month. And that same day, I was supposed to go to an
> interview for a regular job, and they were good enough to
> hold the job open for me. And I had to wait until I could
> find out whether I would be able to work. They decided
> that I could work and so I went to work with my collar
> on, about two and a half, three weeks ago. But they placed
> me in another ward, with new people because there was a
> rule about two people in the same family on the same ser-
> vice and my sister-in-law was working on that service. I'm
> supposedly teamed with two other aides, but they're very,
> very close and are roommates as well so that they're to-
> gether all of the time, and they're actually teaming and I'm
> way off, and I see them only during report.

T: Yes, so you're kind of isolated?

J: Yeah.

The theme of people's letting her down is repeated again: the nurses, nurse's aides, her doctor, and (by inference) this therapist. The therapist gently affirms this feeling by saying that she is isolated, and so she continues with a freer description of how tough things are at work. She says she broke down one day recently but does not reveal what that means. Only in later hours did she describe what had happened. She had grown so irritated with a complaining, senile patient that she slapped him. She was terrified that she would be reported and lose her registration as a paraprofessional, as well as the immediate job. After adding details about work, which seem to smooth out the communicative feeling with the therapist, she continues as follows:

J: But after I got myself upset Tuesday, I couldn't get myself calmed down, and I dragged through Wednesday, and I couldn't make it Thursday, and I stayed off today.

T: Yes. Well, can you tell me what being upset and nervous is like inside you? How is it going in there?

J: It changes. It started just to be stomach trouble, but along with it, my stomach would hurt and my bowels would be loose. The stress would go into my back, and now the small of my back and my hip joints and my neck all hurt, and just about every single muscle hurts by now. I haven't eaten enough in so long that I'm just exhausted, and—

T: How long has it been since you've eaten anything?

J: I eat little bits 'cause every day is like a cycle. In the afternoon, I'm pretty good, and by evening, I might even be able to eat solid food. But in the morning or the middle of the night if I wake up, I can't stomach anything, and I'll just be sick.

T: Will you throw up if you try to eat?

J: Yes. Or right now, I was throwing up on Wednesday before I went to work, and I got it into my nose and I always get sinus problems anyway, and I was sneezing all day and I didn't think about it, but that evening, it drained back down and burned my throat. I haven't been able to shake that yet; I'm still—like I was crying all day yesterday and the night before, and the more I cry, the worse it got. So, last night, I woke up hysterical; I couldn't breathe 'cause I couldn't clear my throat and I had a pain in my chest, and it turned out to be that I was sleeping on my side and a muscle had tightened.

During the therapy, this patient has symptoms related to her joints, bones, muscles, gastrointestinal system, eyes, and upper respiratory system. None of these are malingering; she tends to develop psycho-physiological reactions under stress. Such symptoms should never be regarded unsympathetically. It will be seen that Jane has conflicts between dependency wishes and strivings for independence. She has already presented herself to the therapist as both needing to depend on someone and not wishing to depend on anyone. The somatic symptoms are presented as a reasonable basis for obtaining sympathy and attention, but they are presented in such quantity that the therapist is made uncomfortable with the load. He changes the topic, perhaps too abruptly, but does try to find out more about what may be real aspects of her dependency–independency conflict.

T: Are you staying alone?
J: No, I'm with my father and my stepmother.
T: Yes.
J: But I don't get on with my father. He's an alcoholic, and we have what he decided is a mutual agreement: we talk to each other as little as possible because if we say more than three words, there's an argument.

T: I see. Then it's somewhat of a tense living arrangement.

J: I wanted to get out of it before the accident. I had planned to leave in either August or in October, depending on whether I could sign a contract for September or not or get some other kind of work. I was taking typing lessons in case I couldn't find a job as an aide. But now, I have to stay home until I'm well 'cause I have no place to go and no money.

T: Did you finish training just recently?

The therapist notes with interest that the accident has forced her to stay on with her father. She had planned to separate from him, a more-than-appropriate move for a 23-year-old. The topic deserves further exploration, but the therapist delays this because a therapeutic alliance is not yet established and because she is so distraught. He already believes that her dependency–independency conflicts may be important and that the establishment of a therapeutic alliance in itself will offer enough support to enable her to improve and not require hospitalization and probably not need medications. After details about her current work and training situation, the therapist tries gently to return to the situation of living with her alcoholic father.

T: Do I gather that you had a kind of plan of getting a job and then moving out?

J: Uh-huh pretty soon.

T: Yes, well (*long pause*), so there seems possibilities of that, but getting into the accident really set you back?

J: Yeah, right after the accident when I was pretty medicated, I felt really, really good because the pain hadn't set in; it took a few days. A job possibility came up for just the kind of job I wanted. Only it was a rumor; it was something the nurses were pushing, and the nursing director hadn't set her mind on it yet, and she had just asked around for nurses and aides to transfer into those positions who were already employed in the hospital. And so several people contacted me who had been contacted by her saying, "You really fit into this one." But in the days after that, my neck got tighter. I couldn't drive myself down to Zone City, so I couldn't go to an interview. And since that time, the woman who would have interviewed me committed suicide.

T: Now, what's been on your mind in terms of the accident itself? Does it come back to you at all?

It is advisable to ask directly about intrusive phase symptoms, as the patient knows them consciously but often does not know how to report them.

J: The only time I really think about it is when we're commuting on the freeway and someone changes lanes or does something stupid. Then I feel that it's about to happen because I saw the guy coming when I was hit. I could see him in the rearview mirror, and he was coming too fast. That's the only time I really think much about it.

T: Yes. And you said you don't drive now?

J: Yes, I do. I don't drive to Zone City because it's too far to go, but I drive around the city. Today I'm not driving because I haven't eaten in so long that I'm too weak.

T: And what's keeping you from eating? Is it lack of appetite?

J: Well, I don't have any appetite, and my throat was really sore, and my stomach wouldn't take food except for a few hours, and then it won't take much. But I talked to my doctor again; I talk to him every day, and he prescribed something so that my stomach will remain calm so that I can eat. I just picked it up before I came here.

T: What is that?

J: I'd have to look; it's in my purse. Do you really want to know?

T: No, just if you knew. Are you taking any other medicines besides this one you're going to be taking?

J: Uh-huh; I was taking Valium right after the accident, with the other medications, and then I went off of it last Tuesday. Then he put me on Compazine. That Compazine puts me to sleep. When it hits, I'm out. So today, he put me back on Valium, and he doubled the dose.

T: Does that help you?

J: Yeah, the only thing that bothers me is that it dulls my mind. After having studied medical stuff like anatomy, that just freaks me out because I like to be able to think clearly and know stuff. Like I couldn't even keep my charts. I had them all messed up as to which patients had what temperatures, which had movements, and all like that.

T: So it would be important to get through this stage that you're in—

J: Right. I really don't like to be on any kind of medicine at all, and I usually have to be coerced by the doctor to keep on it. I keep wanting to go off of it and stay off of medication. It scares me because I've seen too many people with problems.

T: And what did you do at home yesterday?

J: Well, first I typed a couple of letters, and the phone was going all day with the doctor trying to find out where he could have me evaluated. And the people were calling me who were concerned.

T: Where he could have you evaluated?

J: For psychiatric help.

T: Oh, I see.

J: He had thought he could put me in Acme.

T: That didn't work out at Acme?

J: No, I'm out of the district. I'm reading a book and was watching TV. And I've got a dog and I usually walk her every day, but when my hip joints hurt, I don't want to walk. Yesterday, by late afternoon, I was feeling good, so I took her for a walk.

T: And do you have difficulty concentrating, like when you try to read or watch television?

J: It depends on what it is. Like I was reading a medical book the other night, and I kept having to put it down because I couldn't imagine the parts that you should imagine as you're reading. But when I'm reading really light stuff, like from the *Reader's Digest* or something, then I have no trouble concentrating.

T: And do you see anybody?

J: My family keeps coming in and out, but most of my friends are—like when I was working full time and she's (her girlfriend) staying hopped up on uppers to keep working. And she doesn't really want to see me★ because I make her unhappy and mess her up. And another friend just took off★ for the country, and another one is leaving★ for back East, and she claims that she's really busy. And really, those are the only people I see much of; I don't see a lot of people.

T: No boyfriends?

J: Not right now.

T: In the past?

J: Not lately, but yeah.

T: So, you're feeling pretty isolated except for your family? Why does your girlfriend say that you mess her up?

J: We act rather strongly against one another; we have different beliefs, but we're willing to be friends. She, right now, is kind of selling what she wants to be and what she wants to do and trying to convince herself. She's going around spouting it out to everybody. She's already tried it out on me and knows that I disagree with it. She doesn't

---

★ More desertion themes.

want to be near me because she's trying to convince everybody that the things she's going to do next are right, and I
don't believe her.

T: How would you characterize—or how would she characterize you; what are your strong attitudes?

J: Most of my friends, including her, say that I'm stable.
Doesn't sound like it now, but I'm usually stable and
very—if I do something one way, like help out in a strange
situation, I can figure out ways to get out of them. And
I'm always there when anybody wants to get out of that
kind of situation. Like the car breaking down; I'm really
mechanically inclined, and if it broke down and I was
there, I would probably open the hood, and if it was
simple, I would put it together or I'd know how to call
for help.

She has added mention of three friends who left her and counters
this with pride at having independent skills.

T: Right. Any other strong attitudes your friends would say
you had that would characterize your personality?

J: People who don't know me very well think I'm an egg-
head or that I'm cold.

T: But it's not true?

J: Well, I've got other friends who say they thought that and
then when they got to know me, they found out that I
wasn't. So I don't think it's true.

T: Okay, let's go back; do you mind talking more about the
accident? It's seems like it's really centrally important.

This is a firm attempt to set a focus for a brief therapy. The
therapist has gathered some general data and tried to foster a therapeutic alliance in the conversation so far. He has some preliminary
concepts about contextual personality issues.

T: You were going to work, and you saw this car coming at you, and you knew it was going to hit you. Could you, could you just tell me all the details from there?

J: I had come to a red light, and one car had stopped in front of me, and I was stopped and waiting. And while I was waiting, I caught an action in the mirror, and so I watched it and saw the car coming at me too fast and tensed up, and then he hit. And the first sensation after the numbness, the first numbness, went away was that my shoulder and neck hurt. And after the person in the front had seen my car jump, he came back and said, "Are you hurt?" I said, "Yes," and he stayed to help us. And the man behind me, the one who had hit me, he took a look around and came up to see me and says, "Are you hurt?" I said, "Yes, my neck is hurt." But I had checked myself out, and I could tell that was the only thing hurting; nothing else was hurting at all. So, I got out of the car and looked at the situation, then I crawled into the back seat and got some flares out 'cause nobody had anything to mark off this accident, and it was in heavy commute traffic and deep fog. So, I used the flares and said, "Has anybody called the police yet?" Nobody had; nobody knew where a phone was; it was really eerie because we were completely fogged in. You could see the road, but you couldn't see anything else because it was really, really fogged in.

Both her willingness to relate the details and her pride in taking charge of the situation are noteworthy. But she became vague and distracted as she said "fogged in," and that prompted the therapist's next remark. She seemed, in a way, to be reenacting the accident.

T: You probably started feeling unreal.

J: Yeah, yeah. Then the man who had hit me decided that I was shaking, and we couldn't decide whether it was cold or pain. I didn't even know which it was, so he put me in his car, and we traded information. Then he left me in his car and went to use the phone, and after he came back, I decided we'd better move the cars, because I kept hearing cars braking to avoid my car. We moved them and I left the engine running and lights on and I moved it into a zone that was painted off, a safety zone next to an island, a right-turn island. And he moved off to the shoulder, and we got back into his car to keep warm. My car was still in a more dangerous position. And a police car came, and he said they had trouble figuring out what county we were. So a police car came and didn't seem to see us. It came from the other direction, and it made a left turn and stopped. And then after a long time, the policeman that we saw came, and he pulled around and came and talked to us and pieced together the accident. Then he put out his flares and was going back to get this report book when we could hear this other car approaching, and we all turned and watched the next collision, which threw my car about eight feet out into the intersection, because he was going mighty fast. And then that man got out of the car and exploded, and he just ran and he swore all over the place. He stomped around—

T: Angrily?

Her facial expression and vocal inflection indicate a great emotional involvement in this new person, and the therapist intuitively picks out a central aspect.

J: Yeah, he was as mad as he could be. I wanted his name before he went anywhere. He said, "I'm going to find a phone." I insisted, and so he threw his license at me and stomped away (she is very indignant). And the officer was out of hearing range by then, and he came back, and they started calling tow trucks and stuff and then they had to decide whether to send for an ambulance for me or whether I knew some-one I could notify, because I was the only one that was hurt. I said, "I'm really not hurt bad enough to call an ambulance; I can walk around, and I can sit without hurt-ing myself. If I think for a minute, maybe I'll figure out somebody I know who can come and get me." And I thought about it and tried my brother-in-law, and he was home because it was finals week and he didn't have a final that morning. So he came to get me, and he handled my towing service and some of the policeman's questions about me and stuff while I wrote out a report. Then after we had checked the car and left it in an empty lot, we called my doctor and took me in. But my doctor had two other emergencies that morning in his office, and they left me sitting in the waiting room for an hour and a half. Then they decided after he looked at me for one minute, he needed an X-ray before he could decide anything. So he sent me over to X-ray, which is in the same building. I'd been there before because I had had back trouble before, and I had X-rays and retakes and stuff. And I went back, and he decided there were no fractures and no nerves pinched; it was just a severe strain. He prescribed tranquilizers and pain killers and a prescription for the collar, and I went downstairs and got the collar, and I got the medications and stayed home. But my insurance com-pany sent a field representative to my house that after-noon. And I was really, really—not the same as I am anx-ious now—but excited more, and I called a friend to stay with me, and my family kept dropping in, and the house was full of people, and they had like a party and joked a lot, having a good time. And then the guy with a tape recorder came and taped my version of the accident, and he wanted a medical release and—

T: And so your family didn't realize, because there was not any big deal like bandages, they didn't realize that you'd been hurt.

The therapist is picking up on her vocal tone, which indicates her hurt and anger that she got so little attention.

J: Right. And then when I started to hurt, it really scared me 'cause I didn't know it was going to start to hurt.

T: Right, and that was really frightening.

J: And then the following Tuesday, I started therapy, physical therapy. But a few weeks later, I had to call my doctor about pains in my hip joint. It was just one at first, and I've had something related to that before, but it wasn't the same; this was stronger. And he didn't understand what it was and couldn't find out, and so he looked up my old X-ray and found out it was in my other hip, so he went for another X-ray. And he then said that the joint didn't show anything, but in the days that followed, it got worse and has gone to the other side. It turned out that I was sleeping on my side. I always slept on my side before this, and so I was sleeping on my side. I was sleeping on my hip, and it was getting irritated. And then I'd turned over to the other side and done it to the other one. So—

T: How did you feel about seeing your doctor repeatedly?

J: Well, he had me down once a week, and it turned out that I made the once-a-week appointment. I might not have a new complaint every week, but I just got in on a once-a-week appointment until this week.

T: How did the relationship go between you and your doctor? Do you know what I mean?

J: Yes. Well, he's almost argumentative in manner, but not that strong. I don't know where—well, if I ask something, then he asks something back, and we go back and forth. And it isn't as if he's trying to explain the whole thing to me; I need to ask him to find out how things are going to go.

T: Right, just like being surprised that it was going to hurt. Doctors sometimes feel, "Well, I won't say anything because I don't want people to imagine it." And then what happens is what usually happens in these things. Delayed symptoms come up, and then you're surprised. But I get the feeling throughout that your feelings are badly hurt, as well as your neck.

For her, this is a major interpretation and also a second round in trying to establish a therapeutic contract for exploring her ideas and feelings. The therapist attempts to focus on the link between the stressor event, internal reactions, and identity, plus relationship issues incorporated in reactions to the trauma.

J: Uh-huh.

Her response is vague, and so the therapist tries gently to rivet her attention to the issue. She has not yet fully agreed to the exploration of psychological issues.

T: Does it make sense to you?
J: My feelings hurt?
T: Yeah.
J: I'm awfully disappointed that all my plans got wrecked.
T: Yeah, but I don't think you've been able to tell anyone that.
J: But I talk to my sister-in-law all the time. Only thing is that she's talking about other things when she talks back, so I don't know if she's hearing (long pause).
T: Well, I think there's some working through to do about talking over these things. That, at least, I see as being real essential for you to do. Anything else?

The therapist is once again working toward establishing a therapeutic contract centered on psychological issues.

J: Oh, on the day before the accident, I hadn't been called to work. And I have a choice; I can call in at the City Hospital where I used to work and say I'm there, or I can do what I please. So, I decided it was about time I got myself another car 'cause I had sold my car about a month before when it was beginning to give me trouble. It was an old Toyota, and parts were really hard to get 'cause mine was made for the Canadian specifications. So I sold it and was still convinced that Toyota makes a good car for an economy car. It's big enough not to scare me. I know that Volkswagens blow around on the freeways; that scares me, and being in an accident scares me. This is before the accident; I went down—I saw an ad in the paper and I made phone calls; then I went down to Danville where there was a good dealer. I won't trust the guy locally 'cause I've heard what happens. And I test drove a car, and I said, "Yeah, I'll put a down payment on it." Then I told him that there were a couple of things that needed work before I would pay for the car, and he wrote them up and then I had the accident the next day. I was supposed to pick it up on Saturday, and I had arranged financing independently on my own through their bank which they had set up for me. But it was my own financing. I got home, and my father said, "Oh, no, I'll pay the whole thing for you; you can just pay me back." Which is the arrangement he did with my sister, and since I'm financially in a rotten position anyway, I decided, well, money is going to help me get out of the house faster; I'll do it. And so I canceled the loan financing, and I got all their correct numbers and had my father write up a cashier's check 'cause he has the money in the bank.

Dependency on her father and the link of cars to her father turns out to be an important dynamic issue in working through this particular stress event.

> *J:* Saturday, I really freaked out about picking up a car 'cause I couldn't drive; I had the collar on, and the pain was getting bad, and I was taking codeine and was too doped up to drive. I convinced my brother and my brother-in-law to come along. They took me down, and they were really nice; and they took me in a car with back rests in it, shoulder harness, and drove real careful. And when we got there, they test drove it for me. They said they'd take it on a rough road and really see how it was doing but the salesman who was selling it to me and told me he'd be there wasn't there, and he turned me over to the manager.

The desertion theme emerges again. Note that she is talking more openly to the therapist and in a pressured manner.

> *J:* And the manager needed all the details because the salesman had left in a hurry. And we made the arrangements finally and signed the papers and gave him all the money and took the car home. And since then, problems that I stated on the first form weren't solved. Today was the day we finally had an appointment to have it done, so I sent my brother down again, and he just got the car back, but I haven't had a chance to ride in it or drive it myself yet to see if it really is repaired or not.
>
> *T:* So you have that hassle. Well, look, we have to stop. I'd like to see you again before we decide anything. But you know, I think we've already decided that whatever else, there is some talking to be done.

Yet another effort to reach agreement on a therapeutic contract.

J: Okay.

T: You know, I hope this won't interfere with you working.

A suggestion that she is well enough to work and should go on rather than regress.

J: I work in the morning only.

T: Oh, well, let's see what we can do in the afternoon.

J: It would have to be after 1:00 o'clock.

T: Um. I could see you if you could come Monday at 2:30. Would that be okay?

J: Okay.

SECOND SESSION

Jane began by saying that she had done quite well over the weekend. She felt that the first hour had helped her: "It just worked; I don't know what it did. I know afterwards, I kept thinking, 'I sure didn't say a lot of details that were there that I could have said,' but at the time, I didn't think." This suggested to the therapist that she was in a denial phase of response. The hour helped both in the sense of socialization, discussing the accident with a therapeutically oriented person, and, in a general way, raising her concerns to a reality-oriented rather than fantasy-oriented level.

She went on to add that she had moved out of her father's house. She had asked her pregnant sister to take her in, and that had been an improvement over eating with her father, who often vomited at mealtimes because of his alcoholism. She indirectly attributed the idea of this move to the therapist's remark in the first hour that the situation at home was tense. Probably the therapist's repetition of what she herself had been saying acted as a permission for her to become more assertive.

She was worried about being a burden on her sister but said, "I'm going to turn it around, and I'm going to help her, and I'm helping because I don't have to be the one that everyone else is helping. It puts me one block away from the person I was commuting with, my sister-in-law. And I'm going to see if I can commute alone pretty soon, 'cause I don't like to be driven. I'm going to try it one time with her sitting beside me and if that doesn't have any problem at all, then I'm just going to commute by myself."

The therapist is pleased to see the reassertion of her striving for independence and activity. He has also been impressed by both regressive forces leading to searches for dependency as a secondary gain from the accident and the loaded but unexplored issue of her deterioration at the accident when yelled at by the driver of the second car. Also, she was at the point that her doctor was considering psychiatric hospitalization, and she was showing many somatic as well as psychological complaints. He favored further work rather than a termination at this point. His feeling that the improvement was in a way a relationship cure added to this decision to continue. First, he asked more about what seemed to be a fear of driving and then asked an open-ended question.

> T: Well, what about cars and driving? How has that been on your mind the last few days?
>
> J: Well, I drove here. I drove all over this morning doing stuff, getting keys made and stuff.
>
> T: Alone?
>
> J: Sure. Ever since the accident, I'm always able to drive short distances alone; no problem at all. The only problem that still scares me is getting on the freeway in heavy commute traffic, where merges are going on. That part scares me. But I think if I was behind the wheel and not having to watch somebody else do it, I could handle it fine, because I did it since January and never had an accident or even a close call. You know, I know how to do it; just whether I'm scared or not.

T: Okay. Well, where should we go from here?

J: I don't know. I'd kind of like to find out why I get into such deep depressions and can't get—well, this time I couldn't get myself out, because I wouldn't want to go into it again. If it ever happened again, it would screw up my career in nursing, being unable to attend or just breaking down like that. I mean, if I couldn't have pulled out this week, my contract probably would have been torn up and destroyed, and my record would have been messed up, you know. And I really would like to get to the root of why I throw myself into depressions.

T: Okay. That's something then that we should explore a little bit more. Maybe we'll have time now. But I wanted to ask you also where the memory is with you right now about the accident.

J: I can remember it fine.

T: Uh-huh. Does it come back to you when you don't want it to at all?

As mentioned earlier, patients often do not spontaneously report intrusive phase symptoms. Risking the danger of suggesting a symptom, the therapist asks pointedly about a common response to accidents.

J: No. I think—I don't usually remember what I dream. But since, like the last week or so, I have had nightmares, usually right when I wake up I remember something, some piece of it, and I think sometimes I have nightmares about the accident because it scared me so bad.

T: Yes. But you don't remember what they are?

J: No. Never have (*laughs*).

T: Do they sometimes wake you up out of your sleep?

J: Well, it's a combination, because I move around if I'm having a nightmare, and then I don't know whether it's the nightmare or laying on a hip joint or bending my back or what it is that wakes me up. But I wake up, and I can remember a piece of bad dream and being in pain at the same time. So, I don't know, is it the night—you know, I'm so wrapped up in too many things at once—I can't say. Like last night, I slept fantastic—no problem at all. And I know I woke up on my side which is supposed to be a no-no until the hips get better. And this morning, this hip joint was irritated, but after I was up and moving around and took a hot shower, after about 45 minutes, it's okay now. So I think pretty soon I'm throwing the book away and forget about it, so I can sleep like I want to sleep.

T: Uh-huh, and during the day, you don't find you're having thoughts about the accident coming in on you when you don't want them to?

J: The only time they'd come in on me is if I associate with something happening right now, like in the car—

T: That might trigger it?

J: Yeah, trigger it.

T: Well, you know, thoughts like that are always surprises.

This is a "moving closer" type of remark, meant to reveal empathy with the patient. The patient responds with associative memories.

J: Yeah, definitely. Well, I know, well, I mean, I kind of compare it with my mother's death a long time ago, and for a long time after that, things would trigger that memory, you know. And now it's so long that—and I used to counsel at the York Avenue place with the kids who had a lot of trouble. A lot of them had fathers who disappeared and people in the hospital dying and things like that, and I could handle that fine for them, too, you know. And I got out of that, and I'm confident that I'll be able to get out of the accident myself. But something else is still triggering depressions on me because I still get into them.

T: Well, there may have been a clue to that in our discussion Friday. It may not be the right one, but it might be there. I kind of got the idea that you experienced the accident, in one way, as just another insult.

J: Yeah.

T: Does that seem to fit with you?

J: Uh-huh.

T: And maybe there have been a number of other ones in your life, and this was just. . . .

J: Another one, yeah.

T: . . . just another one to hit you. Of course, it had that kind of rippling effect in that it interfered with so many of your plans.

J: Yeah. It meant nothing in particular. My car, I hadn't paid for it; I was right in the middle of it. And that afternoon, I was supposed to go for planning for the summer. That particular day, I was doing a million matters of business, and none of them could be done . . . (*long pause*).

In an event-centered therapy, one may not wish to stray too far afield. But she calls her psychological reaction a depression and seems to recognize a recurrent pattern. The therapist believes this must be explored to understand her character, preexisting conflicts, and the meanings attached to this recent event. As she pours out a tale of losses, the therapist realizes the importance of accumulated stresses and the "last straw" effect in this case.

T: Okay. Well, tell me a little bit about some of the other depressions that you've had. What kind of things seem to trigger them?

J: I think most of the other ones were triggered by people dying, because I've watched my mother go into a depression when her mother died. That was when I was 5; I was just a kid, and I don't know what I was doing. I used to throw tantrums, but I don't know what else I was doing. But when I was 12, she was ill, and she had been ill for years and died of cancer and that threw me. They had to take me to a doctor and start giving me vitamin shots to pull me back out because I was wasting away, losing too much weight.

A few years after that, my favorite aunt died, and I went into another one. Shortly after that, one of my best friends died, and then I went into one again. One summer, in fact, I think it was the summer my aunt died, there was a dog we bought the year after my mother's death—and she always thought a dachshund would be a nice kind of dog because they're clean. So my sister helped find one and everything, convinced my father who was against it, and we bought a dachshund. It turned out that the dachshund was pedigreed, and he was overbred, and he had come out with a mean temperament. If a professional had been the breeder, he probably would have been destroyed because of his temperament, but it was a nonprofessional person who sold it to us, and he was like a one-man dog and we didn't know it. He could have been trained maybe to be a watchdog; otherwise, he should have been destroyed because he was mean. But we kept him for six years, and we had to do all kinds of things all over the house so that the family could protect people from him because he was moody and temperamental. He hurt people, and I got into all kinds of trouble because I was sitting for people at the time. I had to take a little girl to the emergency hospital and nearly landed in a lawsuit because her eye got scratched and all kinds of problems with him.

But anyway, that summer he fell down the back stairs and dislocated his back and paralyzed himself from the shoulders back with some control of his internal organs. I had to take care of him 'cause I was the only one home, and I nursed him and nursed him and nursed him, and finally I was just getting really tired of it. My parents were going to be on vacation, and I said, "Is it okay with you if you'll take along the dog? I'm going to take two weeks off and visit a friend in Tahoe." They said fine. And I call, and they say everything is fine, and I came home and found that they had run out of pain killers and didn't know that pill was important and hadn't gotten any, and the dog had been in pain for eight days and just shaking with the pain. So I took him to the vet, and we had to have him destroyed.

We had two dogs at the time—my other dog caught one of the infections that the dachshund had, and she had to be nursed back to health. After all that happened, after I went into a depression—it wasn't very long or very strong, because I had to do so many things right then and get back to school and stuff, but it seems they're all tied up with someone dying.

T: Losing something you like or are attached to?

J: Yeah. And then after that, there was—last summer was different. Last summer, I was taking courses; that's the last thing before you student nurse and go out. One of the people in the courses said, "I know you're really good" 'cause I was helping her out. She said, "I've got a job possibility for you," so I went and followed it up and got the job, only the job was really something I wasn't quite ready for, and it threw me for a loop. I was tense because I had to learn how to deal with unusual patients and all of this as a semi-volunteer, possibly with money coming through and me in debt for a car that I had just bought, all at once.

And so I got all upset, and Dr. Smith treated me then with tranquilizers, and I got through it and we had a glorious summer, no matter what (*laughter*). But about a week before the end of it, my mother's last surviving sister died of a brain tumor, and her daughter is a dwarf, who is slowly becoming—well, now I guess you'd call her a hermit. She's withdrawn from just about every living soul in the world. I happen to be one of the few people alive that she'll talk to. There is a handful of people: my sister, her sister, her brother, and a couple who she'll talk to on a very superficial level. I was trying to see if I could help her out, but of course, she wouldn't accept it. And also having lost my aunt, I went into another tailspin, but I came out of that one quick; it was short. I just got mad at the whole thing and said, "I've got to live for me and get out of this mess."

Since that time, there's just been like little short things like the pressure of substituting. I'd get myself worked up in the morning waiting for that phone to ring and wouldn't be able to eat breakfast until after the phone rang, and I knew what the day was going to be. I was just waiting because at 6:00 A.M. when it could ring, I'd have to wait until 8:30 to know for sure whether it's going to ring. And then on three occasions, they called me for emergencies, so I really was never sure. So, I made it a policy that if it didn't ring by 8:30, I just left and I either did volunteer work or I did something else, 'cause it was driving me crazy to wait for the phone.

T: Well, you're a very strongly motivated person to get out and do things.

J: Yeah, well, I've had to.

T: It's related to what you've said; you've decided that you're going to survive. There are a number of messes in your family.

J: Definitely. Yeah. My mother taught me from the time I was very tiny, because my sister told me not too long ago that my mother had arthritis before I was born. And before she was ever pregnant with me, they told her that she shouldn't carry another child; it would hurt her too much, she had arthritis in her back. When I was very, very small, she would be in bed in the morning, and she would tell me how to do things. I would have to go and do them and then come back to her and see if they were done correctly. Instead of having her show me, she would just tell me, and I would have to go and do them, like getting ready for school in the morning, getting breakfast, and that kind of thing. So, I had to learn how to do things independently.

Then, it got to the point where her arthritis would get worse, and she wouldn't be awake, and I wouldn't want to wake her, so I would do them all by myself, and if something new came up, I would sit down and think and see if I could figure it out so I wouldn't have to wake her up. But the older I got, the arthritis got worse and then—I don't know, something happened when I was about 8. It improved for a while, and she got out and got a job. And then we had to take on the whole thing about fixing dinner and buying food while she was out working. Then the cancer started, and she stopped work. Then she got really, really sick. Finally, because my father doesn't believe in hospitals, he insisted that she die at home, and she died at home from cancer and from all the complications from it.

T: Were you nursing her?

J: No, they wouldn't let me because I was the littlest. They had locked me out. That hurts sometimes (*crying*). They'd send me away, so I couldn't see her very much. Because she was so sick, they didn't want me to be scared, but it's scary not to know.

T: It can be harder than knowing the worst, sometimes.

J: I don't know. She finally died of dehydration, not from the cancer itself, but from what it caused.

T: I get the feeling that you never had a chance to say good-bye.

J: No. She said something once that sounded like good-bye, but they never told her she had cancer, and we knew for a while. She was smart and knew it. 'Cause she was taking cobalt treatment, and anybody would know. But (*silence*) one time she did say something that was like good-bye. But that was months before she died. But I always have to—in my own family—I have to fight for the right to be treated my own age because I'm the littlest. My father wants me to be little and protected.

The accident made her ill and a stay-at-home like her mother. Later material will show that she has an ambivalent attachment toward her father in which they each can play either role: he babies her or she nurses him. Her progressive developmental strivings were leading to a healthy separation from this bond, with external sources of potential gratifications providing the enticements that would allow her to leave her father. The accident upset this forward movement and is a variegated type of loss, as later material will show.

J: I usually win, but it's always a big hassle. Like he didn't want me to go to the funeral. I told him—I was going to a parochial school at the time—I told him they're sending 100 school-age children my age to sing at her funeral, and they're my classmates. And if my classmates can go, there's no good reason why I can't go. He was convinced and I went. Had he left me out of the funeral, I don't think I would have believed that she had died.

T: Yes, I think you were quite right to have gone.

In hope of a rapid restabilization at her most progressive level, the therapist has decided to directly support her independence. He means this support also as a counter to the undercurrent of her potential dependent transference.

J: After that, after my father married Joan; she's fabulous; she came in, and we tried to make her fit and she tried to fit. It was a strain for a while, but it all worked out really beautiful. But then Dad began to drink more and more.

T: That's something more recent then?

J: Well, I can't remember how many years they've been married. He drank heavily after my mother died. My aunt, the one who's dead now, was trying to get all the kids placed somewhere else. They wanted to take me away from my house and place me with family or in an institution or something 'cause he was drinking too badly. But we proved to her that we were old enough to run a household whether he was well or not, and we did, 'cause he couldn't do anything. He was drinking really, really bad.

And then, for a while, he sobered up, and he met Joan and he was well and healthy and doing all kinds of things. Like he's really handy around the house; he fixes everything, or he did. And it was then that she knew him when he was happy, a whole person.

But not long after the marriage, he began to go to pieces again. And a couple of years ago, her son was in Vietnam, and he had a few more months before he came home from Vietnam, and we had a long time to wait before we could see my brother. So we planned a vacation 'cause she was getting so anxious for him to get home. We would drive to Arizona and visit my brother, and by the time we got home, it would be close to the time for her son to get home.

Shortly after we left, they notified our household that her son was killed in action. My sister was the only one there, and she tried to notify us on the road and because it was a military matter, the highway patrol wouldn't help. We got all the way there, and my brother told my father on the phone and Joan collapsed, and we had to carry her

to the car. He knew she was upset; she started saying all
kinds of things against everybody.

She reports another loss. The therapist notes similarities but
cannot be sure whether they are relevant. Joan "said things against
everybody," which may be like the second man's anger. In what
follows, her father insists on sticking to the cars instead of going
with Joan. Cars are very important to him. The therapist recalls that
in the first hour, Jane spoke so proudly about taking care of the car,
putting out flares, but does not yet know what to make of all this.

J: Then we got to the base, and my father wouldn't let us aban-
     don what we were driving, which was a car with a trailer. I
     wanted to abandon the whole thing and take a jet home and
     comfort Joan, and he wouldn't let us do it. So my brother
     got an emergency leave, and we put my stepmother and
     brother on a plane, and they got to San Francisco, and they
     have lots of family and friends here to help them out. But
     then my father and I had to take the car and trailer back home.
     I knew how to drive; I had a license and I was experienced;
     more experienced than he realized because he doesn't hear
     me when I say things—he discounts what I say. But he
     wouldn't allow me to relieve him at the wheel.
T: He tried to drive it all himself?
J: He did. And finally, a gas station attendant took one look
     at him part way down and said, "Hey, you guys need a
     rest." My dad told him, "Yeah, we have to get home to
     a funeral, but I guess I do need a rest." One time, we tried
     to stop and find a motel, but we couldn't. But finally, a
     gas station attendant let us sleep in the back of the gas
     station. I could sleep, but he couldn't and he stayed so
     wound up; he was wide awake waiting for me to sleep so
     that I wouldn't fall apart. I woke up and I had to talk to
     him all the way to San Francisco 'cause I was so scared he

would fall asleep at the wheel. He wouldn't let me relieve him at all, and he knew I could drive the car even with the trailer on it, 'cause I knew how to drive a car. I knew quite well; I had driven tractors and all kinds of things before that. But when we got to San Francisco and got home, he got sick all over the place and collapsed in a big heap; he had no control over his vomiting, diarrhea, and yelling and screaming, and he just fell to pieces.

An important memory contains cars, yelling, and falling apart. This memory was reactivated by her more current accident. Note how the patient is using the hour to go through an association that she may have been warding off in her own thoughts and that would be difficult to talk through with her family members.

J: And he won't allow any doctor to ever touch him, and we didn't have anything in the house that we could calm him with, except alcohol again. And there he went again on alcohol. From there until now, he's become an alcoholic, only he won't admit it and he won't accept any help of any kind, and he won't see a physician of any kind.

Note the implication that she is partly responsible for his resuming drinking by not driving, needing sleep, and giving him alcohol.

J: But, we went to the funeral, and it turned out that my stepbrother's wife had sent him a "Dear John" letter and he had volunteered for a dangerous mission and that's how he had gotten killed. Right after the funeral, she was living with another guy and getting the money from the government for him and buying a hot rod and just running all over. Joan was so upset that the household was just in a turmoil for months and months and months. She was bitter all the time. And even today, we all know that we can't say President Johnson in front of her or she'll become upset, and we can't say Vietnam in front of her or she'll become upset, or we can't say the name of the girl he married or see anybody drive a red sports car or any of that because she's still very upset about it. When things happen to make her upset, she sits and cries about her son who's gone, because her husband died and her son's gone and he was the last one of their family.

T: So, this kind of series of events you think might contribute to your vulnerability to getting depressed when an event happens? And there's another element in it that sounds like it's very important, which is your determination to survive and get out from under.

J: Be independent, is all I want. That's the one thing my family always hesitates about, always, is for me to try something. They're always holding me back, saying, "Well, are you sure, are you sure, are you sure?" I finally get myself convinced and I'm ready and confident, and they put all the doubt back in me.

T: Yeah, but you seem very successful when you do things. Like just moving out now; it seems like it's really an important step.

The patient has been crying at times during her telling of these stories. This expression of her feelings seems to have been a positive reaction for her. The therapist offers an appointment one week off to see how things are going then, implying by inflection that he expects them to go well.

THIRD SESSION

Jane was to return for her next appointment on Monday. But she called sooner, on Friday, asking to be seen because she did not think she could get through the weekend. A brief appointment was scheduled for later the same day.

T: Well, what's up?

J: I'm getting all keyed up again.

T: Uh-huh.

J: And the thing that scared me really bad is in the pediatric ward. I've hit two patients. The first one was before; I hit an old man who kept touching me. And then it happened again this morning with a child. It's just terrible. But this kid kept picking at his burn. I couldn't get his attention because my voice keeps fading. My hearing is also shot. Doctors say I've got both eustachian tubes blocked, so when I get all frustrated and something is about to go, I overreact.

She goes on with details about the patients, crying at times and searching the therapist for his facial responses. He responds neutrally.

T: Yes.

J: And I'm physically getting myself tied up again. This morning I couldn't eat anything again (*spoken very slowly and deliberately*). I don't want to do that Saturday and Sunday and Monday. So when I left work, I decided that I'd call you and see if I could see you. The first time I saw you— after that I could eat again (*long pause*).

T: Yes. Why don't you just try and tell me whatever comes to you right now?

J: Well, I'm shaking (*there are tears in her eyes*).

T: Uh-huh; well, you're also crying, aren't you?

J: Yeah. Okay, this morning I told my doctor that I wouldn't take anything that had any depressants in it, 'cause I was scared of getting depressed again. And I have an infection, but he's treating it with antibiotics. He said, "If you won't take any depressants, will you use steam?" I've got an old vaporizer that I used to use when I'd get these things before. I'm staying at my sister's with her husband in their flat. They put me in the spare room that's going to be the nursery in January when the baby is born. It's just an old flat, but the vaporizer last night was too strong and loosened all the dirt on the wall, and this morning there was just gobs of greasy dirt dripping down on the walls, all around. That's what I woke up to. Stupid stuff that's nobody's fault; just keeps happening, but when it does—

T: Did somebody blame you for that?

J: No, they kidded me about it, but they couldn't laugh about it because I was too tied up already and they knew it.

T: Yeah.

J: And then I woke up even before I saw the walls, with some of the paint which had been doing—and once I saw them, my stomach was out of control. I took stomach medicine that I'd been taking, and I got up and got dressed and went in, and they were having breakfast. I couldn't bring myself to eat anything because I just kept feeling so rotten. After they were gone, I was sick. Then I pulled myself together. My attorney wants me to write a diary, so I wrote an entry in the diary and left for work (*silence*). That's just today. Today's worse than yesterday which is worse than the day before.

T: You have an attorney?

Litigation is always a concern because compensation can be a secondary gain for continued suffering.

J: Yes, he's on vacation this week.

T: What is he going to be doing for you?

J: He's going to handle the medical costs of my accident.

T: Uh-huh.

> *J:* But it's kind of ripped up; we don't know a lot of things yet. Because I was a substitute, we don't know if there's any way to collect compensation for loss of job.
>
> *T:* Yes (*silence*).
>
> *J:* Other things that keep bugging me is on my own ward I don't—can't think of things far enough ahead—can't plan ahead, so many things, I can see how they should go and can't make them go. Things turn my head in another direction and I can't get back fast enough.
>
> *T:* Tell me more about your reaction with your patient.

Jane then gives a detailed description of how frustrating the child patient was to care for. She does not label her affect with words, but the therapist provides the label as the transcript continues.

> *T:* You must have felt angry at him.
>
> *J:* Yeah, repeatedly angry at him. But I have to watch it because he's so destructive of himself and won't let himself heal.
>
> *T:* Yes, but right now, anger is especially hard for you to control because you're also angry at those people who. . . .
>
> *J:* Yes, angry at the nurses who won't help enough.

The patient interrupts the therapist. He had intended to link her anger to the auto accident and to the various people who had blamed and deserted her. Deciding this link is probably correct and that she is warding it off by her interruption, he persists with his intent, feeling that she will be able to tolerate this confrontation.

> *T:* Well, you're also susceptible to anger now because you haven't had a chance yet to work through and work out anger at the people who got you into the accident.
>
> *J:* Yeah. Something happened yesterday that got me started off last night. There was a continuing education thing at

the hospital. Yesterday's film was a thing on policemen and first aid. It was how a patrolman saw an accident happen and what happened after it. I really got upset during it, but I got myself all together before the lights went back on and helped clean up and everything. I've been having lunch with the ward clerk and went out to see a friend of mine in another ward and talked with her. She's going to try and help find me someplace to stay besides where I am.

But that accident flashed back on me again last night during dinner. My sister and brother-in-law had been riding in their car. They witnessed an ambulance accident and right in the middle of dinner, they were telling me about it. They didn't know it, but I couldn't take it and I just stopped eating and right then, I began to get sick. And I don't want to make my sister any more upset, so I just slipped away. They know I don't have any appetite anyway, and they weren't very upset.

Jane's intrusive episodes are now very apparent. Although intrusive signs were present before as bad dreams, the earlier interviews basically represented a denial phase. In the first interview, she was in an unstable denial state with loss of concentration, bodily symptoms, anxiety, and tension. In the second interview, the denial phase was more stable. Now, by the third interview, it appears that ideational repetition has become more prominent and is contributing to her discomfort.

T: But you didn't want them to know that their talking about the ambulance triggered the memory?

J: Yeah.

T: Were you ashamed to let them know, or you thought it would hurt their feelings?

J: No, my sister is pregnant with her first child, and we were very, very scared that she would lose it and she wouldn't let us tell anybody for weeks. She's just—I don't want to upset her that much either, because she was upset already about it, worrying about it.

T: Yeah. But last night they were talking about this ambulance, and then you began—

J: Thinking about the morning I reacted in my own accident. And then I stopped eating and (*silence*) and later—

T: And you were feeling frightened when this happened?

J: Yeah.

T: In fact, very frightened.

J: But I couldn't really say anything because I was also afraid to get her upset.

T: Yes (*silence*). Well, that may have been a trigger to your reaction today, you know.

J: It acted like a trigger.

T: Do you know that this is the sort of thing that happens after accidents?

J: I figured it would, but I never heard it said.

T: Yes. People often go through a period when they put things out of mind. Then they come back, especially if there is something that hasn't been worked through about it. For you, there are a number of things that haven't been worked through. You're frightened. Even though you don't rationally think so, part of your mind thinks that it might just happen again.

This is essentially a supportive remark aimed at reducing her fear of her symptoms and at sharing an understanding of what is going on.

J: Well, it was the kind of accident that could happen again and again because, I was saying, that it was the other man's fault, and I had no way to get out of the way. But I have to commute now because—the only arrangement I had be-

fore was riding with my sister-in-law, and I reached the
breaking point with that. I can't ride with her anymore
because I get just as scared watching her drive as not going
at all. I'm better when I'm in control of the car.

T: Yes, I'm not surprised to hear that.

J: But even like coming over here. A couple of times I
checked the mirrors and ahead in merging traffic, and I look,
and there's somebody too close behind me, and I have no
idea how they can get that close unless they're coming up
too fast, which is what happened before.

T: Yes, so there is this constant expectancy below the surface
that is frightening you. And the other thing I think that
will need some working on is your anger. You feel very
bad about having it, and you're trying to do things, like
with your sister, by not even letting her know that this
reminded you of your accident.

J: That's why I want to stay with somebody else besides her.

T: Are you sure she's so delicate?

This is an indirect challenge directed against what the therapist intuits is her own defective or vulnerable self-image. The remark, at an unconscious level, may be received as "maybe you are
not so delicate and can see yourself once again as a capable, grown-
up woman."

J: Well, she was a few months ago, and she tells me she's not
now. But it's hard to believe.

T: Well, for her to know what you're going through might
not injure her in any way. You might just let her know
what you're going through.

A therapist ordinarily does not give direct suggestions, even
in brief therapy. But in this instance he does, because he believes
that less inhibited communication with her sister may help her to

work through the meanings of the accident more rapidly. As with his previous statement about the delicacy of her sister, this comment has an indirect meaning: "You can take knowing what is going on, and it will also be all right to let others know how you have responded."

> J: The thing is that she's a personnel worker for the phone company, and she's getting people like me all the time and she's always saying she works because she has to. I don't want her to be pressured at home, too. But she really should stay out of that job; it's not doing her any good.
>
> T: Well, we have to stop now. We can continue on Monday at the time we scheduled. So see you then.
>
> J: Okay, at 3:00 o'clock.

FOURTH SESSION

Jane reported feeling gradually better over the weekend, but she was still shaky and awoke early. At the beginning of the hour, she and the therapist again reviewed her reaction to the movie on accidents and her intrusive thoughts about her own accident. She then talked about wanting to avoid discussing the accident because she was afraid that if she did get into it again, she would become upset and not do well at work. The therapist was inclined to deal directly with the accident memory. He wanted to work the memory through to the point that she would not be upset by reminders. The hour proceeded with the following discussion of whether or not to focus further on the accident:

> T: Yes, that's the decision we have to make now. Should we do that [not dwell on it now], while you try and get through, or—sooner or later, I think it has to be talked out.
>
> J: I know it does, because it scares me when it happens.

> *T:* Yes. So I think your intuition might be best. My intuition doesn't say for sure, so let's go on yours. You decide whether we talk about it now or make another appointment and talk more about it.
>
> *J:* It's kind of weird because it's hanging over my head if I don't do it. And then I might just start thinking that way and go round and round again.
>
> *T:* Well, I wonder if you're not in enough control so that we could do a little bit, kind of a small dose, and then just stop.
>
> *J:* Okay.
>
> *T:* Want to try that? Let's say you can stop any time you want.
>
> *J:* Okay.
>
> *T:* Okay? So I'd like you to do this feeling as relaxed in your body as you can. Why don't you try and just see if you can't really relax yourself, okay? Then we can spend a little time talking about it.

The suggestion to relax is used because the therapist believes it will be helpful with this particular person. Other patients tense up with a directive to relax. The implication is that she will be able to talk about the accident with the therapist without getting too frightened. In what follows, the therapist continues talking until he feels the patient is in a mental set in which she can recall and yet retain a sense of control.

> *T:* Okay. Here's what we're going to do and all we're going to do. We're going to go back to the accident and have you remember a little bit of it and just see what springs to mind from it, and perhaps it will be something that will make you reexperience some of those emotions. As it happens, you'll try and keep relaxing, and we'll try and talk about the ideas and feelings as they come to you. You'll try and keep putting the feelings into words, and I'll try and understand them as best I can. We don't have to do a

big chunk of it today; we can do a portion. That way, you'll learn it's safe. I think it might help to put it all in your control, keeping it from coming back when you don't want it to. Does it seem reasonable to you? Any questions? Okay, let's just go back to the accident. One thing that struck me about it was that man who came out yelling at you.

J: Yeah, he was the second guy.

T: Yes, I thought maybe that was upsetting you, especially upsetting. Was that so?

J: I could feel myself just going out of awareness when he was doing it. I mean, just slipping into shock or whatever it is; just the more he yelled, the farther away from him I got until I finally just yelled at him, "You're not leaving the scene of this accident until I get your name!" So he threw his license at me and left anyway. But that was a long, long time because that collision was a half hour after the first collision.

T: Now, try and just go back and remember what he said, and let's just see what comes to you.

J: His thing was how he had appointments to keep, and I couldn't hear a lot of it. He sees the wreck and yelled and screamed, and then he turned to us. But to us, he just says, "I have to go find a phone as fast as I can." And it turned out that he was in very much the same situation as I was in: he works in a hospital the same as I.

T: He was going to work?

J: Uh-huh. He wasn't a nurse, he was a student lab technician. But it's hardly any different. He had the same need to be on time that I had. But then he stomped away from the scene, and I don't even know where he went because you couldn't see in the fog. I was mad because I had stuck to the scene of the accident, and I wanted to see a doctor because my back was hurting, and he stomped away right away! We had the policeman; we could have settled it, and I could have been on my way if he had stuck around. And I was standing around shaking and hurting, and he was gone.

T: And what's this; he threw the license—

J: Threw it at me.

T: At you?

J: Because I was the one that protested.

T: And where did it hit you?

J: I think I caught it.

T: And then what happened to his license? He drove off without his license?

J: No, he couldn't drive his car; his car was demolished. He walked away fast from the scene, but you couldn't see more than twenty feet in the fog, and he went to a phone, which I should have done long before that. But since my neck hurt and I knew I was numb every place else, I was afraid to walk as far as it was to a phone. I didn't know how badly I was hurt.

T: And you never saw him again?

J: No, he came back. In fact, a few minutes later, the policeman had his report and stuff together. I got confused then, and I gave him the other man's license instead of my own because he wanted a license. And then I left to phone Zone City to tell them I couldn't come. By then, they had already talked to me about an ambulance, and I told them I didn't think I needed one. So I called my brother-in-law to come and take me to a doctor.

T: But this other man came back?

J: Well, I missed him somehow. I'm not sure if he came back by the time I came back.

T: And did you have any more to do with him?

J: Yeah. We climbed into the back of a patrol car to fill out all the forms because it was really cold and he kept borrowing pens and being obnoxious to everybody. He had to ask his questions whether you were in the middle of saying something or not, and this kind of thing. I was the last one to finish the report because I had the two collisions to report.

T: How was he obnoxious to you?

J: It was just his general attitude, I would suppose. His standard behavior. Instead of asking for anything politely, he would just demand it. Like if another officer asked a question about the tow cars—I called for a 3-A truck because I know 3-A's come faster and I'm personally in 3-A, even though my Dad's not. So they had three different trucking companies, two trucking companies coming. A tow truck arrived, and he assumed automatically that it was his. And I listened and understood that it had to be mine. But he butted in already, and I couldn't outspeak him; I had to wait until he was finished and then explain it to them that it was my tow truck. Every time there was a question, he was right there for himself.

T: So you feel he was being selfish?

J: Yeah.

T: And his selfishness was hurting you worse.

J: This was the wrong time to be selfish. He should have been—like the police officers; there were two of them there, let them direct it. And before that, when they weren't there and they weren't in charge, he didn't take any effort to lead it, you know, like direct the traffic or put out the flares or that kind of thing. But when somebody else was there, he would compete with them—just standing in our way.

T: So, he was obstructing your getting help?

J: I wanted to get out of there as fast as I could and find out why my neck hurt so bad.

T: Let's try and go back then. We know a lot more about your neck now than then, but let's go back then; let's see if we can reconstruct your thoughts about your neck.

J: Right after the collision, I was numb and in a few seconds, the only feeling I had was my neck on the right side and in my shoulder. And it hurt; I couldn't feel anything else at all. Then the driver in front came back 'cause he could see I was just dazed and looked straight ahead. He had seen through his mirror my car hit. He came back and said, "Are you okay?" And I said, "No." He said, "How bad?" I said, "I think it's only my neck, but I'm not sure." Then I waited and I could tell that the rest of me was okay. I felt okay.

T: What thoughts were going through your mind?

J: Well, I know that if you're hurt and you get into shock far enough, you can be badly hurt and not know it and walk around with it. That's what was going on in my mind. It just feels like my neck, but I'm not sure.

T: So you were thinking that you might be badly hurt and you might not know it, and you might walk around and hurt yourself more.

J: Uh-huh. But then, I looked at the situation and I thought if I don't move this car from where it is right now, somebody is bound to collide into it again. So I got out of the car anyway and got into the back of the car and gave them some flares to pass out. Then I looked at the situation and said to the other man that I think we'd better move our cars because we're at the top of a grade by a red light on a really foggy morning and it's going to be a ten-car pileup if we don't. So I moved into a safety zone near an island, and he moved all the way off to the shoulder. I left my car running with the lights on so that people could see it.

T: Could we go just a little way in your imagination and imagine what didn't happen, but what you might have thought might happen? Which would be that you would walk around and your neck would get hurt worse. Just imagine—

J: My neck or my back?

T: Yeah, imagine that. What would you imagine would happen?

J: Well, I've had back trouble before, and when it got bad enough, I was told not to move until it relaxed. And I would imagine that I would get paralyzed.

T: Where would you be paralyzed?

Because of the patient's neck pain, other somatic complaints, and her mother's severe illnesses, the therapist wishes to explore for cognitive elements of somatic localization that occurred at the time of the accident.

J: I don't know.

T: Your legs?

J: Well, before it would have been my legs, but I don't know about this one.

T: What was the back trouble before?

J: I have one leg shorter than the other, and I repeatedly strained muscles because of the imbalance, so it's been different muscles getting strained. One time I did it real good, strained it on the job and had to stay still for a while until it eased up.

T: And if you didn't, you might get paralyzed?

J: No, just that it would stay, the pain.

T: The paralyzed idea was during the accident?

J: Yeah.

T: Okay. Any other thoughts about your body, anything you can remember? Try and go back in your mind to the accident.

J: Well, after the accident, after the first collision when we were waiting, we were sitting in his car, I got double vision. But that's not unusual for me; I have a muscle problem in my left eye. I wondered about it, because I didn't think my head had gotten hurt.

T: But it might mean that you had a head injury?

J: Right.

T: At least, that was your thought then?

J: Yeah, but I get double vision under stress, no matter what's causing it. Can't think of anything else.

T: So, you were worried then that you might be—your back might be broken or something and you might get paralyzed if you moved. And then you were running around putting out flares.

J: Well, nobody else would do this kind of thing; nobody else was thinking. You know, I'd ask a question, and there wouldn't be a response because they couldn't think of an answer for it.

T: Well, maybe you felt that they were fools. You had to risk yourself because they were so foolish.

From listening to her vocal intonations, the therapist has a growing conviction that she is struggling between impulses to express rage and a need to inhibit such expressions. He is attempting to provoke a clear expression of ideas that might lead to anger as well as ideas that might be threatening, were she fully aware of them. At this point he is trying out certain labels with her and, more importantly, encouraging continued expression by actively receiving her communications and not being critical. In a sense, he has just said, "It would be all right with me if at the time of the accident you thought the people around you were fools or were afraid they would think you were a fool. I'd like you to freely tell me that sort of thing, even if you feel badly about it." As it happens, the label of fool does not exactly hit on a central ideational complex, but the feedback from the therapist sets up a dialogue that promotes fuller expression.

J: Well, I had to save myself anyway, because they weren't going to move their car, his car. Nobody else wanted to—

like—like direct the trucks that were bearing down. You know, I said, "Well listen, I've got a flashlight in the glove box with a red cap on it; if you swing it, they can see it and get around us." Nobody wanted to do it and my arm was stiffening up and I was about to stand out and do it because I—

T: What do you mean, "no one wanted to do it." Who was that?

J: Well, the man in front of us who had stopped and the man who had hit me.

T: Why didn't they want to do it?

J: One man was ready to leave for work because he said nobody is really badly hurt. And the man behind me had to leave to telephone his place of business to tell them he wouldn't be coming in. And nobody was around who wasn't busy.

T: So you were just left. Were you all alone?

J: Yeah. I was sitting in the car of the man that hit me because his was in a better position by then.

T: So you were kind of left alone with no one to take care of you?

J: Yeah, but then I could sit up straight and I knew that if I didn't do anything, nothing horrible was going to happen to me like that.

T: Did you feel it was unfair, though?

J: Yeah, and I asked him to make a phone call for me and he came back and said, "Oh, I forgot."

T: He forgot?

J: Yeah.

T: That must have made you angry.

J: I don't know if I felt angry. I felt like desperate—like how can I make that dumb phone call.

T: Yeah, but you'd been left out again. Do you remember that moment, when he came back and said he forgot?

J: Kind of; he was back in the car again.

T: Now you seem pretty relaxed talking about all of this. Any side thoughts?

J: No.

T: How are you feeling right now?

J: A little bit tense.

T: A bit tense? Where is the tension?

J: It's all over.

T: Yeah, describe it, though.

J: I wouldn't know how.

T: Is it in your muscles?

J: Yeah.

T: Do your muscles feel tight? Okay, try and relax them. Does my asking you about it make you more nervous?

J: About relaxing?

T: Yeah.

J: Well, it's just that that's the one thing that everybody is telling me to do.

T: Everyone tells you to relax?

J: Yeah. You can't exactly do it without knowing how.

T: Have you ever learned how?

J: I don't know. I guess I did a little bit. I used to take yoga for a while, but I can't relax myself when my mind isn't relaxed.

T: Well, let's see if we can find where the tension is in your mind right now. What are you doing now? What are you paying attention to?

J: The back of my head.

T: Uh-huh (*long silence*). Well, one way to find out about such tension, for us to use right here, would be for you to say whatever comes to your mind now.

J: I'm getting scared; I'm not wanting to talk anymore.

T: Yes. What would happen if you were to go on talking? Do you think you'd get more scared?

J: I don't know. This is the same way I feel when I wake up, feeling sick.

T: Uh-huh. Is it a scare that something is going to happen?

J: I think it's more that something is not going to happen that should happen.

T: Uh-huh. That would mean that there'd be no help for you?

J: Yeah.

T: Okay. What do you think should happen?

J: I don't know.

T: You know, the idea of no help for you runs through a lot of this. Nobody being able to help you; your family not being a help to you; the other drivers not helping you; maybe my not helping you.

This labeling of her sense of not being helped seems to make her feel safer, and she continues with considerable additional material, without responses from the therapist.

J: Something else: When I made the phone call, a male operator came on the line, and I didn't recognize the voice as an operator's and I thought it was Bob, which is my brother-in-law, and so I spoke to him as if he were, and then we figured each other out. We were both mixed up. He took the message wrong, too. Then I told him the number, and he connected me so fast that I didn't recognize the change in voice. And so when Bob answered, my message was all confused. I know it made him upset, but the more I said anything, the more confused I got and I couldn't get it straight.

So, it turns out that after he had hung up, he didn't know how badly I was hurt, so he called my sister at work, and all he told her was that Jane's been in an accident and I'm going to pick her up. I'll call you later.

After the accident when we were trying to arrange a doctor and stuff, he told me about it, about her being notified. And I said, "Aren't you going to call her back?" He said, "No, we'll wait and see how you are." When I got to the doctor's office, he had two other emergencies ahead of me, and so I waited in the waiting room for an hour and a half and then I waited in an examining room for fifteen minutes, and then when he saw me, he sent me to X-ray. The doctor in charge of X-ray had to look at the X-rays that were taken.

And it wasn't until after all of that, that my brother-in-law told my sister. She had been sitting there all morning not knowing, just knowing that I was in an accident. That bothers me because there have been other accidents in the family. There was one when my stepbrother died in Vietnam and my sister was the only person in San Francisco, so when the call came through, she knew and we were on our way to Arizona. Nobody would notify us because it was a military matter, and the highway patrol wouldn't stop us so we had to get all the way there where my brother was and he had to tell us. It was just her sitting there again, waiting and not knowing.

T: So that happened to her with your accident.

J: Yeah.

T: That's upsetting for your sister?

J: It's upsetting for both of us because after that I was in Arizona with my father and we put everybody else on a jet; my brother got emergency leave, and my father refused to let the car sit and go back with his wife. He insisted that we drive back to San Francisco. And I had a driver's license and was perfectly capable of driving, but because there was a trailer on the car, he didn't trust my driving and he wouldn't allow me to drive.

Here is a retelling of the story of the trip with her father, discussed in an earlier interview. The timing in this hour and her general demeanor indicate the importance of her father in the associations to the accident.

J: So for the whole trip back, I really was tired and very, very worried, so I kept tuning in radio stations and talking so that he wouldn't fall asleep. And he wouldn't pull over and he wouldn't rest until finally I convinced him that we needed to stop, and we stopped in a town full of motels and all of them were closed for the night. So we had to go on or sleep at the side of the road and he refused to do that. Finally, a gas station attendant let us sleep in the back of the station, but he didn't sleep all night; he only did it for me, and I barely slept and then had to get up again.

T: How do you know he didn't sleep?

J: He told me he didn't and he'd been sick. He had vomited all over the trailer. He told me he hadn't slept at all. I told him I was in better shape to drive, but he wouldn't let me.

T: That still bothers you?

J: (*indignantly*) He still doesn't believe I can drive. He won't ride in the car if I'm driving.

Here is an important meaning of her accident. Her father has criticized her driving. Right after the first collision, one association would be something like "Oh, no, my father will say this is all my fault!" This thought would already be on her mind when the second collision occurred and the driver of that car angrily screamed at her. In a larger sense, she anticipates that her accident will give her father reason to say that not only can she not drive well, but also she is not an effective, grown-up woman and must remain his dependent and subordinate little girl. She anticipates his rage and depreciation of her. Responding to this prophecy, she is hurt by him and angry at him. The various rejections and desertions she experiences from other persons involved in the accident and its aftermath serve to justify these feelings. Frustration, sorrow, and anger are also activated by the disruption in her life plan.

Rage at her father cannot be expressed or experienced directly because that would make her feel guilty. She already feels bad at not having rescued her father from his alcoholism relapse after the long drive following her stepbrother's death. This is part of a general ambivalent attachment to her father. Though these formulations are oversimplified and incomplete, they represent the therapist's working hypotheses at this point in therapy. He follows her statement with an exploratory question relating her father to the recent accident.

> T: He thought that if you drove, you might have an accident?
> J: Uh-huh. Any car that I've bought, he's never stepped foot in.
> T: And now you've had an accident.
> J: Uh-huh.
> T: Maybe you were worried right at the accident about what your father would say. There you'd gone and had an accident, even if it wasn't your fault at all.
> J: Yeah! Later that day, I let my brother tell my father; I didn't want to tell him.
> T: Why didn't you?
> J: Because if I talked to him on the phone, we don't get along very well at all; but if I talked to him on the phone, I would probably get upset enough for him to worry that I was hurt more than I was—just because it's so hard. He doesn't usually hear my voice; he's deaf in one ear and hard of hearing in the other one. He usually—I either shout or he reads my lips. And on the phone, it's impossible with two of us, but it's always a strain for me to talk to him. But on this occasion, I just said, I can't do it at all. Somebody else has to do it.

Her initial response here is probably partly defensive in function. Other evidence suggests that she was primarily afraid of her father raging at her. But she seems to undo that fear by saying that he will worry unduly about her: "I would probably get upset enough for him to worry that I was hurt." This also suggests another defensive operation. If people present signs of physical harm, then one shows concern and does not blame them. She goes on to imply a complaint about her father's neglect: "He doesn't usually hear my voice." After these remarks about her father, she then expresses her own anxiety over confrontation with him: "It's always a strain. . . . I just said I can't do it." The therapist chooses to focus on this self-experience.

T: Were you concerned about what your father would say?
J: Well, I didn't want him to come walking home from the bus stop and see the car all smashed up.
T: Yes, what would he have thought if he had seen the car all smashed up?
J: He would have wondered where in the world I was, what had happened.

Once again, she presents a worried and concerned image of her father rather than that of the enraged accuser. She continues along this line.

J: I didn't think he should do that. I would rather that he be told on the phone than when he comes home—
T: Well, he would think that you'd been in an accident.
J: Yeah. Well, one time before, I messed up the front end of a car, and he went on for hours about "why didn't you tell me." So I knew I had to tell him, otherwise we'd go through that again.

Here is the associative meaning to the man yelling angrily at her. The important and, as yet, undisclosed detail that the car damaged in the current accident belonged to her father follows after the therapist clarifies that the car she dented earlier also belonged to her father.

> *T:* Was that his car?
>
> *J:* Yeah, these were both his cars. Because I had sold my car a few months ago.
>
> *T:* Oh, so this was his car in the accident?
>
> *J:* Yeah.
>
> *T:* And the new car you bought was going to be yours?
>
> *J:* Uh-huh (*very softly*). I sold my car when it started giving me trouble.
>
> *T:* Yes. So maybe you felt badly that it was your father's car that was damaged.
>
> *J:* Yeah. We never agree on that car anyway. He won't keep it up (*very angry*)! He won't, like, put the tires on soon enough when they're wearing out or get stuff done that needs being done. It's always run down. And like he rebuilt the engine and put it back in; he didn't put the transmission back in straight so when you start it, you have to know how to force it into drive to get it started. I usually get frustrated with the engine; you have to sit and wait and then get it started. I am—every time I get into the car, I'd get mad if I couldn't happen to get it started right away because of the way he fixed it; only halfway.
>
> *T:* Yeah.
>
> *J:* He did that to the exhaust system, too. It sounded horrible to drive. They'd give you three clamps; he'd put one clamp on and put the tailpipe on, and it would rattle all over the place. It'd get a hole in it and was worn out.
>
> *T:* Yeah, he really didn't take very good care of the car.
>
> *J:* He took as little care as he could. He insisted that no work be done that needed being paid for. He had to do the work.
>
> *T:* But then he bawled you out when you got in an accident?
>
> *J:* Yeah.

T: What did he say to you that other time?

J: That was the car before this. That was my fault because I had a sinus infection and was all run down.

Once again, physical illness is presented as a way to avert blame.

J: I had a choice of public transportation and getting on the medicine and not being able to drive 'cause it makes me drowsy. So, I decided to drive and not take the medicine, but I got too tired anyway and I missed a turn in the parking lot and hit a cement wall at a low speed and punched in the front end on one side. So we all knew it was all my fault, but he refused to accuse anybody. He just went wandering around junkyards trying to find a replacement for the front end of the car, and he never found one.

T: Huh. What did he say to you though?

J: Well, by the time that he saw me, I was upset enough and my face was swollen enough that he didn't want to say anything. I loosened my front teeth, and I couldn't talk by the time he saw me, 'cause my whole face was swollen.

T: But he was angry?

J: He didn't show anger or anything; he just stomps away and gets a drink because he's an alcoholic, but he doesn't say anything.

It is possibly relevant that she uses the same word, *stomping*, to describe her father as she did to describe the driver of the second car that hit her car, because this accident is a repetition of the earlier accident. Because she is physically hurt, she does not receive the direct brunt of her father's anger but, instead, is made to feel guilty that she has hurt him and caused his drinking.

T: But did you feel worried about how he would react before he reacted?

J: Yeah.

T: Were you very concerned in your mind?

J: But then he doesn't really react; he runs away from it.

T: But beforehand, you were worrying about how he would react?

The therapist is holding here to the topic and trying to clarify her feelings about her father's potential or actual anger at her.

J: Yeah.

T: I wonder if you had any thoughts about your father right during this current accident?

J: I don't remember thinking about him. I do remember thinking, "Well, at least this car is gone now; nobody can drive it; he'll be forced to get rid of it." And it turns out he's not; he's taking money for it and says he's going to put it back together again. Since then, when we got it home, he made me drive it one afternoon. I told him that the doctor told me to leave the collar on and if I needed to drive, to only go a short distance and take the collar off to drive so I'd be able to turn my head. I said I didn't feel like turning my head enough to drive that day, but he insisted.

She is talking about how her father hurts her. The role-relationship model is that of one person hurting another, and she can place herself in either position. She is afraid both of her accusations that he hurts her and of the possibility that he will accuse her of hurting him. Her communication is devoted to obtaining a verdict from the therapist that she is "not guilty," has been hurt more than enough, and deserves tender attention. She may also want the therapist to be angry at her father. This would be anger on her behalf, and she could avoid guilt. She continues with evidence that her father gave her a bad car.

J: So I drove it and I'd been complaining about the car down-shifting suddenly on hills 'cause the transmission still needed work. It took a really good hill to do it, and there weren't any near the house, so I took it to the best hill nearby and it didn't do it. He still doesn't believe me, and he's not going to work on that part of it. But what used to happen was if I took it to work in Zone City, it doesn't have enough speed to make merging easy, so I would go wandering freeway to freeway in a way that I wouldn't need to merge so much. I would get onto highways that weren't freeways. And one of them was Pickwood Drive, which is really steep, and up near the top of it, the car would downshift suddenly and then shift back up and just jerk really, really bad. He had never experienced it because he doesn't drive at all like I drive. I kept telling him that it would happen and that it needed something so that it wouldn't happen, but he wouldn't fix it. So that's why he wanted me to drive it. He said there's nothing wrong with the car. The whole tail end of the car now is out of alignment; it doesn't even travel on a straight line anymore, but according to him, there's nothing wrong with the car anymore. He's going to drive it that way.

But every time his job makes him travel, because his job changes, he takes the other car.

Throughout these sections, she is expressing anger at her father, as shown by her tone of voice and her nonverbal communications.

T: Which other car, the new one?
J: There's another car that he owns.
T: He owns two, a better one and this clunkier one?
J: Yeah.
T: And you got to drive the clunkier one?
J: I was not allowed to drive the better one.
T: Why not?

J: He didn't want me to.

T: He wasn't using it at the time; he was taking the bus.

J: That's right.

T: So why doesn't he want you to use it? Is the idea that you'd get in an accident?

J: I'll do something to it. I'll scratch it in a parking lot or whatever. That one was special; this one is the one that I was allowed to use. It was the one I had driven before that, anyway.

T: But you resented it.

J: I hate that car to begin with! And every time I had car trouble, they'd tell me it's just because you don't like the car and are not willing to put up with it. I said, "Why can't you get me in the situation where I can get another car and I could put up with that." Like I'd wear the battery out trying to start it, and I couldn't keep the transmission in drive long enough to get it started.

T: Okay; well, it seems to me that we were able to talk about the accident, and it wasn't too dangerous to talk about here, so we might go on and schedule another appointment to do that a little bit more.

J: Okay.

T: Does it seem reasonable to you to do that?

J: Yeah.

T: Okay. How about next Monday at this time?

J: I can make it any time; I'm out of work by then. My job ends Friday.

T: Okay, let's make it 3:00 next Monday.

FIFTH SESSION

During the fifth session, Jane indicated that she felt she was back to normal. Her physical symptoms were much improved. She was sleeping and eating well and no longer felt tense and anxious. She did not have intrusive episodes or moments of intense irritability, though she still had some pain in her neck and in her hip joints. She felt that things were going smoothly for her. Three topics occupied the session: her relationships with her father, her mother, and her therapist.

During the week she had begun a dispute with her father that, because of her assertiveness, was resolved to the satisfaction of both of them. Her father wanted her to sign a release so that the payment for damage to his car could be obtained from the insurance company of the other driver. She refused to do this, pointing out that the medical liability was as yet undetermined. She consulted her attorney, who backed up her position. Her father became pleased that someone more responsible than he or she was looking into it. She felt relief at living out of the house, as her father drank heavily during their discussions. She had resolved her guilt feelings over living with her sister by making maternity clothes for her.

The therapist felt that the restoration of Jane's equilibrium was the result of many factors. Time had passed; there had been some working through in the therapy; and with this, her improvement might have been motivated by a desire to reduce the need to explore the relationship with her father. The presence of unresolved conflicts and ambivalent attachments would not, however, indicate the continuation of a brief therapy aimed at restoring a balance disrupted by a stressful life event. She had moved out of her home environment and was continuing her work; she could pursue her life plan. The therapist continued the interview by asking about the status of memories about the accident in order to see whether there were further intrusive episodes. This would be an additional sector of information relevant to a decision about termination.

T: Any memories come to you about the accident?
J: Today's weather reminds me of it: looks the same.

T: But have there been any other events, like the conversation with your sister that triggered it?

J: No. I've been feeling people being more sympathetic because—even though, like I've had to miss some days at the hospital; one of the other aides came up to me and said that her mother had had the same thing. Only she said that her mother had to have special shoes made, and I kind of smiled and said, "I'm wearing special shoes, too." Other things—we had a ward party and people came and talked to me and stuff.

She went on to talk of how her body was feeling better, though she was afraid that any tension might make her stiffen up again. The therapist offered a kind of summing up of one aspect of what had happened:

T: One of the psychological problems for you was that the accident let you know in a way that your body was vulnerable to injury. When you didn't get better rapidly, you got frightened that your body was even more vulnerable.

J: It made me think of something. My mother used to have arthritis in her back and stay in bed in the mornings. I found myself doing the same thing, just like her. I was staying in bed because it was the most comfortable place to be. I didn't want to get up and move and walk around. I just kept thinking of all the things I was doing then and that she was doing that when she hurt from arthritis in her back.

T: Yes. She kept on going also?

As before, this is an implicit encouragement and support of her attempt at independence.

J: Yeah, until she had cancer and she died of cancer.

The therapist believes that one function of this remark is to test him for a transference potential. If he feels sorry for her and gives her attention for being sick, then she may be tempted to adopt that role more durably in order to obtain the gratification of sympathy. The therapist believes Jane is indirectly asking whether she really has to get better. He wants to give her the support of saying "yes," which he does with a repetition of the same type of remark he made when he said, "She kept on going."

> T: So you feel kind of brave at times?
> J: Sometimes, but sometimes I feel dreadful because I know, uh—she used to send us away when she was feeling bad so that she could rest. I can't send my responsibilities away.
> T: Okay. Now, have you had any other thoughts, you know, since we talked a week ago, about getting upset because of the accident? Have any other explanations for that occurred to you?
> J: I think it was a huge disappointment that stopped me from everything I was trying to do. It was at a time when I was trying to plan moving out of the house and getting a permanent job and just changing everything around me. And all of a sudden, I was frozen where I didn't want to be.

The remaining part of the hour dealt with the idea of termination and the possibility of a transfer to long-term therapy if she wished to explore further her vulnerability to depressions after losses and/or dependency–independency issues of personality. Because she did not express feelings about the separation other than gratitude, the therapist asked her directly:

> T: Well, maybe you'll be sad not to see me anymore?
> J: I think so (*pause*). Yeah (*pause*). That's been happening this month to everyone I'm around, though. Well, one friend

who took me out to dinner really doesn't want to see me. It's happening all around me. I'm beginning to get used to it. The patients, you get to know them and they leave. It's okay.

She later entered a personality-development type of psychotherapy and continued to see another therapist for forty sessions. By the onset of that therapy, she had essentially recovered from all symptoms related to the immediate stress event. The physical symptoms that had gone into remission remained absent. The residual pains in neck and hips improved by the end of one month. An exception to this marked improvement was continued difficulty with her eyes, a symptom corrected by a new prescription for glasses. The central issue of the therapy was loss and neglect with the attendant fear of not getting enough care in her relationships with other people, though she kept her angry reactions to frustrations in tight check. These themes were worked on in regard to medical treatment for the eye symptoms, legal manipulations to recover medical costs after the accident, relationships with her family members, and the transference.

DISCUSSION

Had it not been for the accident, Jane may have continued her progress toward independence. By establishing social and professional ties, she may have been able to continue her development throughout her young adulthood. If not beset by stress and the disruption of interpersonal relationships due to her neurotic potential, she probably would not have sought treatment. At a crucial time, however, the accident activated unresolved conflicts about her own bodily integrity, degree of dependency, and the validity of what might be called her character trait of excessive "self-righteousness."

Her concept of bodily integrity was related to her mother and other relatives who had severe bodily misfortunes. She herself had a slight leg deformity and a tendency, when stressed, to a disruption in optic focusing that was also apparently based on a mild congenital anomaly. She was the baby of the family and was raised during a period when her mother was an invalid. Thus, she had a special vulnerability to feeling a defective identity and body image. The physical trauma and fears of even greater injury forced on her awareness by the accident reinforced her defective self-concept as it conflicted with more recently developing womanly and intact self-concepts. Such an accident threatens the sense of invulnerability of all persons, but Jane had a less stable adult self-organization to use to master this threat. Working it through on her own was impossible, and the therapist supported her more competent self-concepts by encouraging her continued efforts to work and cope.

The ambivalent ties with her father were rapidly conceptualized by the therapist in establishing a formulation and plan for the therapy. This rapidity carries more risks of error than do the more temperate inferences possible in a long-term therapy in which more associations, memories, and fantasies are gradually accumulated. Basically, it seemed as if a variety of factors had combined to develop and emphasize a self-schema as "hurt, little, and in need," one that conflicted with her developmental progress toward a more mature self-concept.

Jane's mother had been too ill to provide complete maternal care or even a stable identity model. She might have turned to her father for love. She conceptualized herself as "little and in need" and her father as taking care of her. But at times, she probably felt insufficiently cared for and had a role-relationship model in which she was "little and in need" and her father was neglectful. Rage at her father stemmed from this latter version.

Because of such rage, she also developed a role-relationship model of herself as destructive in her relationship with her father. In conflict with her ideals and morals, this role relationship generated a tendency to feel guilty if she were placed in the role of hurting her father. To avoid guilt, to gain the stronger role for herself, and quite likely also to replace her mother, she often conceptualized herself in the caretaking role and her father in the role of being in need. Later material supported these formulations. Her father turned to her for care at various times, but he also rejected her when she assumed a caretaking role. During her adolescence, he fostered her regression to a preadolescent stage of life and rejected her efforts to care for him. He belittled her attempts at this and, in general, undermined her efforts to gain a sense of womanly competency.

The accident heightened the ambivalence between them. "Cars" and "accidents" were already part of this as a theme because of the previous dented fender, the long, traumatic drive he refused to share with her, and his reluctance to let her drive the "good" car. As soon as the accident happened, she knew that blame would enter the picture. Her father would blame her and she would blame him for blaming her and for giving her a bad car. The second man, who yelled angrily at her, became a symbolic father image for her and gave the ambivalent role fantasy a terrifying reality.

The accident thus became an event that produced fear over her bodily integrity, rage and sorrow over the loss of her plans for independence, and anger and guilt, entangled with a wish to remain attached to her father. Perhaps the most important conflict was that of dependency and independency wishes. The bodily symptoms gave her an excuse to resume dependency and yet led to the frustration of not being taken care of properly. The bodily symptoms also could punish her for her aggressive feelings toward her family. Working through the stress event meant processing these themes. She had to reassure herself, by reexamining the current reality, that her body could still work and was not under continuing threat. She had to consider the possibilities for resumed dependencies and ties to her father (or father substitutes such as her doctor) and reject them. She had to reexamine her work and living situation and continue toward independence. She had to evaluate the accident and decide that it was just an accident, that the angry man was just a nasty stranger who behaved badly, and that it was over.

The therapist fostered this working-through process by providing support while encouraging continued efforts toward independence. The various themes were not interpreted at a deeper level. Rather, there was an effort to process the details and immediate associations to the accident so that reality could be clarified and separated from fantasy elaborations. The major theme of dependency–independency surfaced in the transference as a tension between an "I don't want any help; I can do it myself" attitude, presented largely through her resistant demeanor, and a subsurface clamor for excessive worry and concern by the therapist. This was countered with a steady insistence on working on the immediate meanings of the stress event. That is, the therapist did not appear worried about the patient, guilt driven by her remaining symptoms, or neglectful in offering her help and sympathy.

SUMMARY

Jane drove her father's second, poorly cared-for car to a job that she hoped would enable her to gain her independence. She was rear-ended on a foggy day. The man who drove into her was so polite that she could not be angry with him, but a second car piled into her already-damaged vehicle as it stood by the roadside. That driver, a man, exploded angrily at her. This seemed to induce a dissociative state of shock. Later she had difficulty obtaining medical attention. She then felt that her family neglected her by turning a postaccident visit (to check up on her) into a party that ignored her condition.

She developed a progressively debilitating syndrome combining somatic and psychological signs and symptoms. She had neck and hip pains, eye difficulties, nausea, upper respiratory infections, and sleep disturbances. She was also affected by dazedness, difficulty concentrating, irritability, intrusive and repetitive thoughts, and episodes of anxiety. Her brief psychotherapy began when she was in an unstably defended denial phase in regard to conscious ideas, and then entered an intrusive phase.

When viewed retrospectively, the accident can be seen as an activator of unresolved conflicts. Before the accident, these conflicts caused episodes of what might be a depressive disorder, not severe enough as yet to motivate her to seek psychotherapy. Rather, she was moving forward in her psychological and sociological development. After a turbulent childhood and adolescence, she had successfully completed school and training and was about to engage in a career that would allow her to separate from her family and, especially, to diminish the ambivalent ties binding her to her father. And the therapy enabled her to continue this forward course.

15

SUICIDE OF A PARENT

With Frederick Parris

Margaret, a 25-year-old woman, illustrates denial and the resumption of mourning during psychotherapy and the communicative problems imposed by a style in which isolation and undoing are prominent.

She telephoned the outpatient clinic for an "evaluation of depression" because of suicidal thoughts during a period shortly after her mother committed suicide and because of fear that she might do as her mother did. She was referred to the stress clinic, and an appointment was made. She phoned and canceled this appointment, explaining that she was feeling much better. Contact was renewed several weeks later when Margaret called again, saying she had been feeling better but now wanted help.

FIRST SESSION

She presented herself as composed, unemotional, controlled, intelligent, and personable. As part of obtaining informed consent, she signed a statement containing the words "Research on Stress Response Syndromes." She began the first session by commenting on this phrase.

> *M (Margaret):* It is important to, uh, to study that, and I think the greatest impact has of course, been on my father.

She was referring to her mother's suicide.

> *M:* And ah, I read a research study recently in the paper that said that sudden deaths are extremely hard to get over for a spouse, for him, and after they've been married for 33 years and were very, very close in the relationship, so it affects me most when I'm with him but when I—whereas I'm living my own life out here, and I was living my own life when she died, although we were very close (*pause*).

She said again that her father is the one most affected by her mother's suicide. As is often the case, the first minutes of therapy indicate a character trait of the patient. She used alternative facts ("he is upset") as a way to ward off threatening facts ("I am upset"). She went on to say how days could pass without thinking of it, before disclosing her own distress.

> *M:* So I was just thinking recently that sometimes I'm, I'm pretty sure I, I go whole days without thinking about it— and I'm feeling the more direct problems that I'm confronting, you know in my work, which is difficult. I was standing talking on the phone at work yesterday, and there was this girl behind me who was cracking up, saying to her girl friend she felt like committing suicide, and you know, everything was going wrong. And all the machines weren't working, and you know, I was identifying very strongly because that happened to me a couple weeks ago.

Her identification with one who commits or might commit suicide was inscribed on the therapist's mind as a possible key issue. The "universal" stress response theme of fear of merger with a victim is here colored by another "universal" theme, identification with the parent of the same sex.

M: . . . 'cause all the machines I wanted to use weren't working, or I was doing really stupid mistakes. And ah, it was just before Easter and I had to get something done and, and I was just starting to shake, I was just so uptight, and so when I first called here I, ah, was in a very, uh, very bad situation, you know, emotionally, I just didn't know what was going on, and I was, I was feeling suicidal and ah, just, for the first time in my life that I just couldn't cope with the things that were happening to me. And I couldn't cope with my own feelings, and I was just, I felt like I was getting out of control. And when I started realizing what I was doing to myself and to the people around me, notably to the guy I'm living with, um, I realized I had to get a grip on myself, and I have been, I don't feel like I'm freaking out that much anymore. Sometimes I feel, this is why I didn't follow up too closely after I called, I called and, and ah very very urgent at the time and then, you know, then I got a grip on myself and ah, I, I couldn't really make up my mind whether or not I should come ah, or whether I was getting back on the road, and I didn't have to worry too much any more and still feel alternately one way or the other. Sometimes I feel fine, I feel sane, and sometimes I still feel that ah, I need new perspectives and I really need somebody to um, help, you know put my head right back where it should be, you know. I don't know if I've ever, my head has ever been where it should be. So, um, it, it's also hard. I got kind of nervous this morning when you first saw me because I suddenly tried to put all my problems together, and sometimes I feel I can talk about them very coherently, and I like to, and then it comes out to somebody, whoever I happen to be with at the moment, and then, there, I was just afraid this morning on account I wouldn't be able to talk and I wouldn't be able to put anything together. So, I don't know if I can (*pause*). But I guess it's also hard for me just to sit here and keep talking without any sort of direction, I suppose. So (*laughs*) do you have any advice for me?

She became diffuse and repetitive at an abstract level over the issue of whether or not she was all right.

The therapist asked her to go on with whatever she felt most distressed about. She talked of her current love relationship with Ned but quickly shifted the topic to her work in photography. She graduated from college with a major in literature and then decided to leave her home in suburban New York to come West. She got a very promising job in movie production. It required that she plan her own original work in addition to carrying out certain editing-room routines. For the first time in her life she felt that she was embarked on a satisfying and self-fulfilling career, but she had difficulty concentrating in the darkened editing room. She retraced her history in order to illustrate her feelings during earlier periods, continuing as follows:

M: You know, I really hated myself all through high school. I thought I was ugly and nobody liked me and I went through all these very unstable things, um, that I started getting over finally when I went to New York State and um, I had a couple of relationships and I met a girl who is now very very close to me. I'm very close to Alice, and we lived together for about a year and a half and have been friends for nearly three years now. And then after I graduated as a lit major, um, I worked for a year as a secretary in Central

Bookstore which was, it was fun, it was nice, but I felt I wasn't doing anything with my life, and I wanted to do something more creative and interesting. So I came out here because a friend had this movie studio that was really moving, and then, um, my father, who is a computer designer, he was working for General Labs in New Jersey, and he was working for General Labs in New Jersey, and he was pressured into taking a big important job which would mean moving to Philadelphia for two years, and my mother said absolutely no, I won't go, I'd die sooner. You know, she's a very strong-willed, independent person, and, ah, that upset me a whole lot, like (*laughs*) my God, my parents are splitting up after 29 years, and there was no way my father could get out of it, so, um, my mother would go back and forth. She finally decided to go with him, but she was going to stay home in New York for the summer, and, ah, then she killed herself; it was just as sudden as that. You know, it's very, in a way it's very like her because she wasn't a person to make a big show of trying to ah commit suicide. You know, just she did it (*ha, ha*).

Margaret's laughter was not simply nervousness; it was a way of undoing and averting negative emotional responses. She later revealed that her mother was strongly committed to her own career as a free lance illustrator and had earned substantial sums for many years. For a period immediately preceding her suicide, she had received an unusual number of rejections in competitive circumstances and was not earning any money. Her mother loved their home, friends, and community. She hated Philadelphia and the idea of tagging along with her husband and was sure that he would have a second and fatal heart attack from the enormous pressures of the new job to which he had committed himself.

M: —you know just a total shock to everybody, and so I stayed with my father for a month. Just every day, just trying to

see him through every day, and, ah, then I spent the next
month seeing him and going, arranging things in New York
and, and, ah, relaxing and then going down to Philadelphia, and, and then I came out here, ah, about five and a
half months ago, um, and started work. I was going to work
full time, but I didn't, I'm working part time instead. I'm
working two days a week, taking some courses, um, and
that's about it. I don't know if it's given you any insights.
It's been a, you know, I feel it's been a pretty normal
middle-class existence, and, ah, up till now I feel I've been
coping with everything fairly well (*pause*). So I don't think
it's anything unusual; I don't even think my problems are
anything unusual, and you said it was, um, it was good I
realized that it was all going on inside my head, and I do
know that. I don't feel that the world is doing anything to
me. Um, I feel that the way I see life is that I can sort of
make it whatever I want to, I know that whatever I'm doing
with my life is totally up here (*pause*). So I don't know
where to go from here.

Margaret was in a denial phase. After her mother's death she
devoted herself to her father's grief, and then she continued with
her plans. She was having difficulty at work and with her boyfriend,
though she played down these problems in order to maintain her
sense of esteem. At this point she was not experiencing sadness over
the loss of her mother, although the need to ward off such responses
may have contributed to her problems at work and with Ned.

The therapist then asked a series of questions exploring for signs
of depression, suicidal potential, and any abnormalities in her current mental status. When no material of consequence emerged, he
requested more details on her present interpersonal relationships.
She responded by telling of her difficulties with Ned, her periodic
feeling of jealousy, and her worries about losing him. The therapist
sensed, because of clues in the flow of her remarks, that it was she

who wished to leave Ned but that for some reason she felt bad about
this and could not acknowledge it. But he did not verbalize this,
and she continued to describe how Ned moved in with her.

M: Just after Ned and I started getting a little, very, very slightly
    involved, um he was, he was forced to move out of his
    apartment, and, ah, so in a moment of rashness, you know,
    of generosity, I said, well, you know, stay with me if you
    can't find any other place to stay, as a temporary thing.
    That's how (*laughs*), that's how it started. It was really weird,
    and for a long time, for about a month, I guess, I said, ah,
    you'll just have to find your own place as soon as you find
    a job and can pay for it. And he was saying after a while,
    after we'd been living together for a couple of weeks, he
    was saying, "No, I want to keep living with you," and I
    said, "No, I don't want that. I want to live by myself." Um,
    and so finally, you know, we worked out things to the point
    where I decided, after about a month and a half or some-
    thing, that if if we found different living quarters our rela-
    tionship, which had built to a certain point, that point
    would just be thrown out the window because it wasn't
    the kind of thing that could survive on, ah, two totally
    separate, um, things. It would be a regression, if we lived
    in different places; it would be putting our relationship on
    a lower level, which neither of us thought it would sur-
    vive. So I decided I wanted to continue with it rather than
    just completely throw it out. And that's why we got a larger
    apartment and moved about two months ago.
T: And that's about the time you began to become jealous,
    had fantasies, and worried?
M: Well, it was also the sort of time when I stopped being in
    control of the situation, because as long as Ned was saying,
    "I want you," and I'm saying, "Well I'm not sure," you
    know, I was more in control, and as he was always the one

who was making the efforts to, to adapt to my needs and wants and I needed more time by myself. And, ah, once I, once I, you know, sort of made a turn around and said, "I want you," then sort of like the balance shifted, and, ah, he became, he wanted to become more in control. I've always, I, I, you know, always resist him being in control, you know, and I said I'm the one who's suddenly having to make all the adjustments. I want it to be 50-50, and, ah, that's when it started, um, resisting the security of, the security of the relationship, and, and sort of subconsciously trying to dump on it, and that was when we moved. So now, now I, I sort of resent feeling that I'm the one who has to make most of the adaptations and most of the changes. You know, because he's, he's still, he says, "Well that's the way I am you know. If you don't like it, that's too bad."

T: How do you feel about having to make the changes? Are you feeling very frightened that if you don't, you'll lose him?

The therapist was aware of the parallel between Margaret and her mother. Both were threatened by lowered controls, possible loss of a man, and a loss by moving. He groped for this connection and her possible identification with her mother in what follows.

M: Yeah (*pause*).

T: I'm struck also—I'm trying to tie this in with the "Why now" question I have in my mind. You came West involved with yourself. Everything was going fine. You had your independence, but for some reason things have regressed.

M: Mm-hmh.

T: Perhaps you feel now the way you did back in high school, that you doubt your own value.

M: No, not, God forbid if I could ever doubt that again. No,

I still have a basic sense of my own value and my own worth, and, and the person I am. I still have, you know, about 300 percent more self-confidence, down basically than I, than I, did, then, um.

T: What I was really driving toward was closing the circuit. I was wondering if your mother's death had any effects on you. Here was this case where *she* wanted to retain some control, in a sense of not having to make the move, was forced into a corner, and as you said, "She wouldn't make the move even if it killed her," and that's apparently how it occurred. Would you identify with this part, or would you prefer to—

M: Ah, I respect her a lot, and ah, ah, I respect, you know, the, the strength that she always had and the independence and the, the person that she was. You know, she was just a really beautiful person, and, ah, I suppose the fact that I had to come to terms with her suicide, the fact that she deliberately took her life in the sense that I respect her so much. You know, so I've got to respect what she did, you know.

Margaret did not quite connect with the therapist's communication about identification. Instead she reacted as if the therapist had suggested that she might feel critical of or angry at her mother for committing suicide. She was protesting too much about how wonderful her mother was and how much she respected her. She not only was avoiding negative feelings, but she also was avoiding them by stating opposite ones. This was a characteristic style for her, akin to the switching described in Chapter 10. She did this so emphatically and repetitiously, while seeming ill at ease, that the therapist approached it in a very gingerly manner.

T: In fact you almost had to respect what she did, so as not to interfere with your image of her as a. . . .

M: Mm-hmh.

T: Not to place a value on suicide, but you had it in your mind as respecting her suicide because if you didn't respect that, you would have to question the image. . . .

M: Yeah. Also, um, like she couldn't, you know, I can see how after decades of of living with one man and loving him and having a very close, good relationship that they did, she couldn't turn around and say, I'm leaving you. You know that. I don't see how any person could really do that.

Hence she also could not break up with Ned, although later in therapy she felt able to do so. One reason for coming to therapy was her conflict over how to terminate an unsatisfactory but close relationship.

M: Whereas knowing how much she hated Philadelphia and the pressure-cooker existence, that and the fact that she, she was also very sure that my father, you know, was going to die of a heart attack because he almost did five years ago. And put in a similar situation, she was positive he was going to drop dead anyway, once he did that, once he moved, um. So having made that decision, and she, she also felt that he betrayed her by doing this when he knew that she, she would hate moving so much. But I respected that fact that she wanted to retain her independence and, and that it was hurting her pride to have to follow somebody else. You know, like just to be an appendage to my father, um (*pause*). So she, she wrote in her note, you know, to my father, "You did what you have to do. I'm doing what I have to do." And uh, I, you know, I've never, I haven't thought of suicide at all since I was about 16 years old. And you know, the fact that, you know, my mother's, you know, doing it brought it to my attention so much and having to respect the fact.

Like I, I'm, I'm almost positive that's why it seems like an alternative to me now. Um—although I'm, I'm, I'm pretty positive that I wouldn't do it. Because I, I don't think that I could face hurting my father that much. I mean, I wouldn't have to face it, obviously, but um, I just don't think I could. You know, knowing, how much it hurt him for her to die. You know, I just feel it would be another blow that he couldn't bear.

T: I wonder if what makes it even triply hard for you, as sad as you feel just trying to respect and love your mother, is the fact that she did hurt your father very much in the final analysis.

This was a fairly direct interpretation of her hostile thoughts toward her mother and of a warded-off hostile component in her reaction to her mother's suicide.

M: No. I know she was a very selfish person, and I knew that when she was alive, and I knew it when she was dead. Um, it was a selfish thing to do, you know, and she was a very self-centered person, and she, I knew, I always knew that (*pause*). So I don't respect her for being so, you know, that self-centered, you know. I certainly don't blame my father, either (*pause*).

The therapist inferred here an unspoken thought, "I don't blame my mother" before she said, "I don't blame my father either." This was a sequence of undoing: "I don't respect her (I do blame her). (I don't blame her), (I blame father), I don't blame my father." She ended by denying the impact of her mother's death.

M: But I do feel that I've come to terms with, you know, with her death about as much as I ever will. I don't feel that it's, it's really disturbing me so much now, you know, emotionally, except that there are situations that I find myself in now that I, I just say (*laughing*) you know "I wish you were here." You know, because she, you know, she was always a great support for me. She was somebody who really, really did believe in me and always said so. And she always tried to put some backbone into me, you know, and she really did. I absorbed a lot of things from her. When I was in a situation where I'd say, "Oh mommy I like this guy, and he won't ask me out," and she'd say, "Well go ask him out. What are you waiting for?" You know, she was a very aggressive person, and she, she pounded that into me. Um, and she was, she was an extremely proud person, and she pounded that into me as much as she could too (*pause*).

T: Okay. We're going to have to end for today.

SECOND SESSION

Margaret came in expressing ambivalence about her need for therapy. She denied any relationship between her problems and what had happened to her mother and said that she had come back only because she felt obligated to discuss whether or not she needed therapy. She did not like the way the therapist just listened to her and offered nothing of himself. In various ways, she asked for more support and direction. However, in doing so she became provocative and accusatory. The therapist felt that she was testing him to see whether he would collapse (have a heart attack as her father did), become angry and wish to be rid of her, or approach her more intimately and socially (which would frighten her), or try to control her. But he continued with the same concerned, tactful, and objective professional manner as in the first interview. She announced that she was going on a visit to see her father for a few days.

THIRD SESSION

Margaret dealt superficially and unemotionally with the visit to her father. She felt that she was much better and believed that her fears of being flooded were related to "a period of identity problems in adolescence." She gave additional history, including a suicidal gesture as an adolescent when depressed. She was agreeable and intellectual during the hour, using undoing, negation, and disavowal to avoid anxiety.

FOURTH SESSION

Margaret spoke of an episode of sadness that occurred while she was developing her own pictures in the darkroom at work. She had taken these pictures during a recent visit home and had also brought back a picture of her mother that she had found there. She talked longingly of missing a girlfriend, but to avoid intensifying her sad feelings, she switched to discussing both difficulties and successes with her editing work, focusing on mechanical issues. In summarizing her remarks over the hour, the therapist mentioned an idea she had spoken of earlier in the hour, about going home to be closer to old friends of hers and her mother.

She responded that introspection on such ideas made her "massively oversensitive to any little thing." She related this oversensitivity to Ned and continued as follows:

M: . . . like, um—even if, if I feel, ah, I feel affectionate toward Ned and he just doesn't happen to feel that way at that moment, it just sends me, I mean, right to the bottom, or just looking, you know, at a picture of my mother will just send me into a fit of crying, and this doesn't happen normally. But things that don't normally upset me do, things that I just can't, I can't deal with them rationally. I can't shrug them off, and I feel—in a way I feel a huge loss of self-esteem—whereas on the other hand, if somebody said, "Do you like yourself"—I would say "yes." It's just one of, one of the main characteristics of my depression is just feeling unable to cope with the complexities and the demands of life and the future and making a living and achieving something or accomplishing something. It just seems too complicated and too difficult, and the whole thought of it just appalls me.

T: It's only a hunch, but I would think some of those feelings come to mind when you look at a picture of your mother and have some realization of her loss and talent.

The therapist noted the defensive maneuver of abstract generalization, attention to peripheral details, and expansion to issues too large to contemplate, such as "the complexities and the demands of life and the future." By giving this interpretation, he tried to hold her to a topic she had brought up and was also warding off.

M: Well, one of my, one of my strongest fantasies, or actually I have very, very few fantasies that, that I wish, but one of the things that has been recurring since she died is wishing that I'm little again—very little—you know like about 5 years old. And I brought back from the East two pictures, one was of my mother when she was in college, and one was of me when I was 5 years old, and I'm, I'm planning to put them together in a frame because that is my strongest fear (a slip of the tongue), ahh, fantasy, you know, I want to go back to the time that everything was taken care of for me and I didn't have to worry about finances and supporting myself and, and, ah, trying to accomplish something in life. Although I suppose you know, the little things I was going to try and survive were just as traumatic as the things I, I might go through now. But that's, that's how I feel. You know, it's not so much that I hate myself, I hate myself, but a feeling of just being unable to cope with all these things because I, I think that the self-esteem, and the, ah, the feeling I like myself, or I wouldn't be anybody else, um, I think that those feelings are very solid in myself. I don't question them, I, I feel in that sense, I always feel very together. . . .

She was switching from her wish to be little and dependent, an idea that made her feel too infantile, self-critical, and controlled, to assertions that she liked herself. When this undoing operation restored a sense of safety, she could resume her self-critical statements.

M: . . . But my main, the the main characteristic of my depression is just I hate to get up. I hate to face each day. I hate to—um, I feel that every single day is a struggle, and I never want to wake up in the morning, or when I wake up, I never want to get up. I just dread every day. And that's, those are, that's the massive feeling that my depression consists of. And, ah, I relate this to the pressure that has been put on me by my father to succeed—it's not that he's pressuring me. . . .

She was using her characteristic switching maneuver again. She switched to describing her father and was also using the topic of her father to switch away from ideas and feelings related to her mother. As will be seen, the "mother" topic will return.

M: . . . but (sighs) he wants me to, you know, for my own sake, be, because he knows, or he's instilled in me, I suppose, the need to feel that I'm accomplishing something in life. But at the same time I've gone through four years of liberal arts college, and movies are such an overloaded market that it's very difficult, and you have to be extremely aggressive to be able to succeed, and ah, much as I want, I still have these ambiguous feelings. I have tremendous fear of not being able to. And ah, it's just really, that is, that is another thing that's very, very difficult for me to cope with. And you know, when I got these feelings from him, my mother was always the person I was able to go to. She wanted the same things from me, but she, she didn't express them in a pressurized way. She expressed them in a much more sympathetic way that I could identify with, and I've, you know, I always turned to her. And in the years when I was closest to her, I was farthest from my father.

T: When were those years?

The therapist, sensing she was about to switch away from the train of thought involving her mother, tried to hold her to this topic by asking a relevant question about her mother.

M: Oh, my college years and, and, ah, up until she died—well after I'd left home. She was, ah—um, I feel a lot of sympathy for her, because she, I don't think she was a very good (*pause*) mother. . . .

This "I feel a lot of sympathy" was a kind of premonitory undoing of the angry feelings that were incipient and emerged clearly in her voice when she subsequently spoke of her mother's terrible temper. Both feelings were really present.

M: . . . She didn't want to be really (a mother). My father told me this after she died. Especially when both my sister and me were little. She hated having two little kids around, and, I mean, she loved us, but I remember she had the worst temper, you know, she used to—I remember when she grabbed me by my hair and shook me like that. Um, I mean she never beat me or, you know, anything like that but she, you know, she had a terrible temper. And this died away very, very much after I left home. And she and my sister, ah, my sister was very unstable and really hated my mother for years even after she went to college, and ah, I don't think their relationship ever really got close, even after that. But after I left home, very quickly I started growing back closer to my parents, and, and my mother always, um (*pause*), she, she always needed me, and I, I understood that, you know, without ever really talking about it. And you know, sort of a feeling she really wanted me to have all the freedom that I could possibly have, even though she needed me, and she wanted me to be near, you know, on vacations and stuff like that. You know, and she urged me to move to California, even though you know, she would've much rather had me (*pause*) closer (*pause*).

The therapist tried to hold her to this topic with another question, but she deflected to other topics until the end of the hour.

FIFTH THROUGH SEVENTH SESSIONS

The next two hours, the fifth and sixth sessions, dealt with ordinary matters at work and with Ned and avoided mention of her mother. In the seventh hour Margaret talked in a general way about everyday work frustrations. She then told of how strongly she had felt that she had to get away from Ned and be with a girlfriend, not to "sob on her shoulder but to get her energy." She "accepted it with equanimity" when the girlfriend was too tired to have her come over. She immediately returned to work topics and expressed righteous anger with her boss. She then criticized her editing machine for being defective and talked abstractly about artistic tasks. One purpose of discussing the boss and the equipment was to show that she was not at fault or to blame for her anger.

She then talked, dejectedly, of eventually showing her film work. The therapist said that she might be asking if it were all right to show not her work but her feelings, for he could sense that she was depressed. She said she was sad that she had only her work to attest to her worth, and she was uncertain about it. She came close to tears at the end of the hour, but the cause was unclear, concealed by intellectualized generalizations.

EIGHTH SESSION

Margaret began the next session by saying that she had been feeling unstable for the last two days. She had been reluctant to do darkroom work because she was afraid she would be unable to focus her thoughts while there. The first half of the interview was occupied with a long soliloquy about the uncertainty of her future plans and her ambivalence toward accepting financial support from her father. When the therapist attempted to focus her attention on the unstable feeling, she deflected toward continuing these generalizations and abstract ruminations. But she then went on to mention her mother, as illustrated in the following transition:

M: . . . ah, like last night I got terribly depressed about what I was saying, and I was going through one of my sort of panics, and this time I said, "I'm not going to run over to anybody," and in a way I didn't want to, I wanted to just figure it out. And I couldn't. I mean, I just couldn't figure out why I was feeling so completely down. I knew when it started though, and, and I have an absolute progression of what happened because I'd been sort of down for two days. It all started with a thought of my mother, and, ah, I mean everything was fine. I was feeling really good one evening, and Ned and I were just sitting around talking and a song of Joni Mitchell's came on the radio, and all of a sudden I flashed back to this conversation I had with my mother about Joni Mitchell about two or three years ago, a long time ago, when, um, my mother was just saying, "Oh, it's just her publicity people that say she writes and sings and plays the guitar and she does everything." I said, "Mother, cut it out, she really does." And my mother said, "Oh." You know, she was, she was just thinking I was being naive. And I flashed on that, and I got really depressed and into my own thoughts and I sat down and I wrote a long letter to this woman back East, who, um, was my mother's closest friend, and who's like, you know, another mother to me. I just haven't, I haven't been writing letters lately, but I wrote her a long letter, and (*sighs*) it was just, you know, I just went into the bedroom and, and sort of sat and thought for a long time. I was, I was feeling down but not, not really terribly bad. I was just thinking and I wanted to be by myself (*sighs*), and I was still down with the flu, and I was sick of being sick and, ah, and so on. And the next day, the next evening, a couple of friends of Ned's came over. I've talked to you about the problem I have of relating to his friends, and this is his friend Tom, who's a total freak and Tom's, a woman that he lives with. I mean it's a really weird situation; she's a call girl.

T: Can I ask you what the letter was like that you wrote to the friend of your mother?

Although the associations may possibly be relevant, the therapist noted the reference to her ambivalence about her mother, and so he chose to help Margaret hold onto that aspect of the topic, that is, the issue of missing her mother, feeling frustrated, and wishing for a substitute mother. If Margaret were on her own, as she would be alone at home, she would probably not continue to develop this ideational line because it evoked painful feelings.

> M: Oh, yeah, um (*pause*). I wanted to explain to her, you know, what was going on between Ned and me because I'd talked to her about it when I was back East. What I mainly, what I expressed right away, was the fact that I needed, um (*pause*), ah, somebody sort of to function as my mother, and, you know, she is the closest to me. But she doesn't have the background in my life, and the, the things that you always go through with your parents (*sounds about to cry*).
>
> T: I asked you that very directly because I think you're experiencing a lot of feeling right here and now.
>
> M: (*Long pause, sighs*). I just don't know if I can really talk about it (*almost crying, sniffs long pause*).
>
> T: What sort of thoughts are you having?
>
> M: I'm not really having any thoughts. I'm just trying to pull myself back together again so that I can talk. You know, it's like I said, I don't want to come in here and and break down, you know, although you said that does serve a purpose (*cries*). Um, I really want to use these sessions very constructively for my head (*sniffs*). But we are getting very close to my emotions recently, because I've noticed this several times when I've come in here and started talking, just talking, you know, but not about my mother, not about anything, but I feel like crying, and it's not as as hard, I mean it's not hard to hold back, but, but I feel that I'm very close to my emotions (*sighs, pause, sniffs*).
>
> T: I think that there's something very constructive going on, expressing emotions here.

This patient had been warding off crying, not only because her sadness is painful, but also because she believes it is humiliating to give way to her emotions. The therapist said this to counter her humiliation. With other types of patients it would be a gratuitous remark that could be used transferentially.

> M: (*Pause*) um, it's not that I've been holding back. The emotions that I'm feeling are reactions to what I'm saying, um. Thoughts of my mother have been very much with me. Well, one way of showing this is a photograph I wanted to make, a self-portrait for my father. What I chose to do (*sighs*), was use time exposure on my camera, you know, you can set it, and about ten seconds later it goes off so you have a chance to get into a pose or something, do it by yourself. So I chose to try to take a picture of myself studying myself in the mirror and in the mirror are two pictures; the two pictures that I mentioned once to you very briefly before: one of my mother and one of myself when I was little, and the one of my mother when she was about say 20. And to show that I'm looking at myself very strongly these days and that these two pictures are, um, well, pictures of the little girl, I mean myself as the little girl because that's, as I've said before, that's sort of almost how I wish that I were, was, and the picture of my mother, and it's an old picture. She'd, she just didn't like to have her picture taken so we have very few pictures of her that are recent and of those my father has them. My father's coming this weekend, by the way. . . .

She was expressing the thought "I miss my Mommy, I wish I were a little girl with her again." She modulated the rate of the idea's emergence by using other thoughts. In effect, these thoughts partially filled cognitive channels so that the previously warded-off thought could not rush out all at once and overwhelm her sense of control. The other thoughts, such as "my father's coming," might also have been antidotes to her compelling sense of loss. She continued talking about her father, using his sadness as a vehicle to externalize her own similar feelings, identifying with both his feelings and his capacity to cope with them and savoring the continued attachment. Note that she will say that she warded off ideas of her mother for his sake.

> M: . . . So, I'm hoping that we, as always I'm hoping that we'll, we'll just enjoy each other's company and not (*sighs*), um, bring too many old ghosts back in. Um, this past week was their anni——, their wedding anniversary, and ah, I was afraid my father was going to be really down, so I called him up, and he was, he had friends over for dinner, which really made me happy, he wasn't by himself and depressed. He had been very depressed lately. I knew that, but he was really pleased and touched that I had remembered and that I had called and that made me really happy, and we're both looking forward to seeing each other. But, um, when we're together, I try to keep as far away from any mention and thoughts of my mother as possible because it (*sighs*) amplifies the feelings so much when the two of us are together. I mean I can talk about my mother, and I can cry about my mother in front of Ned or you or any one of my friends. . . .

As far as the therapist knew, this was the first time she had cried. To reduce her embarrassment she declared that she was comfortable with crying and did it all the time.

> M: . . . but with my father, his pain is just so great and so is my own that we just increase each other's feelings. So with him, I just try to avoid every mention of her, every thought, and whether this is good or bad I don't know. . . .

One reason that she might feel bad is that she might have been predisposed to feeling guilt over an oedipal victory. She now had her father and excluded (mention of) her mother. This would be only one factor in an overdetermined behavior pattern.

> *M:* . . . (*sniffs, pause*). There are, there is this one lady, ah, Marion, who is my mother's closest friend. I've known her all my life. She has a daughter who's a year younger than I am, and (*pause*) you know, it's like back home. I have a lot of people who who want to function as my special friends and parents, and they do, but she's, she's very much the closest . . . (*pause, cries, clears throat*).

Stabilized by discussing her father and perhaps growing anxious about that topic, she returned to her wish to attach herself to a woman friend as a mother replacement. The woman could not replace her mother; she must give up her mother, and so her sadness came out again.

> *M:* . . . But what I feel that she has been, she's missing in her role with me (*cries*) is, you know, all the things that are, that go between a mother and a daughter when they're growing up. All the little problems, all the, you know, the ado——, especially adolescence, which has got to be the worst period of anyone's life, but all the things that, you know, I went through with my own mother, and I have never experienced with Marion (*pause*). So one of, I expressed that in my letter to her, saying that I wanted, that there were questions that I wanted to ask my mother about her experiences in life that I had never had a chance to or had never run up against and ah . . . (*sniffs, pause*).
>
> *T:* What sort of questions would those be?
>
> *M:* Well they're mainly, ah, with regard to, ah, her marriage. Like I know that my parents went through difficult times, and I, I wanted to know how much do you, should you go, I mean it's crazy, nobody can tell you this, but I wanted

to know from my mother's experience (*sighs*) how do you, how long do you hold on to a relationship when it's not good? How hard do you work for it? How, like, like Ned said to me once that there are going to be times in our relationship when we'll hate the sight of each other, you know, and, and trying to show that that's, you know, that if you really, that a relationship will go through good times and bad times—and the bad times will be awfully bad, but if you can hold on, I mean, the relationship will be very much strengthened, and this is something that my mother had also said to me. She'd, when we'd discussed the relative merits of marriage you know, I've said, you know, what am I supposed to push marriage for, you know, for nothing (*said rapidly and vehemently*).

She continued talking in generalities about one person hurting another. She then recalled a family scene in which she had said she did not want to have children. Her mother took her side, but her father was horrified. She went on to talk of her parents' ambivalence toward each other. The therapist summarized by saying that she was talking about expressions of both tender and angry feelings between persons and added that she too may have angry feelings that cannot now be shared with her mother. She denied this:

M: Um, not so much share feelings with her because I always did, and I always did tell her how much I loved her. But I think (*sighs*), when my mother died, I must have been the only person on earth who didn't have guilt feelings, who didn't say "If only I had done this" or, um, I had no feelings that I could have prevented or, or, ah, I don't know, just plain guilt that, that she had done it, she had committed suicide, and I still don't have any. I don't have any feelings that I wish that I had said that I loved her because, you know, I did. I said it many many times you know, starting I remember even years ago. Must have been when I was just about 17 or 18 and, and, ah, either just off to college, or about to go off to college, I said, I remember very distinctly saying to her, that she had given me so much love and understanding and it was the kind of love and understanding that you can't give back. I mean, I can't turn to her and say "Now, you know anytime you want advice, come to me," but it was some, something that I could, that I had learned and could hand on to somebody else. And, ah, even way earlier than that I remember when I was about probably 12 or 13, I had said something meaning to be funny, and it was actually very malicious. I said, she was, no I, I must have been about 14, 'cause I remember the house we were living in, and it's one of my really clearest memories (*cries*). She was, she was doing the laundry and I was sitting at the table and she was singing and I said, "Mother have you ever listened to yourself sing" and she said "no," and I said, "Well you're lucky," and I was just, it was a stupid joke, and years, I remember, for years later, I always said if there was one thing that I could call back in my life it was that, because it started her crying. I had made my mother cry, and I was just, I, I apologized, I said I'm sorry, I didn't mean it that way; that was really stupid.

She continued with memories of her mother and then spoke of wanting to talk to her father about her mother but being afraid to do so. Finally she talked again of longing to see her mother's friend Marion and of being envious of Ned, who could still call up his mother whenever he had a problem. At the end of the hour she gestured to the box of tissues and said, "Do you always keep these by the chair?" The therapist suggested that she was asking him to say that it was all right with him that she cried during the hour, and it was all right.

REMAINING SESSIONS

This stress-oriented treatment continued for seven more sessions. The above session marked the beginning of Margaret's open mourning for her mother. Her grief process was marked by her loving attachment as well as her resentment and fear of over-identifying with her mother. She had a model of her mother that she had never before clearly conceptualized; she saw her mother as superficially strong and powerful but as weak underneath. The refusal to move with her father, for example, she saw as strong in her first conscious thoughts, but she was warding off ideas that it was weak to have to commit suicide. Her mother was dependent on her father and could not live independently from him. But the attachment was ambivalent and unsatisfactory; her mother did not feel fulfilled by the marriage or by the children or by her creative work.

SUMMARY

Margaret was afraid that she was too much like her mother. Her relationship with Ned was a psychological parallel for the relationship between her parents. Like her mother, she believed, she could not give up Ned because she would then drown in a sense of abandonment. On the other hand, she feared marrying Ned because he was self-centered and in some ways unstable, and she did not love him enough. As she could deal more authentically with her separation and independence from her mother, while also accepting the painful reality of the loss, she could risk separation from Ned. She engineered this separation and tolerated it well, while using the therapist as an interim relationship.

In the therapy she also worked through her feelings of being neglected by her father, especially when she heard of his plans to remarry a woman younger than himself, who was about her age. Rage at all abandoning figures, including the therapist, with whom termination was impending, was an important topic for working through in the therapy, in which she continued to use her style of switching topics or attitudes toward the same topic. The therapist's awareness of this defensive style allowed him to help her temper its use, that is, to use it when her emotions were too threatening at a given moment or to not use it and stay with a topic when her emotions were anticipated to remain within tolerable limits.

16

SUICIDE OF A FRIEND

With Robert Hammer

Tim is a 31-year-old single man whose friend committed suicide shortly after a plea for help. During the weeks that followed, Tim felt so haunted by his dead friend that he was motivated to seek treatment. He was unable to sleep, was afraid of the dark, and had startle reactions and unbidden images. During a brief psychotherapy these symptoms were relieved. The suicide of his friend was also linked associatively with the death of his father several years earlier. When the therapist established a situation of safety through a tactful maintenance of Tim's self-esteem, it initiated a mourning process not begun at the time of the father's death.

Jack was Tim's friend and in some ways his leader for several years. His was the role of a man who knows women and is successful at work. Then for about a year while each was involved in other activities, they seldom met. Recently, Jack had called Tim, and they had spent a long evening together. Jack spoke of feeling depressed and meaningless. He asked Tim to spend more time with him and hinted at moving in with Tim. Tim inwardly recoiled. He was aware of a strong feeling that he did not want to be sucked in. He did not want to rescue Jack; they had not been that close recently. But on the surface he presented a friendly demeanor and tried to cheer Jack throughout the evening.

A few days later, Tim received a telephone call from Carol, a woman who was a close friend of Jack's and a person Tim had recently dated. Carol was worried. Jack was missing and had left a note that suggested a possible suicide. Once again Tim was concerned but did not want to become involved. Over the next four days Tim periodically felt anxious that Jack might be playing some type of trick to get back at him for not being more concerned. Then on the fifth day Carol called again to say that Jack had shot himself and that his body had been found in some nearby hills.

Carol asked Tim to join some friends in a funeral service. Feeling pressured, he refused but then felt that he had acted in an aloof and callous manner. Within days he developed insomnia, a phobia of the dark, and intrusive thoughts about Jack that at times were so vivid that he could feel his presence as a menace within the room. Below is the opening of the first interview in which he described some of these symptoms.

FIRST SESSION

Tim: A friend of mine shot sh-shot and killed himself; I don't know, about ten days ago; since that time I was afraid of the dark and I'd keep a light on. At first it took me forever to get to sleep; I kept, I'd keep wanting to open my eyes to look around to see if anyone were around in the apartment. I experienced periods during the day when I was frightened, felt very empty, extremely alone (*pause*); every time I drive by the hills I hate to look in the direction to where I think he was when he shot himself (*pause*). I don't even want to know the specifics, but

I have general information about it (*pause*). His body was taken to a funeral home which happens to be very near where I live. Every time I go by there I hate to. I just get very uncomfortable, and (*pause*) I don't like dealing with a woman whom he was involved with, who I happen to work with somewhat now. I felt like she was going to suck me in this thing, into a funeral and extend it, and that was very upsetting. I had a talk with her last night about how I don't want to have anything else to do with her whatsoever (*pause*), and then on top of that, I started thinking about my own life and how I'm not happy with it. I dislike it, how I want to change certain things in it (*pause*), how I'm lonely, want to get closer to somebody, thinking about having a family, and having a job that I would like to put energy into (*pause*), but mainly right now I just want to get rid of all these feelings about him (*pause*). I can't stand it, it's hard for me to, he crops up when I'm alone all the time. . . .

T (*Therapist*): You mean sort of intrudes on your mind?

Tim: Yeah, this morning, washing my face, I have soap in my eyes, with my eyes closed, I keep thinking all of a sudden somebody is going to touch my arm, and there's no one in the apartment (*pause*). I don't know why I freak out on that; I just force myself to finish washing my face, and then I open my eyes and I'm okay, look around; it's daylight, and everything's fine. . . .

T: How have you been sleeping lately?

Tim: I was sleeping a little better—at first I had all the lights in the apartment on; now I'm down to one in the living room which I'm very much aware of from my bedroom. Until last night I was definitely sleeping much better each night. I wasn't feeling much. I was better, and then I had this confrontation with this mutual friend, this woman, and that upset me and I felt nervous in my stomach, and it was hard for me to get to sleep. It makes me a little angry, the whole thing, that it should bother me.

T: It makes you angry.

Tim: Angry. I figure the way to get rid of the stress, for me, is to start doing things I want to do that make me happy and to stop sitting around on my ass 'cause then I just think about him. But I feel I move like a snail toward things I want to do.

During the beginning of the first hour, the therapist noted that Tim in his display of earnestness seemed pronounced and displayed a kind of charm that invited smiles, nods of agreement, and reassurances. There were unusually frequent requests for the therapist's interpretations and personal responses, all of which would have been premature or inappropriate. The therapist thus found it necessary to make some effort not to react with either a feigned warmth or a withdrawal from the patient.

Tim had obtained psychotherapy on several previous occasions. He had entered both individual and group treatment after his father's death several years before, when he had felt not so much sad as empty, alienated, and aimless. These therapies had focused on his difficulties in maintaining intimate attachments with both men and women. Since developing the intrusive images of Jack, Tim had already gone to a gestalt therapy group. There he had worked on this symptom, and he described it during the interview.

Tim: I took a gestalt therapy group which I haven't found helpful. I wanted more personal attention.

T: You wanted what?

Tim: I wanted more personal attention. This thing was so stressful for me; I felt that I had to get on it now and work on it closely, work on improving my life closely with somebody, and I felt that it wasn't going to happen at the gestalt therapy.

T: Have you been able to talk about this in the gestalt therapy?

Tim: I talked about it yesterday. I had Jack on a pillow, you know, this guy on a pillow, and I yelled at him. I said: "I don't want to think about you anymore. I want to get on to living." Did that whole thing. And I didn't get what I wanted out of there. I was leaving, and one of the senior consultants there, I went up to him and I had wanted to ask him for a hug, but I hadn't been able to in the group, well, he said, that was fine, he would give me a hug afterward, anyway. And then he said, you know—he didn't know what to say. And I interpreted that to mean that he couldn't offer me any help about this thing. And that was, I didn't like that; I felt lonely. I felt like saying (*angrily*): "Hasn't anyone died in your life or something, and haven't you had to work it through? Can't you even tell me that?" I didn't say that, though.

Tim criticized the gestalt therapist for behavior he felt bad about in his own relationship with Jack. "He couldn't offer me any help." Tim also seemed to denigrate the gestalt therapy in order to win the approval of the present therapist, to whom he related rapidly, superficially, and projectively. Tim appeared ready to idealize the present therapist as a shaman who would exorcise Jack's ghost and diminish Jack as a person with the power to hurt him.

Tim watched the therapist intently. If he talked about his problems to an extent that might be embarrassing, he would then switch to another version of the story that put him in a better light. In telling of his relationship with Jack, Tim spoke alternately of caring and not caring, as if trying to move from a blameworthy to a praise-worthy position. The danger of an uncaring and strong self-concept was that he would in that role-relationship model feel criticism of self for hurting or using others. The danger in a role-relationship model of self as responsibly caring was the associated sense of weakness and personal vulnerability. The therapist did not comment on these shifting self-concepts. He concentrated instead on trying to develop a shared model of the sequence of events and a therapeutic alliance in which his role would be defined as giving neither blame nor praise but, rather, clarification of what had happened and was happening now.

Later during the first hour, the therapist was surprised by Tim's expression of intense anger toward Carol, the Gestalt therapist, and others in general. In essence, Tim regarded Jack's death and its aftermath as an imposition on him, which had weakened him by depleting his energies. This imposition was personified by others who made demands on him or did not contribute to his well-being. He was especially intense in his anger with Carol, who he felt was trying to "milk Jack's death for all it was worth" and to "move in on him" in doing so. He minimized all of his own questionable attitudes and displayed Carol in a bad light.

SECOND SESSION

The second hour can be summarized as one of transference testing. Tim reported feeling much better. His phobia of the dark had improved, and he could sleep with fewer lights on in the house. This was followed by a eulogy about Jack's good qualities. He then attempted to engage the therapist in sweeping theoretical reviews of his current life problems and to communicate a nonspecific readiness for an "in-depth" approach. His wish to please the therapist was clearly apparent but, because of his vulnerability to shame, was not interpreted. Instead the therapist diligently leaned toward a continued reconstruction of the stress event, Tim's state before it happened, and the sequence of subsequent events. His benevolent nonreaction to the patient's provocations for expressions of closeness seemed to be reassuring. Tim then went on to review his life history, commenting on various patterns and meanings himself.

THIRD SESSION

In the third hour Tim seemed to be dejected and closer to the therapist, and again solicited sympathy. He described general feelings of fear and helplessness and gradually related these to an identification with Jack. The next associations led to Tim's first discussion of his father, who had died of cancer some years previously, and from whom Tim had inherited some money. His mother had tried to get closer to him and also felt that she should have a greater portion of the money from the father's will. His feelings that his mother was trying to suck him in and being selfish the therapist linked to Tim's reactions to Carol as trying to suck him in after Jack's death.

FOURTH SESSION

During the fourth hour Tim was more defensive than he had been throughout the first three hours. He maintained an aloof, overmodulated state of mind. Even in such a state, however, he gave useful information. He talked glibly about his conflicted attitudes toward women. He enjoyed fantasies replete with sadistic but harmless play. But in his actual relationships with women, he tended to be so submissive that he felt they soon lost interest in him. There was a certain exhibitionistic quality about his stories of sexual relationships, as if he were saying pointedly that he was heterosexual rather than homosexual. The therapist accepted these demonstrations at face value and did not interpret them. Rather, he worked to maintain a steady and nondirective interest in Tim in order to stabilize his self-esteem and gain empathy for what might be going on beneath the defensive surface.

FIFTH SESSION

A few weeks had now passed since Jack committed suicide. Carol called to invite Tim to join several friends at the site of the death, where they would have a final farewell ceremony for Jack. But Tim was determined not to go and tried to make other plans for that day, of a concrete and defiantly pleasurable nature. In this, the fifth hour, Tim spoke with some pressure of how he wanted to avoid thinking of Jack because it "would drive me crazy." The therapist sensed that it was necessary to ask him what this meant. Tim, with embarrassment bordering on a sense of deep humiliation, reported that although he had said he was feeling better, he had still been having recurrent intrusive images of Jack. Though he could not describe this quite as directly as it is stated here, he had not talked about these intrusions because he was afraid the therapist would withdraw from him because he had not improved rapidly enough.

In the intrusive images Tim saw Jack, still alive and bleeding from his wound, having second thoughts and crying out for help. The therapist quietly said, "Jack felt alone." Tim then related "alone" to himself and talked of his own suicidal ruminations and his identification with Jack. He then worked on the association to himself of "having second thoughts." He had second thoughts that he ought to have been more willing to reestablish his closeness to Jack and thereby prevent Jack's need for such a desperate escape from loneliness. This line of thought was repeated throughout subsequent therapy sessions, and as Tim reviewed his acts and decisions, he confirmed for himself that though he did feel guilty, he was not responsible for rescuing either Jack or Carol.

As he returned to the idea of suicide and whether or not persons should be rescued, Tim revealed for the first time that his father had contemplated suicide and had himself entered therapy. Tim had felt then the way he had felt with Jack, that he should give more affection to his father but did not want to drain himself. He used the treatment as an excuse; he did not have to get close to his father because it might interfere, in some nebulous way, with the therapeutic process. His father had, at this time, tried to get closer to Tim, but in a needy rather than paternal way. This abortive effort at intimacy or, as Tim experienced it, at using him, had been repeated after the diagnosis of cancer.

In more normal times, the father had treated Tim imperiously. A successful businessman, he regarded Tim as an appendage rather than a successor whom he might groom to take on adult work. Tim thus had been placed in a need–fear dilemma. He felt dependent on his father and lonely without his love, but whenever he got close to him, he felt used.

SIXTH SESSION

At the sixth session, Tim reported feeling more depressed. After the last hour he had felt like talking with his mother. In a long telephone conversation with her, he had had both positive and negative feelings. His mother seemed to make herself more available to him and to want more contact, but he was uneasy about becoming closer to her and being used. The similarity of his images of his mother and Carol and his fears of being "sucked in" were worked on. Although he feared being used, he also had bad self-images when he backed off from people.

He then spoke of feeling bad when he approached women. He felt as if he were too strong, inappropriately taking over his father's or Jack's woman. The emotions of these "strong" images were isolated; he did not feel virile and competitive, only vaguely

disturbed over issues of right and wrong. Avoidance of the imagined blame in the therapist's eyes seemed to Tim to be an important motive for how the information about these meanings was
processed. For example, he readily changed the designation of attributes, sometimes labeling the one in need as himself and other
times as Carol. The therapist's interventions were to clarify gradually who had any given attribute in a specific interchange.

Tim became uncomfortable talking of his mother and Carol and,
as an avoidance, began to discuss sports. He described his enthusiasm
and vitality while playing ball. He imagined that the therapist was "a
fellow jock" who empathized with this and felt warm and close. The
therapist asked if this reminded him of anyone. He then spoke of how
he and his father had played ball and of how it was the only time of
sharing between them. He entered an undermodulated crying state,
which became more modulated. He spoke of continuing with sports
as some kind of celebration of his father's memory.

SEVENTH SESSION

The following hour was characterized initially by flat affect and
his aloof, overmodulated state of mind. Tim talked vaguely of current work and dating problems. The therapist commented that he
"seemed to have more difficulty getting started this hour" and asked
in a kindly way if they might reflect on it together to see why this
might be. With hesitation, Tim entered a shimmering state with
both signs of earnest expressivity and warding-off behaviors. In this
state he reported that he was having "difficulty thinking about his
father." This acquisition of the therapist's word usage (*difficulty*) was
noteworthy. The implicit shield of certification seemed to enable
him to contemplate warded-off ideas without feeling like a bad
person for having them.

He went on to say that he had been stopping himself from
thinking about his father when he was alone. As he spoke, Tim

checked the therapist with penetrating glances to see whether he felt that such avoidance of therapeutically endorsed topics was blameworthy. When he seemed reassured that the therapist was not angry with him, he expressed anger with his father. He questioned the need to let himself feel sad; his father did not deserve his positive and sad feelings because he had given Tim so little during his life. Tim should be selfish too, a person who needs no one. The same held true for Jack. Tim was angry that he had been made to feel as though he ought to be a rescuer. He did not know how to be of help to anyone else and did not want to be expected to try.

REMAINING SESSIONS

In the nine ensuing hours, Tim and his therapist worked through his fear of being "sucked in," his anger, and his fear of retaliation for neglecting Jack. A mourning process had been initiated. As part of this process they worked on his feelings toward his father and his father's death, as well as on the symbolic connections between his father and Jack and between Carol and his mother. The process in relation to his father can be summarized as follows.

DISCUSSION

During Tim's mourning process, the threat of injury to his self-concept was prominent in the themes that were warded off and in the transference attitudes that were activated by approaching these themes. Rage at neglect was the central theme, and it had to be viewed in terms of self-experience as both the neglected person and the person to blame for the neglect. Tim placed himself in both roles in relation to Jack and his father.

When Tim saw his father as healthy and powerful and when he saw Jack as the masterful leader, he felt anger at their lack of interest in him. When he saw his father and Jack as in need, Tim felt withdrawn and even found them repugnantly weak. He then feared that they would in turn be angry with him. If he were to give of himself, he feared that he would be drained, lose independence, and be doomed to serve the identity of another. By dying, his father and Jack seemed to confirm to Tim that he was at fault.

His problem was warding off this blame. He expected the rage of others in the form of either angry demands on him or revenge for neglect. This fearful expectancy was represented in the intrusive images of Jack who had, symbolically, come back to haunt or assault him.

As Tim recalled and related memories of being with his father during his terminal illness, he realized that he felt bad that he had not been more giving to his father, just as he regretted not being more supportive of Jack. But this awareness emerged in stages. He softened the potential injury to his self-esteem by first presenting material about how others were to be blamed. By implication he was then not to blame, or not completely to blame. For example, he explained to the therapist that the reason he had not told his dying father that he loved him was because his mother had told him not to do so. Her rationale was that if he told his father that he loved him, it would be an unusual event, and so his father would then realize that he must be terminally ill.

As he spoke of his regret for not telling his father of his feelings, he expressed rage at his mother. He pointed out to the therapist that she was also to blame for making his father uncomfortable when, because she was worried about money, she would not provide luxuries for the hospital room. Only when he was further along in the working-through process could he acknowledge that as a person in his late twenties, he was independent enough to decide for himself what to say or to do for his father and that his holding back was related to his own discomfort with his closeness to his father and his fear of his father's illness.

As Tim dealt with the issues of himself as self-centered and related this to his mother's and father's selfishness, he experienced the therapist in such roles. He felt that the therapist would be critical and angry with him for neglecting the therapy and at times tested the therapist for this countertransference potential.

At the height of this transference, Tim usually regarded the therapist's interpretations as reprimands rather than insights. He would feel more aloof from the therapist when he thought the therapist was enthralled with the theory that Tim's reaction to Jack's death was connected with his reaction to his father's death. Tim could then disavow that such feelings were his own by believing that he was manipulating the therapist as he continued the theme only in order to make the therapist happy. If he did not feel praised for such continuation, then he would feel that the therapist was angry with him. During this period, he felt that he and the therapist were each, in some way, neglecting the other. Rage would be vaguely in the air, never fully attached to either person.

It was necessary for the therapist to avoid direct interpretation of the externalization of blame during the period when Tim's defense to preserve his self-esteem was paramount. A premature comment that Tim blamed his mother for what he blamed in himself would have been taken as a slur, as Tim was not yet ready to tolerate the experience of bad attributes in himself. He first had to contemplate the idea of blame for neglect at a distance, to see whether it was safe. Then, gradually the attribution could move from others to himself.

Although the therapist avoided overly direct interpretations, he did encourage this working-through process. For example, when Tim talked about not saying that he loved his father, the therapist helped clarify which persons communicated what ideas, what his mother said about not telling his father, what Tim felt like saying but did not say, what he said to his mother, what he said to his father, and so on.

With such work Tim made contradictory statements. When he felt too bad about not expressing affection, he said that he had shown his father that he cared. But when he felt less threatened, he said that he had not expressed himself to his father. A tactful approach meant avoiding confronting Tim with contradictions but, rather, encouraging a gradual movement along a train of thought that he had been inhibiting and distorting.

With this rudimentary outline of some themes, it is possible to put them into a sequence of thought. Some of the principal concurrent defensive operations are indicated below in parentheses.

- My father (and Jack) is a powerful man. He does not do enough for me; I like him but I hate him for that.
- I would like to be powerful like father (and Jack); then I would not need him.
- I will model myself after him while watching out for the danger of being used by him or being sucked in by him.
- He (father, Jack) is not omnipotent; he can feel pain, weakness, and death.
- I must move further away from him (father, Jack) to avoid contamination with death or extreme need. I am afraid it is too late; the same thing may happen to me.
- By moving further away, I did not save him (father, Jack) or even help him during his suffering.
- Jack, like my father, will be enraged and get back at me.
- These images and my feeling that he is present are either evidence he is out to get me or show I am weak and going crazy.
- But I am not to blame. I refuse to believe I should have done more. People are wrong to expect anything of me. I refuse to think any more about this (denial, suppression, disavowal).
- It is not true that I moved away from Jack or my father (slides meanings to alter the story).

- Even if it is true, then others did it too, more than me. They are to blame (externalization).
- Even though others moved away and bear their responsibility, I am responsible that I moved away from him (father, Jack).
- Although I did not do all that I might have, I am still not a terrible person. My neglect did not directly kill them.
- I miss my father and am sad that it was not better between us.
- I am sorry that he (father, Jack) died; I wish I had done more. But even though I did not do as much as I would have liked, it is not true that they are now enraged at me.
- Even though it is true that I felt an inner rage that my father did not do more for me, that rage did not kill him (or Jack). So I do not have to bear total responsibility for his death (father, Jack).

As indicated by the later items in this condensed ideational line, Tim began to grieve not only for the father he had lost but also for an ideal father he had never had. As one example of this mourning process, he had a kind of restitutional fantasy in which he was a surgeon operating on his father and saving his life. This fantasy condensed many feelings: his anger (cutting open his father), his rescue wishes (saving him), his need to be strong and admirable (the brilliant surgeon), and his need to be omnipotent against death.

Tim's symptoms were relieved. With the cessation of intrusive images of Jack entering or being present in his apartment, he was able to go to bed with the lights off and to sleep through the night. His anxiety attacks stopped, and he felt confident that he had worked through the stress event. He had shown a readiness to deal with his character problems and a wish to advance from his less-than-optimal prestress level of character development. For these personality problems, long-term psychotherapy was recommended as a possible future choice for him to make.

References

Abraham, K. (1924). A short study of the development of the libido, viewed in the light of mental disorders. *Selected Papers*, pp. 418–501. London: Hogarth.

Adler, A. (1916). *The Neurotic Constitution: Outline of a Comparative Individualistic Psychology and Psychotherapy*, trans. B. Gluck and J. Lind. New York: Moffat Yard.

Agee, J. (1957). *A Death in the Family*. New York: McDowell, Obelinsky.

Aldrich, C. K. (1974). Some dynamics of anticipatory grief. In *Anticipatory Grief*, ed. B. Schoenberg, A. C. Carr, A. H. Kutscher, et al. New York: Columbia University Press.

Aldwin, C. M., Sutton, K., and Lachmann, F. M. (1996). The development of coping resources in adulthood. *Journal of Personality* 64:837–871.

Antonovsky, A. (1987). *Unraveling the Mystery of Healing: How People Manage Stress and Stay Well*. San Francisco: Jossey-Bass.

Archibald, H. C., and Tuddenham, R. D. (1965). Persistent stress reaction after combat. *Archives of General Psychiatry* 12:475–481.

Baker, G. W., and Chapman, D. W. (1962). *Man and Society in Disaster*. New York: Basic Books.

Barnett, J. (1972). Therapeutic intervention in the dysfunctional thought processes of the obsessional. *American Journal of Psychotherapy* 26:338–351.

Barr, H. L. (1972). *LSD: Personalities and Experience*. New York: Wiley.

Basch, M. (1980). *Doing Psychotherapy*. New York: Basic Books.

Beck, A. T. (1976). *Cognitive Therapy and Emotional Disorders*. New York: International Universities Press.

—— (1985). *Cognitive Therapy of the Anxiety Disorders*. New York: Basic Books.

Becker, S. S., Horowitz, M. J., and Campbell, L. (1973). Cognitive response to stress: effects of demand and sex. *Journal of Abnormal Psychology* 82:519–522.

Bibring, E. (1943). The conception of the repetition compulsion. *Psychoanalytic Quarterly* 12:486–519.

Bilodeau, C. B., and Hackett, T. P. (1971). Issues raised in a group setting by patients recovering from myocardial infarction. *American Journal of Psychiatry* 128:73–78.

Boehnlein, J. K., Kinzie, J. D., Ben, R., and Fleck, J. (1985). One year follow-up study of post traumatic stress disorder among survivors of Cambodian concentration camps. *American Journal of Psychiatry* 142:956–959.

Bourne, S., and Lewis, E. (1984). Pregnancy after stillbirth or neonatal death: psychological risks and management. *Lancet* 2:31–33.

Bowlby, J. (1961). Process of mourning. *International Journal of Psycho-Analysis* 42:317–340.

——— (1969). *Attachment and Loss.* Vol. 1. New York: Basic Books.

——— (1980). *Attachment and Loss.* Vol. 3: *Loss: Sadness and Depression.* New York: Basic Books.

Bowlby, J., and Parkes, C. M. (1970). Separation and loss. In *International Yearbook for Child Psychiatry and Allied Disciplines*, vol. 1: *The Child in His Family*, ed., E. Anthony and C. Koupernik, pp. 197–217. New York: Wiley.

Breger, L., Hunter, I., and Lane, R. (1971). Effect of stress on dreams. *Psychological Issues* 73:1–213.

Breger, L., and McGaugh, J. C. (1965). Critique of reformulation of "learning theory" approaches to psychotherapy and neurosis. *Psychological Bulletin* 63:338–358.

Bretherton, I., and Waters, E., eds. (1985). *Growing Points in Attachment Theory and Research: Monographs of the Society for Research in Child Development.* Chicago: University of Chicago Press.

Brett, E. A., and Ostroff, R. (1985). Imagery and posttraumatic stress disorder: an overview. *American Journal of Psychiatry* 142(4):417–424.

Breuer, J., and Freud, S. (1895). Studies on hysteria. *Standard Edition* 2:1–17.

Brill, N. Q. (1967). Gross stress reactions II: traumatic war neuroses. In

Comprehensive Textbook of Psychiatry, ed. A. M. Freedman and H. J. Kaplan, pp. 1031–1035. Baltimore: Williams & Wilkins.

Brill, N. Q., and Beebe, G. W. (1955). *A follow-up study of war neuroses.* Veteran's Administration Medical monograph. Washington, DC: U.S. Government Printing Office.

Broadbent, D. E. (1971). *Decision and Stress.* London: Academic Press.

Brom, D., Kleber, R. J., and Defares, P. B. (1989). Brief psychotherapy for post-traumatic stress disorders. *Journal of Consulting and Clinical Psychology* 57:607–612.

Burgess, A. W., and Holstrom, L. (1974). Rape trauma syndrome. *American Journal of Psychiatry* 131:981–986.

———— (1976). Coping behavior of the rape victim. *American Journal of Psychiatry* 133:413–418.

Calhoun, L. G., and Tedeschi, R. (1990). Positive aspects of life problems: recollections of grief. *Omega* 20:265–272.

Caplan, G. (1961). *An Approach to Community Mental Health.* New York: Grune & Stratton.

———— (1964). *Principles of Preventive Psychiatry.* New York: Basic Books.

Cartwright, R. D., Bernick, N., Borowitz, G., and Kling, A. (1969). Effect of an erotic movie on the sleep and dreams of young men. *Archives of General Psychiatry* 20:262–271.

Chodoff, P. (1970). German concentration camp as psychological stress. *Archives of General Psychiatry* 22:78–87.

Christianson, S., and Nilsson, L. (1987). Functional amnesia as induced by a psychological trauma. *Memory and Cognition.*

Clayton, P. J. (1974). Mortality and morbidity in the first year of widowhood. *Archives of General Psychiatry* 30:747–750.

Cobb, S., and Lindemann, E. (1943). Neuropsychiatric observation after the Coconut Grove fire. *Annals of Surgery* 117:814–824.

Coelho, G. V., Hamburg, D. A., and Adams, J. E., eds. (1974). *Coping and Adaptation.* New York: Basic Books.

Cohen, F., and Lazarus, R. (1973). Active coping processes, coping dispositions, and recovery from surgery. *Psychosomatic Medicine* 35:375–389.

Cohen, J. (1979). *Power Analyses for the Social and Behavioral Sciences.* New York: Academic Press.

Crits-Christoph, P., Luborsky, L., Dahl, L, et al. (1988). Clinicians can agree in assessing relationship patterns in psychotherapy: the Core Conflictual Relationship Theme method. *Archives of General Psychiatry* 45:1001–1004.

Dahl, H. (1977). Considerations for a theory of emotions. Introduction to J. DeRivera, A structural theory of emotions. *Psychological Issues* 10:1–8.

Danieli, Y. (1982). Families of survivors of the Nazi holocaust: some short and long term effects. In *Stress and Anxiety*, vol. 8, ed. C. Spielberger, N. Sarason, and N. Milgram, pp. 405–423. New York: Hemisphere.

Davidson, J., Kudler, H., Smith, R., et al. (1990). Treatment of post-traumatic stress disorder with amitriptyline and placebo. *Archives of General Psychiatry* 47:259–266.

Davis, D. (1966). *An Introduction to Psychopathology*. London: Oxford University Press.

De Fazio, V. J. (1975). Vietnam era veteran: psychological problems. *Journal of Contemporary Psychotherapy* 7:9–15.

De La Torre, J. (1972). The therapist tells a story: a technique in brief psychotherapy. *Bulletin of the Menninger Clinic* 36:609–616.

Derogatis, L. R., Rickels, K., and Rock, A. F. (1976). The SCL-90 and the MMPI: a step in the validation of a new self-report scale. *British Journal of Psychiatry* 128:280–289.

Deutsch, H. (1937). Absence of grief. *Psychoanalytic Quarterly* 6:12–22.

DeWitt, K., Kaltreider, N., Weiss, D., and Horowitz, M. (1983). Judging change in psychotherapy: the reliability of clinical formulations. *Archives of General Psychiatry* 40:1121–1128.

Diagnostic and Statistical Manual of Mental Disorders (1952). Washington, DC: American Psychiatric Association.

———— 2nd ed. (1968). Washington, DC: American Psychiatric Association.

———— 3rd ed. (1980). Washington, DC: American Psychiatric Association.

———— 4th ed. (1994). Washington, DC: American Psychiatric Association.

Dickinson, E. (c. 1862). Poem #341. *The Poems of Emily Dickinson*, ed. T. H. Johnson. Cambridge, MA: Belknap/Harvard University Press, 1955.

Dimsdale, J., and Hackett, T. (1982). Effect of denial on cardiac health and psychological assessment. *American Journal of Psychiatry* 139:1477–1480.

Easser, R. R., and Lesser, S. R. (1965). Hysterical personality: a re-evaluation. *Psychoanalytic Quarterly* 34:390–405.

Eaton, W. W., Sigal, J. J., and Weinfeld, M. (1982). Impairment in Holocaust survivors after 33 years: data from an unbiased community sample. *American Journal of Psychiatry* 139:773–777.

Egendorf, A., Kadushin, C., Laufer, R., et al. (1981). *Legacies of Vietnam: comparative adjustment of veterans and their peers.* Washington, DC: U.S. Government Printing Office.

Eisenbruch, M. (1984). Cross-cultural aspects of bereavement. I: a conceptual framework for comparative analysis. *Culture, Medicine and Psychiatry* 8:283–309.

Eitinger, L. (1969). Psychosomatic problems in concentration camp survivors. *Journal of Psychosomatic Research* 13:183–189.

Engel, G. L. (1975). The death of a twin: mourning and anniversary reactions. *International Journal of Psycho-Analysis* 56:23–40.

Engel, G. L., and Schmale, A. (1967). Psychoanalytic theory of somatic disorder: conversion specificity and disease onset situation. *Journal of the American Psychoanalytic Association* 15:344–365.

Epstein, S. (1992). Coping ability, negative self-evaluation, and overgeneralization: experiment and theory. *Journal of Personality and Social Psychology* 62:826–836.

Erickson, K. (1976). Loss of communality at Buffalo Creek. *American Journal of Psychiatry* 133:302–305.

Fairbairn, W. R. D. (1952). *War Neuroses: Their Nature and Significance.* Boston: Rutledge, Kegan Paul.

——— (1954). *An Object-Relations Theory of the Personality.* New York Basic Books.

Fenichel, O. (1945). *The Psychoanalytic Theory of Neurosis.* New York: Norton.

——— (1954). The concept of trauma. In *The Collected Papers of Otto Fenichel*, vol.2, pp. 49–69. New York: Norton.

Ferenczi, S. (1926). *Further Contributions to the Theory and Technique of Psychoanalysis.* London: Hogarth Press and Institute of Psychoanalysis, 1950.

Festinger, L. (1957). *A Theory of Cognitive Dissonance.* New York: Row, Peterson.

Figley, C. R., ed. (1978). *Stress Disorders among Vietnam Veterans: Theory, Research and Treatment.* New York: Brunner/Mazel.

——— (1984). *Trauma and its Wake.* New York: Brunner/Mazel.

Figley, C. R., and Leventman, S., eds. (1982). *Strangers at Home: Vietnam Veterans since the War.* New York: Praeger.

Finn, J. D. (1972). *Multivariance: Univariate and Multivariate Analysis of Variance, Covariance, and Regression.* Ann Arbor, MI: National Education Resources.

Fischer, R. (1971). A cartography of the ecstatic and meditative states: the experimental and experiential features of a perception-hallucination continuum are considered. *Science* 174:897–905.

Fleming. D., and Altschul, S. (1963). Activation of mourning and growth by psychoanalysis. *International Journal of Psycho-Analysis* 44:419–431.

Foa, E. B., Davidson, J., and Rothbaum, B. O. (1995). Posttraumatic stress disorder. In *Treatment of Psychiatric Disorders*, 2nd ed., vols. 1 and 2, ed. G. O. Gabbard, pp. 1499–1535. Washington, DC: American Psychiatric Press.

Foa, E. B., and Kozak, M. J. (1988). Emotional processing of fear: exposure to corrective information. *Psychological Bulletin* 99:20–35.

Foa, E. B., and Rothbaum, B. O. (1998). *Treating the Trauma of Rape: Cognitive Behavioral Therapy for PTSD.* New York: Guilford.

Foa, E. B., Rothbaum, B. O., Riggs, D. S., and Murdock, T. B. (1991). Treatment of posttraumatic stress disorder in rape victims: a comparison between cognitive-behavioral procedures and counselling. *Journal of Consulting and Clinical Psychology* 59:715–723.

Frank, J. B., Kosten, T. R., Giller, E. L., and Dan, E. (1988). A randomized clinical trial of phenelzine and imipramine for posttraumatic stress disorder. *American Journal of Psychiatry* 145:1289–1291.

French, T. (1952). *The Integration of Behavior*, vol. 1: *Basic Postulates.* Chicago: University of Chicago Press.

Freud, A. (1936). *The Ego and the Mechanisms of Defense.* New York: International Universities Press.

Freud, S. (1893). On the psychical mechanism of hysterical phenomena. *Standard Edition* 3:24–41.

————— (1899). Screen memories. *Standard Edition* 3:302–322. London: Hogarth Press, 1962.

————— (1900). The interpretation of dreams. *Standard Edition* 4 and 5:1–310 and 339–630.

————— (1909). Notes upon a case of obsessional neurosis. *Standard Edition* 10:155–318.

————— (1912). The psychodynamics of transference. *Standard Edition* 12:97–108.

————— (1914a). On narcissism: an introduction. *Standard Edition* 14:69–102.

————— (1914b). Remembering, repeating and working through. *Standard Edition* 12:145–150.

————— (1915). The unconscious. *Standard Edition* 14:172–205.

————— (1917). Mourning and melancholia. *Standard Edition* 14:243–260.

————— (1920). Beyond the pleasure principle. *Standard Edition* 18:1–68.

————— (1926). Inhibitions, symptoms and anxiety. *Standard Edition* 20:77–175.

————— (1937). Constructions in analysis. *Standard Edition* 25:255–269.

Friedman, O., and Linn, W. (1957). Some psychiatric notes on the *Andrea Doria. American Journal of Psychiatry* 114:426–432.

Furst, S. S. (1967). Psychic trauma: a survey. In *Psychic Trauma*, ed. S. S. Furst, pp. 3–50. New York: Basic Books.

Gallagher-Thompson, P., Hanley-Peterson, P., and Thompson, L. W. (1990). Maintenance of gain versus relapse following brief therapy for depression. *JCCP* 58:371–374.

Garmezy, N. (1985). Stress resistant children: the search for protective factors. In *Recent Research in Developmental Psychopathology*, ed. J. Stevenson, pp. 213–231. Oxford: Pergamon.

Glick, I., Parkes, C., and Weiss, R. (1975). *The First Year of Bereavement*. New York: Basic Books.

Glover, E. (1929). The "screening" function of traumatic memories. *International Journal of Psycho-Analysis* 10:90–93.

————— (1931). The therapeutic effect of inexact interpretation: a contribution to the theory of suggestion. *International Journal of Psycho-Analysis* 19:457–459.

Goldberg, A., (1978). *The Psychology of the Self*. New York: International Universities Press.

———— (1980). *Advances in Self Psychology*. New York: International
      Universities Press.

Goldstein, M. J., Alexander, E C., Clemens, T. L., et al. (1965). Coping
      style as a factor in psychophysiological response to a tension arous-
      ing film. *Journal of Personality & Social Psychology* 1:290–302.

Gorer, G. (1965). *Death, Grief, and Mourners in Contemporary Britain*. New
      York: Doubleday.

Grayson, H. (1970). Grief reactions to the relinquishing of unfulfilled
      wishes. *American Journal of Psychotherapy* 24:287–295.

Green, B. (1982). Assessing levels of psychological impairment follow-
      ing disasters. *Journal of Nervous and Mental Disease* 170: 544–552.

Green B. L, Grace, M. C., and Glesser, G. C. (1987). Identifying survi-
      vors at risk: long-term impairment following the Beverly Hills
      Supper Club fire. *The Journal of Consulting and Clinical Psychology*
      53(5):672–678.

Green B. L., Wilson, J. P., and Lindy, J. D. (1985). Conceptualizing
      posttraumatic stress disorder: a psychosocial framework. In *Trauma
      and Its Wake: The Study and Treatment of Post-traumatic Stress Disor-
      der*, ed. C. R. Figley, pp. 53–69. New York: Brunner/Mazel.

Greenacre, P. (1952). *Trauma, Growth, and Personality*. New York:
      Norton.

Grinker, K., and Spiegel, S. (1945). *Men under Stress*. Philadelphia:
      Blakeston.

Haan, N. (1977). *Coping and Defending*. New York: Academic Press.

Hackett, T., and Cassem, N. (1970). Psychological reactions to life threat-
      ening illness. In *Psychological Aspects of Stress*, ed. H. Abram, pp. 121–
      135. Springfield, IL: Charles C Thomas.

Haley, S. A. (1974). When the patient reports atrocities. *Archives of Gen-
      eral Psychiatry* 30:191–196.

Hartman, E. (1967). *The Biology of Dreaming*. Springfield, IL: Charles C
      Thomas.

Hartmann, H. (1939). *Ego Psychology and the Problem of Adaptation*. New
      York: International Universities Press.

Hendin, H., and Haas, A. P. (1984). *Wounds of War*. New York: Basic
      Books.

Hendin, H., Haas, A. P., Singer, P., et al. (1983). The influence of precombat personality on post-traumatic stress disorder. *Comprehensive Psychiatry* 24:530–534.

Higbee, K. L. (1969). Fifteen years of fear arousal: research on threat appeals: 1953–1969. *Psychological Bulletin* 72:426–444.

Hilberman, E. (1976). *The Rape Victim*. Washington, DC: American Psychiatric Association.

Hinsie, L. E., and Campbell, R. J. (1960). *Psychiatric Dictionary*, 3rd ed. New York: Oxford University Press.

Hocking, F. (1970). Extreme environmental stress and its significance for psychopathology. *American Journal of Psychotherapy* 24:4–26.

Horowitz, M. J. (1969). Psychic trauma: return of images after a stressful film. *Archives of General Psychiatry* 20:552–559.

——— (1970). *Image Formation and Cognition*. New York: Appleton-Century-Crofts.

——— (1973). Phase oriented treatment of stress response syndromes. *American Journal of Psychotherapy* 27:606–615.

——— (1974a). Microanalysis of working through in psychotherapy. *American Journal of Psychiatry* 131:1208–1212.

——— (1974b). Stress response syndromes: character style and brief psychotherapy. *Archives of General Psychiatry* 31:768–781.

——— (1975a). Intrusive and repetitive thoughts after experimental stress: a summary. *Archives of General Psychiatry* 32:1457–1463.

——— (1975b). Sliding meanings: a defense against threat in narcissistic personalities. *International Journal of Psychoanalytic Psychotherapy* 4:167–180.

——— (1976). *Stress Response Syndromes*. New York: Jason Aronson.

———, ed. (1977a). *Hysterical Personality*. New York: Jason Aronson. Second edition, 1991.

——— (1977b). Hysterical personality: cognitive structure and the process of change. *International Review of Psycho-Analysis* 4:23–49.

——— (1979a). *States of Mind*. New York: Plenum.

——— (1979b). Depressive disorders in response to loss. In *Stress and Anxiety*, ed. I. G. Sarason and C. D. Spielberger, pp. 235–255. New York: Hemisphere.

——— (1981). Self-righteous rage and the attribution of blame. *Archives of General Psychiatry* 38:1233–1238.

———— (1983). Post-traumatic stress disorders. *Behavioral Sciences and the Law* 1:9–23.

———— (1986). *Stress Response Syndromes*, 2nd ed. Northvale, NJ: Jason Aronson.

———— (1987). *States of Mind*, 2nd ed. New York: Plenum.

———— (1988). *Introduction to Psychodynamics: A New Synthesis*. New York: Basic Books.

———— (1989a). *Nuances of Technique in Psychodynamic Psychotherapy*. Northvale, NJ: Jason Aronson.

———— (1990). A model of mourning: change in schemas of self and other. *J Am Psychoanal Assoc* 38:297–324.

———— (1991). *Hysterical Personality and the Histrionic Personality Disorder*. Northvale, NJ: Jason Aronson.

———— (1995). Histrionic personality disorder. In *Treatment of Psychiatric Disorders*, 2nd ed., ed. G. O. Gabbard, pp. 2311–2326. Washington, DC: American Psychiatric Press.

———— (1997a). Stress, post-traumatic and adjustment. In *Textbook of Psychiatry*, eds. J. Cavenar et al. Philadelphia: Lippincott.

———— (1997b). *Stress Response Syndromes*, 3rd ed. Northvale, NJ: Jason Aronson.

———— (1997c). *Formulation as a Basis for Planning Psychotherapy*. Washington, DC: American Psychiatric Press.

———— (1997d). Organizational levels of self and other schematization. In *Personality Development*, ed. P. Westenberg, A. Rogers, L. Cahn, and A. Blasi, pp. 79–113. Mahwah, NJ: Lawrence Erlbaum.

———— (1998). *Cognitive Psychodynamics: From Conflict to Character*. New York: Wiley.

———— (1999). *Essential Papers on Posttraumatic Stress Disorders*. NY: NYU Press.

———— ed. (1992). *Person Schemas and Maladaptive Interpersonal Patterns*. Chicago: University of Chicago Press.

Horowitz, M. J., Adler, N., and Kegeles, S. (1988). A scale for measuring the occurrence of positive states of mind. *Psychosomatic Medicine* 50:477–483.

Horowitz, M. J., and Becker, S. S. (1971). The compulsion to repeat trauma: experimental study of intrusive thinking after stress. *Journal of Nervous and Mental Disease* 153(1):32–40.

———— (1971a). Cognitive response to stress and experimental demand. *Journal of Abnormal Psychology* 78:86–92.

———— (1971b). Cognitive response to stressful stimuli. *Archives of General Psychiatry* 25:419–428.

———— (1971c). The compulsion to repeat trauma: experimental study of intrusive thinking after stress. *Journal of Nervous and Mental Disease* 153:32–34.

———— (1973). Cognitive response to erotic and stressful films. *Archives of General Psychiatry* 29:81–84.

Horowitz, M., Becker, S. S., and Moskowitz, M. L. (1971). Intrusive and repetitive thought after stress: a replication study. *Psychological Reports* 29:763–767.

Horowitz, M., Becker, S. S., Moskowitz, M. L., and Rashid, K. (1972). Intrusive thinking in psychiatric patients after stress. *Psychological Reports* 31:235–238.

Horowitz, M. J., Field, N., and Classen, C. (1993). Stress response syndromes and their treatment. In *Handbook of Stress: Theoretical and Clinical Aspects*, 2nd ed., ed. L. Goldberger and S. Breznitz, pp. 757–773. New York, Free Press.

Horowitz, M., and Kaltreider, N. (1979). Brief therapy of stress response syndromes. *Psychiatric Clinics of North America* 2:365–378.

Horowitz, M., Krupnick, J., Kaltreider, N., et al. (1981). Initial psychological response to parental death. *Archives of General Psychiatry* 38:316–323.

Horowitz, M., Marmar, C., Krupnick, J., et al. (1984a). *Personality Styles and Brief Psychotherapy*. New York: Basic Books.

Horowitz, M., Marmar, C., Weiss, D., et al. (1984b). Brief psychotherapy of bereavement reactions. *Archives of General Psychiatry* 41: 438–448.

———— (1986). Comprehensive analysis of change after brief psychotherapy. *American Journal of Psychiatry* 143:582–589.

Horowitz, M. J., Milbrath, C., Bonanno, G., et al. (1998). Predictors of complicated grief. *Journal of Personal and Interpersonal Loss* 3:257–270.

Horowitz, M. J., Milbrath, C., and Stinson, C. (1995). Signs of defensive control locate conflicted topics in discourse. *Arch of Gen Psychiatry* 52:1040–1057.

Horowitz, M., Schaefer, C., Hiroto, D., et al. (1977). Life event questionnaires for measuring presumptive stress. *Psychosomatic Medicine* 39:413–431.

Horowitz, M., Siegel, B., Holen, A., et al. (1997). Diagnostic criteria for complicated grief disorder. *American Journal of Psychiatry* 154:904–911.

Horowitz, M., Simon, N., Holden, M., et al. (1983). The stressful impact of news of premature heart disease. *Psychosomatic Medicine* 45:31–40.

Horowitz, M. and Solomon, G. F. (1975). A prediction of stress response syndromes in Vietnam veterans: observations and suggestions for treatment. *Journal of Social Issues* 31(4):67–80.

——— (1978). A prediction of stress response syndromes in Vietnam veterans. In *Stress Disorders among Vietnam Veterans*, ed. C. F. Figley, pp. 67–80. New York: Brunner/Mazel.

Horowitz, M., Sonneborn, D., Sugahara, C., and Maercker, A. (1996). Self regard: a new measure. *American Journal of Psychiatry* 153:382–385.

Horowitz, M., Weiss, D., Kaltreider, N., et al. (1984). Reactions to death of a parent: results from patients and field subjects. *Journal of Nervous and Mental Disease* 172:383–392.

Horowitz, M., and Wilner, N. (1976). Stress films, emotions and cognitive response. *Archives of General Psychiatry* 30:1339–1344.

Horowitz, M., Wilner, N., and Alvarez, W. (1979). Impact of Event Scale: a study of subjective stress. *Psychosomatic Medicine* 41(3):209–218.

Horowitz, M., Wilner, N., Kaltreider, N., and Alvarez, W. (1980a). Signs and symptoms of post traumatic stress disorders. *Archives of General Psychiatry* 37:85–92.

Horowitz, M., Wilner, N., Marmar, C., and Krupnick, J. (1980b). Pathological grief and the activation of latent self images. *American Journal of Psychiatry* 137:1157–1162.

Horowitz, M., and Zilberg, N. (1983). Regressive alterations in the self concept. *American Journal of Psychiatry* 140(3):284–289.

Hoyt, M. (1980). Therapist and patient actions in "good" psychotherapy sessions. *Archives of General Psychiatry* 37:159–161.

Hoyt, M., Marmar, C., Horowitz, M. J., et al. (1981). The Therapist Action Scale and the Patient Action Scale: instruments for the assessment of activities during dynamic psychotherapy. *Psychotherapy: Theory, Research, and Practice* 18:109–116.

Janis, I. L. (1958). *Psychological Stress: Psychoanalytic and Behavioral Studies of Surgical Patients.* New York: Wiley.

—— (1962). Psychological effects of warnings. In *Man and Society in Disaster,* ed. C. W. Baker and D. W. Chapman, pp. 55–92. New York: Basic Books.

—— (1967). Effects of fear arousal on attitude change: recent development in theory and experimental research. In *Advances in Experimental Social Psychology,* vol. 3, ed. L. Berkowitz, pp. 166–224. New York: Academic Press.

—— (1969). *Stress and Frustration.* New York: Harcourt Brace Jovanovich.

Janis, I. L., and Leventhal, H. (1968). Human reactions to stress. In *Handbook of Personality Theory and Research,* ed. E. F. Bergatta and W. W. Lambert, pp. 1041–1085. Chicago: Rand McNally.

Janis, I. L., and Mann, J. (1977). *Decision Making.* New York: Free Press.

Johnson, J. E., Leventhal, H., and Dabbs, J. M. (1971). Contribution of emotional and instrumental response processes in adaptation to surgery. *Journal of Personality and Social Psychology* 20:55–64.

Jones, D. R. (1985). Secondary disaster victims: emotional effects of recovering and identifying remains. *American Journal of Psychiatry* 142:303–308.

Jones, E. (1929). Fear, guilt, and hate. *International Journal of Psycho-Analysis* 10:383–397.

—— (1953). *The Life and Work of Sigmund Freud,* vol.1. New York: Basic Books.

Kaltreider, N., Becker, T., and Horowitz, M. J. (1984). Relationship testing after parental bereavement. *American Journal of Psychiatry* 141:243–246.

Kaltreider, N., DeWitt, K., Weiss, D., and Horowitz, M. J. (1981). Pattern of individual change scales. *Archives of General Psychiatry* 38:1263–1269.

Kaltreider, N., and Mendelson, S. (1985). Clinical evaluation of grief after parental death. *Psychotherapy: Theory, Research and Practice* 22:224–230.

Kaltreider, N., Wallace, A., and Horowitz, M. J. (1979). A field study of the stress response syndrome: young women after hysterectomies. *Journal of the American Medical Association* 242:1499–1503.

Kandel, E. (1983). From metapsychology to molecular biology: explorations into the nature of anxiety. *American Journal of Psychiatry* 140: 1277–1293.

Kaplan, D., Grobstein, R., and Smith, A. (1976). Predicting the impact of severe illness in families. *Health and Social Work* 1:71–82.

Kardiner, A., and Spiegel, H. (1947). *War, Stress and Neurotic Illness.* New York: P. Hoeber.

Keiser, L. (1968). *The Traumatic Neuroses.* Philadelphia: Lippincott.

———— (1969). Accidents create opportunities. *Contemporary Psychology* 14:434–435.

Kernberg, O. (1967). Borderline personality organization. *Journal of the American Psychoanalytic Association* 15:41–68.

———— (1970). Factors in the psychoanalytic treatment of narcissistic personalities. *Journal of the American Psychoanalytic Association* 18:51–85.

———— (1974). Further contributions to the treatment of narcissistic personalities. *International Journal of Psycho-Analysis* 55:215–240.

———— (1975). *Borderline Conditions and Pathological Narcissism.* New York: Jason Aronson.

———— (1976). *Object Relations Theory and Clinical Psychoanalysis.* New York: Jason Aronson.

Klein, G. S. (1967). Peremptory ideation: structures and force in motivated ideas. In *Motives and Thought: Psychoanalytic Essays in Honor of David Rappaport*, ed. R. Holt, *Psychological Issues* 5:80–128.

Klerman, G., and Weissman, M., eds. (1993). *New Applications of Interpersonal Psychotherapy.* Washington, DC: American Psychiatric Press.

Kohut, H. (1966). Forms and transformations of narcissism. *Journal of the American Psychoanalytic Association* 14:243–272.

———— (1968). The psychoanalytic treatment of narcissistic personality disturbances. *Psychoanalytic Study of the Child* 23:86–113. New York: International Universities Press.

———— (1971). *The Analysis of the Self.* New York: International Universities Press.

———— (1972). Thoughts on narcissism and narcissistic rage. *Psychoanalytic Study of the Child* 27:360–400. New Haven, CT: Yale University Press.

———— (1977). *The Restoration of the Self.* New York: International Universities Press.

Kolb, L. C. (1982). Healing the wounds of Vietnam. *Hospital and Community Psychiatry* 33:877.

————(1983). Return of the repressed: delayed stress reaction to war. *Journal of the American Academy of Psychoanalysis* 11:531–545.

———— (1984). The post-traumatic stress disorders of combat: a subgroup with a conditioned emotional response. *Military Medicine* 149:237–243.

Koranyi, E. A. (1969). Psychodynamic theories of the "survivor syndrome." *Canadian Psychiatric Association Journal* 14:165–174.

Kosten, T. R., Frank, J. B., Dan, E., et al. (1991). Pharmacotherapy of posttraumatic stress disorder using phenelzine or imipramine. *Journal of Nervous Mental Disease* 179:366–370.

Krueger, D. W. (1984). *Emotional Rehabilitation of Physical Trauma and Disability.* New York: Spectrum.

Krupnick, J., and Horowitz, M. (1981). Stress response syndromes: recurrent themes. *Archives of General Psychiatry* 38:428–435.

Krystal, H. (1968). *Massive Psychic Trauma.* New York: International Universities Press.

———— (1985). Trauma and the stimulus barrier. *Psychoanalytic Inquiry* 5:236–241. Hillsdale, NJ: Analytic Press.

Krystal, H., and Niederland, W. C. (1971). Psychic traumatization. *International Psychiatric Clinics* 8:11–28.

Kubie, L. S. (1958). *Neurotic Distortion of the Creative Process.* Lawrence: University of Kansas Press.

Kübler-Ross, E. (1969). *On Death and Dying.* New York: Macmillan.

Langley, K. M. (1982). Post traumatic stress disorder among Vietnam combat veterans. *Social Casework* 63:593–598.

Lazare, A. (1971). The hysterical character in psychoanalytic theory. *Archives of General Psychiatry* 25:131–137.

Lazarus, R. S. (1966). *Psychological Stress and the Coping Process.* New York: McGraw-Hill.

Lazarus, R. S., Averill, J. R., and Opton, E. M. (1969). *The psychology of coping: issues of research and assessment.* Paper presented at *Coping and Adaptation,* Stanford University, Stanford, CA.

Lazarus, R. S., and Folkman, S. K. (1984). *Stress, Appraisal and Coping.* New York: Springer.

Lazarus, R. S., and Opton, B. M. (1966). The use of motion picture films in the study of psychological stress: a summary of experimental studies and theoretical formulations. In *Anxiety and Behavior*, ed. C. Spielberger, pp. 225–261. New York: Academic Press.

Lewin, K. (1935). The conflict between Aristotelian and Galilean modes of thought in contemporary psychology. In *A Dynamic Theory of Personality*, pp. 1–43. New York: McGraw-Hill.

Lewis, C. S. (1961). *A Grief Observed.* London: Faber.

Lewis, N. D., and Engel, B. (1954). *Wartime Psychiatry.* New York: Oxford University Press.

Lidz, T. (1946a). Psychiatric casualties from Guadalcanal. *Psychiatry* 9:143–213.

——— (1946b). Nightmare and the combat neuroses. *Psychiatry* 9:37–49.

——— (1996). *Doors Close, Doors Open, Widows Grieving and Growing.* Old Tappan, NJ: Grosset/Putnam.

Lifton, R. J. (1967). *History and Human Survival.* New York: Vantage Books.

——— (1973). *Home from the War.* New York: Simon & Schuster.

Lindemann, E. (1944). Symptomatology and management of acute grief. *American Journal of Psychiatry* 101:141–148.

——— (1960). Psychosocial factors as stress agents. In *Stress and Psychiatric Disorders*, ed. J. Tanner, pp. 13–17. Oxford, England: Blackwell.

Lindy, J. D., Green, B. L., Grace, M., and Titchener, J. (1987). Prevention of long-term psychopathology following disaster. *The Journal of Preventive Psychiatry*.

Linville, P. (1987). Self-complexity as a cognitive buffer against stress-related illness and depression. *Journal of Personality and Social Psychology* 52:663–676.

Luborsky, L. (1984). *Principles of Psychoanalytic Psychotherapy: A Manual for Supportive-Expressive (SE) Treatment.* New York: Basic Books.

Luisada, P. V., Peele, R., and Pittard, E. A. (1974). The hysterical personality in men. *American Journal of Psychotherapy* 131:518–521.

Malan, D. H. (1963). *A Study of Brief Psychotherapy.* London: Tavistock.

———— (1976). *Toward the Validation of Dynamic Psychotherapy*. New York: Plenum.

———— (1979). *Individual Psychotherapy and the Science of Psychodynamics*. London: Butterworth.

Mandler, C. (1964). The interruption of behavior. *Nebraska Symposium on Motivation* 12:163–220. Lincoln: University of Nebraska Press.

Mann, J. (1973). *Time Limited Psychotherapy*. Cambridge, MA: Harvard University Press.

Marks, I., (1981). *Cure and Care of Neuroses: Theory and Practice of Behavioral Psychotherapy*. New York: Wiley.

Marmar, C., Marziali, E., Horowitz, M. J., and Weiss, D. (1987). The development of the therapeutic alliance rating system. In *Research in Psychotherapy*, ed. L. Greenberg and W. Pinsoff. New York: Guilford.

Marmor, J. (1953). Orality in the hysterical personality. *Journal of the American Psychoanalytic Association* 1:656–675.

Marmor, J., and Woods, S., eds. (1980). *The Interface between the Psychodynamic and Behavioral Therapies*. New York: Plenum.

Marris, P. (1958). *Widows and Their Families*. London: Routledge.

Marziali, E., Marmar, C., and Krupnick, J. (1981). Therapeutic alliance scales: development and relationship to therapeutic outcome. *American Journal of Psychiatry* 138:361–364.

McFarlane, A. C. (1989). The etiology of post-traumatic morbidity: predisposing, precipitating, and perpetuating factors. *British Journal of Psychiatry* 154:221–228.

———— (1994). Individual psychotherapy for post-traumatic stress disorder. *Psychiatric Clinics of North America* 17:393–408.

Meichenbaum, D. (1977). *Cognitive-Behavior Modification: An Integrative Approach*. New York: Plenum.

———— (1980). *Cognitive Behavior Modification*. New York: Plenum.

Menninger, K. (1954). Regulatory devices of the ego under major stress. *International Journal of Psycho-Analysis* 35:412–420.

Miller, G. A., Galanter, E., and Pribram, K. H. (1960). *Plans and the Structure of Behavior*. New York: Holt, Rinehart & Winston.

Moffatt, M. J., ed. (1982). *In the Midst of Winter: Selections from the Literature of Mourning*. New York: Vintage.

Monat, A., and Lazarus, R. S. (1977). *Stress and Coping*. New York: Columbia University Press.

Moore, B. E., and Fine, B. D. (1968). *A Glossary of Psychoanalytic Terms and Concepts*. New York: American Psychoanalytic Association.

Moos, R. (1976). *Coping with Physical Illness*. New York: Plenum.

Murphy, W. F. (1961). A note on traumatic loss. *Journal of the American Psychoanalytic Association* 9:519–532.

Myerson, P. G. (1969). The hysteric's experience in psycho-analysis. *International Journal of Psycho-Analysis* 50:373–384.

Nomikos, M. S., Averill, J. R., Lazarus, R. S., and Opton, E. M. (1968). Surprise versus suspense in the production of stress reaction. *Journal of Personality and Social Psychology* 8:204–208.

North, C. S., Smith, E. M., and Spitznagel, E. L. (1994). Posttraumatic stress disorder in survivors of a mass shooting. *American Journal of Psychiatry* 151:82–88.

Oppenheim, H. (1905). *Textbook of Nervous Diseases*. Berlin: S. Karger.

Oremland, J. D. (1972). Transference cure and flight into health. *International Journal of Psychoanalytic Psychotherapy* 1:61–75.

Orne, M. T. (1962). On the social psychology of the psychological experiment: with particular reference to demand characteristics and their implications. *American Psychologist* 17:776–783.

Ornstein, P. (1978). *The Search for the Self in Selected Writings of Heinz Kohut*, vols. 1 and 2. New York: International Universities Press.

Osterweiss, M., Solomon, F., and Green, M. (1984). *Bereavement Reactions, Consequences and Care*. Washington, DC: National Academy Press.

Ostwald, P., and Bittner, E. (1968). Life adjustment after severe persecution. *American Journal of Psychiatry* 124:87–94.

Park, C. L., Cohen, L., and Murch, R. (1996). Assessment of stress related growth. *Journal of Personality* 64:71–105.

Parkes, C. M. (1964). Recent bereavement as a cause of mental illness. *British Journal of Psychiatry* 110:198–204.

——— (1970). The first year of bereavement: a longitudinal study of the reaction of London widows to the death of their husbands. *Psychiatry* 33:444–467.

———(1972). *Bereavement*. New York: International Universities Press.

Parkes, C. M., and Weiss, R. S. (1983). *Recovery from Bereavement*. New York: Basic Books.

Pearlin, L., and Schooler, C. (1978). The structure of coping. *Journal of Health and Social Behavior* 19:2–21. Also in McCubbin, H. I., ed., *Family Stress, Coping and Social Supports*. New York: Springer, 1982.

Pollock, C. (1972). The mourning-liberation process and creativity: the case of Kathe Kollwitz. *Annual of Psychoanalysis* 10:333–354.

———— (1978). Process and affect: mourning and grief. *International Journal of Psycho-Analysis* 59:255–276.

———— (1989). *The Mourning-Liberation Process*, vols. I, II. New York: International Universities Press.

Popovic, M., and Petrovic, D. (1965). After the earthquake. *Lancet* 2:1169–1171.

Prigerson, H. C., Frank, E., Kasl, S. V., et al. (1997). Complicated grief and bereavement-related depression as distinct disorders: preliminary empirical validation in elderly bereaved spouses. *American Journal of Psychiatry* 152:22–30.

Rado, S. (1948). Pathodynamics and treatment of traumatic war neuroses (trauma-phobia). *Psychosomatic Medicine* 4:362–368.

Raphael, B. (1983). *The Anatomy of Bereavement*. New York: Basic Books.

Rees, W. D. (1970). *Hallucinatory and paranormal reactions to bereavement*. Unpublished M.D. Thesis.

Resnick, H. S., Kilpatrick, D. C., Best, C. L., and Kramer, T. L. (1992). Vulnerability-stress factors in development of posttraumatic stress disorder. *Journal of Nervous and Mental Disorders* 180:424–430.

Rexroth, K., ed. (1970). *Love and the Turning Year*. San Francisco: New Directions.

Richardson,J. T. E. (1979). The post-concussional syndrome. In *Research in Psychology and Medicine*, vol. 1, ed. D. J. Oborne, M. M. Gruneberg, and J. R. Eiser, London: Academic Press.

Robertson, J., and Robertson, J. (1969). *John, Seventeen Months: Nine Days in a Residential Nursery* (film). London: Tavistock Institute of Human Relations, Tavistock Clinic.

Robins, L. N., Smith, E. M., Cottler, L. B., et al. (1985). *Impact of disaster on mental health*. Paper presented at the Annual Meeting of the American Psychiatric Association, Dallas, May.

Rosenbaum, R., and Horowitz, M. (1983). Motivation for psychotherapy: a factorial and conceptual analysis. *Psychotherapy: Theory, Research and Practice* 20:346–354.

Rosenblatt, P. C., Walsh, R. P., and Jackson, D. A. (1976). Grief and mourning in cross-cultural perspective. New Haven, CT: Human Relations Area Files Press.

Rosenthal, R. (1966). *Experimental Effects in Behavioral Research.* New York: Appleton-Century-Crofts.

Rutter, M. (1987). Psychosocial resilience and protective mechanisms. *American Journal of Orothopsychiatry* 57:316–331.

Sachs, O. (1967). Distinctions between fantasy and reality elements in memory and reconstructions. *International Journal of Psycho-Analysis* 48:416–423.

Saltz, E. (1970). Manifest anxiety: Have we misread the data? *Psychological Review* 77:568–573.

Salzman, L. (1968). *The Obsessive Personality.* New York: Science House.

————— (1980). *Treatment of the Obsessive Personality.* New York: Jason Aronson.

Sampson, H., and Weiss, J. (1972). Defense analysis and the emergence of warded off mental conflicts: an empirical study. *Archives of General Psychiatry* 26:524–532.

Sandler, J. (1960). The background of safety. *International Journal of Psycho-Analysis* 41:352–356.

Schank, R., and Abelson, R. P. (1977). *Scripts, Plans, Goals, and Understandings.* Hillsdale, NJ: Lawrence Erlbaum.

Schur, M. (1966). *The Id and the Regulatory Process of the Ego.* New York: International Universities Press.

Schwartz, E. K. (1972). The treatment of the obsessive patient in the group therapy setting. *American Journal of Psychotherapy* 26:352–361.

Sears, R. R. (1936). Functional abnormalities of memory with special reference to amnesia. *Psychological Bulletin* 33:229–274.

Selye, H. (1976). *Stress in Health and Disease.* Boston: Butterworth.

Shapiro, D. (1965). *Neurotic Styles.* New York: Basic Books.

————— (1981). *Autonomy and Rigid Character.* New York: Basic Books.

Shapiro, F. (1989). Efficacy of the eye movement desensitization procedure in the treatment of traumatic memories. *Journal of Traumatic Stress* 2:199–223.

Shatan, C. (1973). The grief of soldiers: Vietnam combat veterans' self-help movement. *American Journal of Orthopsychiatry* 43:640–653.

Shestatsky, M., Greenberg, D., and Lerer, B. (1984). A controlled trial of phenelzine in posttraumatic stress disorder. *Psychiatry Research* 24:149–155.

Shore, J. H., Tatum, E., and Vollmer, W. M. (1985). *Psychiatric findings of Mount St. Helens disaster*. Paper presented at the Annual Meeting of the American Psychiatric Association, Dallas, May.

Sifneos, P. (1966). Psychoanalytically oriented short-term dynamic or anxiety-producing psychotherapy for mild obsessional neuroses. *Psychiatric Quarterly* 40:270–282.

——— (1972). *Short-term Psychotherapy and Emotional Crisis*. Cambridge, MA: Harvard University Press.

Silver, S., and Iacono, C. (1984). Factor analytic support for *DSM-III* post traumatic stress disorder for Vietnam veterans. *Journal of Clinical Psychology* 40:5–14.

Silverman, J. S. (1972). Obsessional disorders in childhood and adolescence. *American Journal of Psychotherapy* 26:362–377.

Singer, J. L., and Pope, K. S., eds. (1978). *The Stream of Consciousness: Scientific Investigations into the Flow of Human Experience*. New York: Plenum.

Smith, E. M., Robins, L. N., Cottler, L. B., et al. (1985). *Psychosocial impact of a double disaster*. Paper presented at the Annual Meeting of the American Psychiatric Association, Dallas, May.

Solomon, G. F., et al. (1971). Three psychiatric casualties from Vietnam. *Archives of General Psychiatry* 25:522–524.

Southwick, S. M., Krystal, J. H., Morgan, C. A., et al. (1993). Abnormal noradrenergic function in posttraumatic stress disorder. *Archives of General Psychiatry* 50:266–274.

Spielberger, C. D. (1966). Theory and research on anxiety. In *Anxiety and Behavior*, pp. 3–20. New York: Academic Press.

Stern, M. M. (1961). Blank hallucinations: remarks about trauma and perceptual disturbances. *International Journal of Psycho-Analysis* 42:205–215.

Stevens, S. S. (1966). A metric for the social consensus. *Science* 151:530.

Stone, L. (1951). Psychoanalysis and brief psychotherapy. *Psychoanalytic Quarterly* 20:215–236.

Strauss, A. (1975). *Chronic Illness and the Quality of Life*. St. Louis: C. V. Mosby.

Strupp, H., and Binder, J. (1984). *Psychotherapy in a New Key: A Guide to Time-limited Dynamic Psychotherapy*. New York: Basic Books.

Sutherland, S., and Scherl, P. J. (1970). Patterns of response among victims of rape. *American Journal of Orthopsychiatry* 40:503–511.

Sutherland-Fox, S., and Scherl, P. J. (1975). Crisis intervention with victims of rape. In *Rape Victimology*, ed. L. G. Schultz, pp. 232–245. Springfield, IL: Charles C Thomas.

Tart, C. T. (1969). *Altered States of Consciousness*. New York: Wiley.

Taylor, J., and Spence, K. (1952). The relationship of anxiety level of performance in serial learning. *Journal of Experimental Psychology* 44:61–64.

Taylor, S. E. (1983). Adjustment to threatening events: a theory of cognitive adaptation. *American Psychologist* 38:1161–1173.

Tedeschi, R., Park, C. L., and Calhoun, L. G., eds. (1998). *Post-Traumatic Growth: Positive Change in the Aftermath of Crisis*. Mahwah, NJ: Lawrence Erlbaum.

Terr, L. (1981). Psychic trauma in children: observations following the Chowchilla school-bus kidnapping. *American Journal of Psychiatry* 138:14–19.

——— (1983). Chowchilla revisited: the effects of psychic trauma four years after a school-bus kidnapping. *American Journal of Psychiatry* 140:1543–1550.

Thompson L., Gallagher, D., and Breckenridge, J. S. (1987). Comparative effectiveness of psychotherapies for depressed elders. *Journal of Geriatric Psychiatry* 21:133–146.

Thompson, L., Gallagher-Thompson, D., Fullerman, A., et al. (1991). The effects of late-life spousal bereavement over a 30-month interval. *Psychology and Aging* 6(3):434–441.

Titchner, J. L., and Kapp, F. T. (1976). Family and character change at Buffalo Creek. *American Journal of Psychiatry* 133:295–299.

Tomkins, S. S. (1962). *Affect, Imagery, Consciousness*, vol. I: *The Positive Affects*. New York: Springer.

——— (1978). Script theory: differential magnification of affects. In *Nebraska Symposium on Motivation*, ed. H. E. Howe, Jr., and R. A. Diensbier, 26:201–237. Lincoln: University of Nebraska Press.

Trimble, M. R. (1981). *Post Traumatic Neuroses*. New York: Wiley.

True, W. R., Rice, J., Eisen, S. A., et al. (1993). A twin study of genetic and environmental contributions to liability for posttraumatic stress symptoms. *Archives of General Psychiatry* 50:257–264.

Updegraff, J. A., and Taylor, S. E. (in press). Vulnerability to growth: positive and negative effects of stressful life events. In *Handbook of Loss and Trauma*, ed. J. Harvey and E. Miller. New York: Brunner-Mazel.

Ursano, R. J., Fullerton, L. S., Vanco, K., and Kao, T. (1999). Posttraumatic stress disorder and identification in disaster workers. *Annals of Disaster Psychiatry* 156:353–359.

Vaillant, G. E. (1977). *Adaptation to Life*. Boston: Little Brown.

van der Kolk, B., Blitz, R., Burr, W., et al. (1984). Nightmares and trauma: a comparison of nightmares after combat with lifelong nightmares in veterans. *American Journal of Psychiatry* 141:187–190.

van der Kolk, B. A., Dreyfuss, D., Michaels, M., et al. (1994). Fluoxetine in post-traumatic stress disorder. *Journal of Clinical Psychiatry* 55:517–522.

Veith, I. (1965). *Hysteria: History of a Disease*. Chicago: University of Chicago Press.

––––––– (1977). Four thousand years of hysteria. In *Hysterical Personality*, ed. M. J. Horowitz, pp. 7–95. New York: Jason Aronson.

Veronen, L. J., and Kilpatrick, D. G. (1983). Stress management for rape victims. In *Stress Reduction and Prevention*, ed. D. Meichenbaum and M. Jaremko, pp. 341–375. New York: Plenum.

Wallerstein, R. S. (1967). Development and metapsychology of defensive organization of the ego. *Journal of the American Psychoanalytic Association* 15:130.

Weiss, D., DeWitt, K., Kaltreider, N., and Horowitz, M. (1985). A proposed method for measuring change beyond symptoms. *Archives of General Psychiatry* 42:703–708.

Weiss, D., Horowitz, M., and Wilner, N. (1984). Stress response rating scale: a clinician's measure. *British Journal of Clinical Psychology* 23:202–215.

Weiss, J. (1967). The integration of defenses. *International Journal of Psycho-Analysis* 48:520–524.

––––––– (1971). The emergence of new themes: a contribution to the psychoanalytic theory of therapy. *International Journal of Psycho-Analysis* 52:459–467.

Whitty, C. W. M., and Zangwffl, O. L. (1977). Traumatic amnesia. In *Amnesias*, 2nd ed., pp. 104–117. London: Butterworth.

Wilkinson, C. B. (1983). Aftermath of a disaster: the collapse of the Hyatt Regency hotel skywalks. *American Journal of Psychiatry* 140:1134–1139.

Wilner, N., and Horowitz, M. J. (1975). Intrusive and repetitive thought after a depressing film: a pilot study. *Psychological Reports* 37:135–138.

Wilson, J. (1982). Conflict, stress and growth: the effects of war on psychosocial development among Vietnam veterans. In *Strangers at Home: Vietnam Veterans since the War*, ed. C. Figley and S. Leventman, pp. 123–165. New York: Praeger.

Wilson, I., and Krauss, C. (1982). *Predicting post traumatic stress syndrome among Vietnam veterans*. Paper presented at the 25th Neuropsychiatric Institute, Veterans Administration Medical Center, Coatesville, PA, October.

Windholz, E. (1945). Observations on psychiatric rehabilitation of veterans. *Bulletin of the Menninger Clinic* 9:121–133.

Windholz, M., Marmar, C., and Horowitz, M. J. (1985). A review of research on conjugal bereavement: impact on health and efficacy of intervention. *Comprehensive Psychiatry* 26:433–447.

Witkin, H. A. (1969). Influencing dream content. In *Dream Psychology and the New Biology of Dreaming*, ed. M. Kramer, Springfield, IL: Charles C Thomas.

Witkin, H. A., and Lewis, H. B. (1965). The relation of experimentally induced presleep experience to dreams. *Journal of the American Psychoanalytic Association* 13:819–849.

Wolfenstein, M. (1966). How is mourning possible? *Psychoanalytic Study of the Child* 21:93–123. New York: International Universities Press.

Zaidi, L. Y., and Foy, D. W. (1991). Childhood abuse and combat-related PTSD. *Journal of Traumatic Stress* 4:325–343.

Zients, A. B. (1986). Identification and its vicissitudes as viewed in adolescence: object loss and identification. *International Journal of Psycho-Analysis* 67:77–85.

Zilberg, N., Weiss, D., and Horowitz, M. J. (1982). Impact of Event
    Scale: a cross validation study and some empirical evidence. *Journal
    of Consulting and Clinical Psychology* 50:407–414.
Zisook, S., Schneider, D., and Schucter, S. (1990). Anxiety and bereave-
    ment. *Psychiatr Med* 8:583–596.
Zisook, S., and Schucter, S. R. (1991a). Depression through the first year
    after the death of a spouse. *Am J Psychiatry* 148:1346–1352.
——— (1991b). Early psychological reaction to the stress of widowhood.
    Psychiatry 54:320–333.

JOURNAL ABBREVIATIONS

Am Psychol	American Psychologist
Psychosomatic Med	Psychosomatic Medicine
Am J Psychiatry	American Journal of Psychiatry
J Pers Soc Psychol	Journal of Personality and Social Psychology
JCCC	Journal of Consulting and Clinical Psychology
J Am Psychoanal Assoc	Journal of the American Psychoanalytic Association
Int J Ment Health	International Journal of Mental Health
Arch of Gen Psychiatry	Archives of General Psychiatry
J Clin Psychiatry	Journal of Clinical Psychiatry
J Affect Disord	Journal of Affective Disorders
Br J Psychiatry	British Journal of Psychiatry
Psychol Med	Psychological Medicine
Psychiatr Annals	Psychiatric Annals
J Am Acad Child Adolesc Psychiatry	Journal of the American Academy of Child and Adolescent Psychiatry
J Psychiatr Res	Journal of Psychiatric Research
J Consult Clin Psychol	Journal of Consulting and Clinical Psychology
J Clin Epidemiol	Journal of Clinical Epidemiology
J Nerv Ment Dis	Journal of Nervous and Mental Disorders
Psychiatr Med	Psychiatric Medicine

Index

441

ABOUT THE AUTHOR

Mardi Jon Horowitz, M.D., is Professor of Psychiatry at the University of California, San Francisco. He has directed (in the Langley Porter Psychiatric Institute) a series of programs including the Psychotherapy Evaluation and Study Center, Center for the Study of Neuroses (an NIMH-supported clinical research center), and Center on Stress and Personality. For a decade, he formed and directed the Program on Conscious and Unconscious Mental Processes of the John D. and Catherine T. MacArthur Foundation.

Dr. Horowitz's published books include *States of Mind: Configurational Analysis of Individual Personality, Person Schemas and Maladaptive Interpersonal Patterns; Nuances of Technique in Dynamic Psychotherapy; Image Formation and Psychotherapy; Hysterical Personality Style and the Histrionic Personality Disorder; Personality Styles and Brief Psychotherapy; Introduction to Psychodynamics: A New Synthesis; Formulation as a Basis for Planning Psychotherapy Treatment;* and *Cognitive Psychodynamics.*

For his achievements in developing the diagnoses of Post Traumatic Stress Disorder and disorders of complicated grief, working out the stress by personality interaction in symptom formation, developing new research methods focused on stress measurement and observation of emotional control processes, and formation of new treatments, Dr. Horowitz has been awarded the Pioneer Award of the International Society for Traumatic Stress Studies, the Royer Award of the University of California, the American Psychiatric Association and Foundation's Fund Prize for Research in Psychiatry, the Hibbs Award for best contribution by the American Psychiatric Association the Strecker Award from the Institute of the Pennsylvania Hospital, and the Outstanding Contribution Award of the Northern California Psychiatric Society.